THE MASSEY LECTURES SERIES

The Massey Lectures are co-sponsored by CBC Radio, House of Anansi Press, and Massey College in the University of Toronto. The series was created in honour of the Right Honourable Vincent Massey, former Governor General of Canada, and was inaugurated in 1961 to provide a forum on radio where major contemporary thinkers could address important issues of our time.

This book comprises the 2017 Massey Lectures, "In Search of a Better World: A Human Rights Odyssey," broadcast in November 2017 as part of CBC Radio's *Ideas* series. The producer of the series was Philip Coulter; the executive producer was Greg Kelly.

PAYAM AKHAVAN

Payam Akhavan is a Professor of International Law at McGill University in Montreal, Canada, a Member of the International Court of Arbitration, and a former UN prosecutor at The Hague. He has served with the UN in conflict zones around the world, including Bosnia, Cambodia, Guatemala, Rwanda, and Timor-Leste, and as legal counsel in leading cases before the International Court of Justice, the International Criminal Court, the European Court of Human Rights, and the Supreme Courts of Canada and the United States. His prior academic appointments were at Oxford University, University of Paris, the European University Institute, University of Toronto, and Yale Law School. He earned his Doctor of the Science of Jurisprudence at Harvard Law School, and his widely cited academic publications include *Reducing Genocide to Law,* from Cambridge University Press. He served as Chair of the Global Conference on Prevention of Genocide and is a founder of the Iran Human Rights Documentation Centre; his groundbreaking human rights work has been featured on BBC World's *Hardtalk,* CBC's *Ideas,* and Brazil's TV Globo, and in *Maclean's* magazine and the *New York Times.* In 2005, he was selected by the World Economic Forum as a Young Global Leader. Payam Akhavan was born in Tehran, Iran, and migrated to Canada with his family in his childhood.

IN SEARCH OF A
BETTER WORLD

A Human Rights Odyssey

PAYAM AKHAVAN

ANANSI

Copyright © 2017 Payam Akhavan and
the Canadian Broadcasting Corporation

Published in Canada and the USA in 2017 by House of Anansi Press Inc.
www.houseofanansi.com

All rights reserved. No part of this publication may be reproduced or
transmitted in any form or by any means, electronic or mechanical, including
photocopying, recording, or any information storage and retrieval system,
without permission in writing from the publisher.

House of Anansi Press is committed to protecting our natural environment.
As part of our efforts, the interior of this book is printed on paper that
contains 100% post-consumer recycled fibres, is acid-free, and is processed
chlorine-free.

21 20 19 18 17   1 2 3 4 5

Library and Archives Canada Cataloguing in Publication

Akhavan, Payam, author
In search of a better world : a human rights odyssey / Payam Akhavan.

(Massey lectures)
Issued in print and electronic formats.
ISBN 978-1-4870-0200-8 (softcover). — ISBN 978-1-4870-0201-5 (EPUB). —
ISBN 978-1-4870-0202-2 (Kindle)

1. Human rights. 2. International law and human rights. 3. Akhavan,
Payam. I. Title. II. Series: CBC Massey lectures series

JC571.A343 2017   323   C2017-901295-9
                          C2017-901296-7

Library of Congress Control Number: 2016958331
U.S. ISBN: 978-1-4870-0339-5

Cover design: Alysia Shewchuk
Text design: Ingrid Paulson

*We acknowledge for their financial support of our publishing program
the Canada Council for the Arts, the Ontario Arts Council, and the Government of
Canada through the Canada Book Fund.*

Printed and bound in Canada

For K & K, the light of my eyes.

CONTENTS

ONE

THE KNOWLEDGE OF SUFFERING

FROM TEHRAN TO TORONTO

"I SPEAK A LITTLE ENGLISH." "I like Canada." "Nice to meet you." I had rehearsed those words carefully, repeating them like a sacred mantra. It was a long journey from Tehran to Toronto. At first, the hours went by quickly. Like all children flying in airplanes, I was in a euphoric trance. But I was growing impatient to arrive. I needed to meet those foreigners called "Canadians" and practise the English phrases I had memorized.

There was no in-flight entertainment in those days, except the view from the window seat. I persuaded my older brother, Dariush, to vacate the prized location, using the time-tested technique

・ IN SEARCH OF A BETTER WORLD ・

of incredibly annoying behaviour. I didn't take the opportunity lightly. As the self-appointed sentry for Iran Air, I kept a vigilant watch, observing each and every object visible from those sublime heights, ready to report suspicious activity to the control tower.

Thirty thousand feet is an ideal altitude to wander and dream. When explored from a safe distance, the world is an enchanting but deceptive place. The word "exile" was not yet part of my linguistic repertoire. The idea of "religious persecution" was still beyond the realm of my experience. I didn't know at the time that I was about to enter the crucible of suffering that teaches us the true meaning of words. As the land of my birth slowly disappeared over the horizon, I glanced one last time at an innocent past. I had a vague premonition that I would never return to the home I once knew.

"When setting out on a journey, do not seek advice from someone who never left home." That was the timeless wisdom of Rumi, the mystical poet of ancient Persia, the land of my ancestors. As children, we needed a safe home so our imagination could wander to distant places, unconstrained by fear. Adventures could be had, effortlessly and endlessly, without expectations and calculations, until it was time to sleep, and even then, our dreams would sustain us until the light of morning. But one day I would awaken to find myself in a strange place, far from home, desperately lost in the wilderness. In that place, I would struggle to find the words, to explain where I had come from, and why part of me was left behind; it seemed that nobody understood what I was trying to say. Knowledge, I was told, was a theoretical abstraction, and purpose a liberal platitude. There was no need to feel deeply, no need to be broken open.

The fate of modern times, the German philosopher Max Weber wrote, "is characterized by rationalization and intellectualization and, above all, by the disenchantment of the world." Emancipated from the mimicry of irrational traditions, the demystified mind was poised to conquer the truth, looking down from the commanding heights of utilitarian objectivity. The man of the European Enlightenment was no longer part of the universe; he was on top of it. Henceforth, intellectual ideas would substitute intense experiences, and reason rather than reflection would discover reality through detached observation. By the twentieth century, the unprecedented catastrophes of total war and genocide had exploded modernity's myth of progress. Just as the scientific mind had dispassionately discovered the secrets of the outward universe, the horrors of the Holocaust forced a chastened humanity to rediscover the mystical universe of the inner self. The cornerstone of the new postwar civilization was the idea of human rights — of a being with an intrinsically noble essence. In a secular world, it was a reminder of that which must remain sacred.

The Universal Declaration of Human Rights was adopted on December 10, 1948. The UN thereby proclaimed, without empirical verification, that "All human beings are born free and equal in dignity and rights." It professed as a self-evident truth that "They are endowed with reason and conscience and should act towards one another in a spirit of brotherhood." In light of the appalling cruelty of our collective past, this would seem more a naive aspiration than a logical proposition. The eighteenth-century English historian Edward Gibbon famously wrote: "History is indeed little more than the register of the crimes, follies, and misfortunes of mankind." Yet human rights remain an idea at the core of our self-conception. Today we demand justice for the oppressed. We no longer accept atrocities as the inescapable fate of the defenceless. We desire and expect a better future. But when confronted with the enormity of injustice and what it demands of us, we retreat into the familiar ritual of intellectualization and moral posturing, recycling lofty liberal ideals from a safe distance. We avoid the intimate knowledge of suffering without which we will never understand the imperative of human rights.

The problem with the world is not a shortage of brilliant theories or feel-good slogans. The problem is that we confuse proliferation of progressive terminology with profound empathy and purposeful engagement. We say the right things, but we fail to act on them because we want to feel virtuous without paying a price. This book is about worthy human rights causes, from the local to the global, of which we speak so often: refugees and multiculturalism; bringing war criminals to justice before the Hague Tribunal; the "Responsibility to Protect" victims of genocide; global governance and world peace through a strong UN; grassroots activism and speaking truth to power. This book is about all of those things, but above all, it is about why we cannot remain comfortably detached from the painful realities and urgent challenges that these ideas convey. There can be no meaningful change if we choose to look down at the arena of anguish from thirty thousand feet.

Looking back at my journey, from that fateful airplane voyage where I first learned about the pain of separation from that place we call home, to the lecture halls of the academy and the tribunals of the UN where I went in pursuit of justice, I have come to the conclusion that instead of a triumphant truth, human rights are a thousand humble stories. Suffering is not some big idea in the sky. It is a lived experience, a profound knowledge, scattered across the many sites of sorrow that I have witnessed. Feeling injustice is the only means of understanding justice; stories, both enchanting and heartbreaking, are the only means of knowing why our dignity matters. This then is a story among stories, a glimpse of our shared longing to redeem irredeemable loss, a tale of how wounds open us to search in darkness for the dawn of a better world.

THE PERILS OF PROSPERITY

I was nine years old when I was first told that we would soon leave Tehran. Our destination was an exotic place called Toronto. It was a strange name. It didn't sound English to me. I found it on my desktop globe, on the other side of the world. It was a small empty circle above a blue lake called "Ontario," in a big country coloured pink that stretched from the United States to the North Pole. I had heard it was very cold, and people lived in igloos. I couldn't understand why we had to leave our beautiful life for a frigid dot on a map. I loved to go on journeys, but only if at the end I could return to my own home.

There had not been much time to say goodbyes. In search of closure, I reminisced about the world I was about to leave behind: playing cops and robbers with my hyperactive brother in our backyard; adoring grandparents, affectionate aunts and uncles, generous and loyal family friends, irritating but indispensable cousins; an endless stream of guests and visitors, parties and celebrations filled with delicious meals and sweets, delightful gifts and games. It couldn't get any better.

There were also the family vacations: hiking under the snow-capped peaks of the Alborz Mountains north of the bustling city, building sandcastles by the Caspian Sea in the lush Mazandaran Province, and the ten-hour road trip to the fabled city of Shiraz, during which my brother and I wrestled non-stop in the back seat, driving our parents insane. There were also my favourite toys. What I missed most was the Märklin model railroad set that my parents had brought back from a trip to Europe with my uncle, Dr. Naïmi. The toy trains were amazingly detailed; I would play with them for hours, intrigued by distant voyages into the unknown. And then there was my beautiful honey-coloured Persian cat, Asal. Leaving her behind was the hardest of all.

The idyllic family orchard in Karaj was the site of my best memories. It was our weekend retreat, a bucolic paradise, with generous fruit trees and limpid streams; a respite from the terrible smog and unbearable noise of Tehran. On a hot summer day, our exhausted parents would repose in the cool shade of the giant cherry trees, lulled by the soothing sound of flowing water, and my rowdy cousins would dutifully disrupt their tranquility by being as obnoxious as possible. The mischief took a discernible turn for the worse after we watched Bruce Lee's *Enter the Dragon*. Henceforth, the songbirds of the orchard were drowned out by random kung fu screams as we practised leaping tiger kicks on each other, our parents begging us to stop before somebody got hurt.

Of all the trees in the orchard, my favourite was an old mulberry tree. Its majestic arms danced gently in the wind, writing mysterious poems in the sky. I would sit on its mighty branches with my best friend, a girl named Sepideh, lost in conversation about nothing in particular. The gentle breeze caressed the leaves as our minds drifted to distant places, oblivious that the coming storm would rip out our roots from this ancient land.

The Iran that I knew was a place of prosperity. I lived an enchanting life, sheltered from the world beyond the walls of my home. Ours was an ancient, complex, and multi-layered country, full of contradictions. My early childhood coincided with a period of profound transformation. In 1973, the shah of Iran had persuaded the OPEC petroleum cartel to dramatically increase the price of oil. The petrodollars were pouring in, transforming the country at a bewildering pace. This new wealth financed the Pahlavi monarchy's ambitious plans for rapid modernization, to restore the past glory of the 2,500-year-old Persian Empire.

This intense fusion of money and technology brought with it new, unimaginable possibilities. For one thing, it dramatically improved the living standards of Iranians. There was a significant increase in literacy rates, public health, and life expectancy. My parents' generation had lived through a terrible famine during the Anglo-Soviet occupation of the Second World War. My paternal grandmother had sold her jewellery to feed her children. My father had lost half of his infant siblings to typhoid and other now-curable diseases. Their lives had been suddenly thrust from survival to prosperity. There was a building boom, with new roads and airports, schools and hospitals, automobile factories and electric dams. Having struggled as a starving student at the University of Tehran, my father had become a much-sought-after engineer. Now he spent most of his time in the wilderness, building the infrastructure that would accelerate his country's progress, while giving his young family the life he never had.

Another side of this rapid modernization was a profound transformation of cultural values. Amidst new riches, the affluent, educated elites of Tehran developed a hedonistic lifestyle. Young Iranian couples sipped whiskey in smoke-filled cabarets, shedding sentimental tears to the melancholic songs of Googoosh, Iran's answer to Édith Piaf. Mini-jupes and shag haircuts were all the rage for sophisticated women, while stylish men sported bell-bottom pants with horseshoe moustaches and sideburns. The bustling city, replete with fashionable nightclubs and casinos, became known as the "Paris of the East." It was a glamorous and happening place, frequented by the likes of Frank Sinatra and Tom Jones.

Not everybody welcomed these changes. The privileged classes were so intoxicated with Western consumerism that one incensed intellectual coined the term "Westoxication" to describe their blind imitation of foreign materialistic cultures. To the south of Tehran, the combination of rising inequality and ostentatious displays of wealth by the nouveaux riches created resentment among the working poor. Marxist movements of various stripes clamoured against oppression and some even resorted to violence. More significant, however, was the increasing alienation of the traditional circles in both the bazaar and the mosque. The historic Grand Bazaar in central Tehran was much more than a shopping mall. It was a meeting place where different social classes mingled, debating politics and exchanging gossip. Within this conservative community, merchants were expected to be as pious as they were shrewd. Symbols of religious devotion were conspicuously displayed to buttress a reputation for moral virtue. The Islamic clerics, known as the *ulama*, had great influence among the traditional bazaars. This was an alliance that would become a central force in the overthrow of the shah, and the religious persecution that would push us into exile.

My family belonged to the Bahá'í religious minority. We went about our lives like anyone else, but we were always aware of our vulnerable situation. The Bahá'í faith first emerged in nineteenth-century Iran. In a time of great ferment, its vision of a world-embracing civilization, combined with an egalitarian ethos and modern mysticism, appealed both to messianic expectations and reformist aspirations. Its ideal of democratizing spiritual knowledge, free from control of the clergy, attracted a significant following. The rapid spread of this revolutionary theology became an existential threat to the conservative clerical establishment. The *ulama* branded the Bahá'ís as "apostates" and incited ruthless massacres against them. By the time of my childhood in the 1970s, the shah tolerated the Bahá'ís because of his need for international legitimacy. But being the traditional scapegoats in Iran, we knew that any political turmoil would not end well for us. Even as a child,

I understood our precarious existence; that there were people who wanted to harm us.

Like elsewhere in the Middle East, Iran was a highly complex ancient civilization with deeply rooted identities. My classmates were mostly Muslim, but they were also Armenian, Assyrian, Jewish, and Zoroastrian. In a tightly knit, traditional society, we were defined first and foremost by our communal belonging, but as children we had other priorities. Playing sports in the schoolyard, we hardly cared about the religion of our teammates.

My first encounter with the idea of religious tolerance was learning ancient history at school. All Iranian children read about the first Persian emperor, Cyrus the Great, and the glorious civilization based in Persepolis that stretched from the Balkans to Central Asia. The most celebrated symbol of this imperial past was the Cyrus Cylinder from circa 539 B.C. It was a clay tablet written in Babylonian cuneiform, discovered in 1879 during an excavation in Mesopotamia for the British Museum. It was arguably the first declaration of human rights in history.

Having defeated the Babylonian king, Cyrus called for the repatriation of displaced peoples and the restoration of their temples. Although a Zoroastrian, the emperor proclaimed that his new subjects could worship the god of their choice, rather than the god of their conqueror. This proclamation was revolutionary by the standards of antiquity. It signalled a new beginning for the ancient Near East. Such was its historical legacy that the Cyrus Cylinder influenced the American Declaration of Independence in 1776. Thomas Jefferson had studied it with admiration in *Cyropaedia*, written by Xenophon, a contemporary of Socrates. Many years later, in university, I would learn that human rights was a Western idea, a unique product of the European Enlightenment.

The Hebrew Bible also praised Cyrus profusely, as the deliverer of the exiled and enslaved Jewish people. Following the Persian conquest of Babylonia, he decreed that the Jews be allowed to return to the Holy Land and even helped them rebuild the Temple in Jerusalem. Many Persian Jews chose to stay, which profoundly shaped Iranian history. A notable instance was the marriage of the Persian king Xerxes I to the Jewish queen Esther. This fateful union helped foil the evil plot of Haman, the king's minister, to exterminate the Jews. Thereafter, Esther's uncle Mordecai became the prime minister.

For centuries this episode of deliverance has been celebrated by the holiday of Purim. Imagine that, Iran with a Jewish prime minister!

Today, in the city of Hamadan, where my father was born, the tomb of Esther and Mordecai remains a place of pilgrimage for Iran's dwindling Jewish community. My paternal ancestors traced their lineage to those Jews that remained in Persia thanks to Cyrus's policy of religious tolerance. Twenty-five hundred years later, in the modern world, the Islamic Republic of Iran's religious persecution would turn their descendants into refugees and exiles.

The myth of 2,500 years of historic continuity, combined with Iran's emergence as the leading regional power, gave the Pahlavi monarchy an air of invincibility. Every morning at school, we would sing "Long Live the King of Kings!" and salute the imperial flag. The photos of the shah, the empress, and the crown prince decorated all our textbooks and classrooms. There were regular shows of military might, the Imperial Guards parading in their regal uniforms while the most advanced American fighter jets flew overhead. The shah was the father of a proud and prosperous nation. But just beneath the surface, there was another reality. The benevolent despotism was maintained by a shadowy secret police. The SAVAK, as it was known, had eyes and ears everywhere. It repressed all dissent, ruling through fear.

Against the looming threat of Soviet expansionism, one of the regime's principal foes was communism. In fact, in 1946, the occupying Red Army had attempted to annex northwest Iran by supporting local pro-Soviet insurgents. This was one of the earliest episodes of the Cold War, two years before the Berlin blockade of 1948. It was also one of the first debates before the UN Security Council. It was only after intense diplomatic pressure by the Americans that the Soviets withdrew, restoring Iran's territorial integrity.

The relationship between Iran and the West was complex. During the Great Game of the nineteenth century, the Persian Empire had been divided into spheres of influence between the competing British and Russian Empires. For the British, Persia, like Afghanistan, was a buffer zone to protect British India, the "jewel in the crown" of the Empire, from Russian ambitions. The foreign domination of Iran, together with the extravagance of the Qajar monarchy, created contempt and opposition. By 1906, there was a Constitutional Revolution. A parliament was elected and the shah placed under the rule of law. Iran had become a constitutional monarchy. This didn't last long. The imperial powers preferred a corrupt and docile monarchy, rather than a viable democracy, so they could exploit the country with a free hand. By 1907, an Anglo-Russian Agreement had divided Iran into spheres of influence. The following year, in 1908, the parliament was bombarded by pro-monarchist military forces with British and Russian support. A factor that helped the imperial powers was the conflict between modern liberals and religious clerics on whether secular laws should prevail over the Sharia. This power struggle, between tradition and progress, kept the country weak and divided.

It was also in 1908 that Iran's geopolitical significance changed dramatically after the first major oil discovery. With rapid industrialization in Europe, oil had become a vital commodity. Soon after, the Anglo-Persian Oil Company was established. It would be renamed British Petroleum in later years. The company made massive profits in Iran. But the Iranian people received only a small fraction of revenues. Even the Iranian oil workers, in the sweltering heat of Abadan, on the Persian Gulf, lived in horrible conditions while their British bosses lived in luxury. In 1950, news emerged that the Americans had agreed to a fifty-fifty profit split with Saudi Arabia's Aramco. By 1951, the popular anger in Iran had boiled over. The Iranian parliament voted to nationalize the Anglo-Iranian Oil Company, as Anglo-Persian was then called. Their nationalist cause found a champion in the incorruptible prime minister, Mohammad Mossadegh, a Swiss-educated scholar of international law.

In 1951, faced with a British naval blockade and threats of war, Mossadegh visited New York to defend Iran at the UN Security Council. He pointed out that Britain's profits from Iranian oil in 1950 alone had been greater than what it paid Iran over the preceding half century. He then went on to defend Iran before the International Court of Justice at The Hague. With India's independence in 1947 signalling the end of the colonial period, the Anglo-Iranian affair became one of the first assertions of sovereignty by a developing nation over its natural wealth and resources.

In Washington, the Iranian prime minister had received a cordial welcome from President Truman. The American leader had opposed British prime minister Winston Churchill's calls for intervention against Iran. Mossadegh also visited the

Liberty Bell in Philadelphia. There, he drew parallels between the American Revolution and Iran's resistance against British imperialism. Inspired by his idealism, some Americans called him the "Iranian George Washington." In fact, he was so popular that *Time* magazine selected him as the 1951 "Man of the Year." It was a world away from the chants of "Death to America" and the clash of civilizations narrative that would emerge in the years that followed.

By 1953, when Dwight Eisenhower had become president, America had assumed a more hawkish foreign policy aimed at Soviet containment. Circumstances in Iran had also changed. There was increasing economic turmoil and political instability because of the British blockade of Iranian ports. The British had finally persuaded the Americans that Mossadegh should be overthrown to avoid a communist takeover. Soon, the secret Operation Ajax would succeed in ousting him through mob violence by hired thugs and bribery of senior military officers. It would become the first of many American *coups d'état* around the world. Cynical foreign meddling would become a constant feature of the Cold War. It was called "keeping the world safe for democracy," or at least safe for corporate capitalism.

In their campaign of subversion, the CIA agents in Iran could count on the help of influential religious clerics to incite the traditional masses. The *ulama* feared Mossadegh more than they feared the young and inexperienced shah, Mohammad Reza Pahlavi. A charismatic nationalist leader who would replace the Sharia with secular laws was a harbinger of their rapid demise. Given the historic relationship between state and religion under the monarchy, they could more easily maintain their traditional powers under the shah — or so they thought at the time.

By 1954, Mossadegh was a prisoner in solitary confinement. A consortium of American oil companies had concluded a commercial deal with the shah, who had returned from a brief exile in Italy. Iran's democratic spring had come to an abrupt end. In 1955, Iran joined the controversial Baghdad Pact, a regional military alliance with the British. To gain the support of the religious clerics, the Bahá'ís were offered as low-cost pawns to appease popular anger. During the holy month of Ramadan, the forty-day fasting period for Muslims, a preacher by the name of Sheikh Falsafi, who had supported the overthrow of Mossadegh, made a series of incendiary anti-Bahá'í sermons that were broadcast on

the national radio. What followed was mob violence by fanatics who unleashed their fury against
the Bahá'ís. In one instance, in a village outside the
city of Yazd, seven people were hacked to pieces
with spades and axes. The Bahá'í National Centre
in Tehran was also demolished, with the help of
senior military officials, in the presence of Falsafi.
The leading Islamic clerics, known as ayatollahs,
sent congratulatory messages to the shah. One of
the allies of Falsafi was a fanatical cleric named
Ruhollah Khomeini.

Following the 1953 *coup d'état*, a period of
authoritarian rule and rapid modernization began.
A decade later, in 1963, the shah announced the
White Revolution, aimed at land reform, literacy,
the right of women to vote, and the right of religious minorities to hold public office. Instead of
welcoming these measures, the conservative clerics responded with consternation. They feared that
social modernization would undermine their traditional powers. Khomeini, in particular, issued a
declaration from the holy city of Qom, denouncing the White Revolution as an attack on Islam.
He condemned the shah as a puppet of the U.S.
and Israel. He warned that the Jews were taking
over the country and castigated the Bahá'ís as a

"secretive organization" collaborating with SAVAK and the Zionists. Angry mobs desecrated the Bahá'í cemetery in Tehran. Thousands poured onto the streets in violent riots, chanting, "Death to the dictator."

By 1964, the shah had exiled Khomeini to Iraq. In 1967, the ageing Mossadegh died in his modest home, where he had been under house arrest. By then, under the shadow of Anglo-American geopolitics and commercial interests, autocratic modernism imposed from above was on a collision course with reactionary fanaticism from below. In between these two opposing forces, secular democracy became the biggest casualty. Without an open society, politics went underground. Western-educated nationalists and Marxists plotted to overthrow the shah. But most significant was the retreat of grassroots politics into the bazaars and mosques of Iran, where it would re-emerge in the 1979 revolution. The masses understood the familiar language of Islam better than the foreign ideologies of Europe. An opportunity for Iran's genuine progress had been squandered. The cynical statesmanship and corporate greed of men a world away had changed the destiny of a nation, and with it, the course of many lives.

WELCOME TO CANADA

After a long and exhausting journey, our flight finally arrived in Toronto. "Welcome to Canada," the sign at the airport declared; "Bienvenue au Canada." As the immigration officer finished stamping our passports, my excitement became palpable. The anticipation of new adventures tempered my nostalgia for Iran. My father had preferred Canada to the United States, where other relatives had gone. He kept on talking about this Frenchman named "Pierre Trudeau" who stood up to the Americans, who wouldn't be pushed around. I had quickly learned, even prior to my arrival, that part of being Canadian was not to be American.

In my new home, I found a new and fascinating world. I was ecstatic that television was in colour. Prior to that, I had only seen John Wayne in black and white. I had no idea that, in addition to Persian, he also spoke English, fluently. What is more, television was not limited to a single channel with those boring soap operas that made my grandmother cry. There was so much to choose from; I didn't know where to start. Armed with a remote control and multiple channels, I sat on the couch, a devotee of endless entertainment, filled with remorse at those wasted years before I discovered Bugs Bunny.

Despite these precious liberties, I found the Canadians somewhat curious. For one thing, they were obsessed with this bizarre game called ice hockey. It involved men with missing teeth chasing a rubber disk, after which they would take off their gloves and punch each other senseless. I also failed to understand why Canadians scrupulously obeyed traffic regulations. It was simply unnatural. There was a certain normative clarity to the survival of the fittest in the chaotic streets of Tehran. The size of the vehicle determined who had right of way. The Canadian shopping malls were also impressive and luxurious, but the stubborn cashiers refused to haggle over the price of merchandise.

I realized further that Canadians were totally ignorant of *taarof*, the Persian ritual of excessive politeness. This fundamental rule of social etiquette was quite simple: you communicate your intention to others by never saying what you actually mean. It was based on the logical proposition that "no" means "yes." If your host offered you food, you as the civilized guest must refuse three times, and they in turn must insist three times, after which you could reluctantly accept and eat like a virtuous barbarian. This social practice reflected the ancient Persian wisdom that the shortest distance between two points is a labyrinth. When my Canadian friend's mother offered me a sandwich for the first time, I said, "No thank you," with smug self-satisfaction at my exemplary politeness. She was hardly impressed. There was no second or third offering; just a long, uncomfortable silence. I went hungry that day. It was a rude introduction to the art of cultural adaptation.

My comparative methodology also extended to school discipline. I was told, much to my pleasant surprise, that teachers in Canada were not allowed to strike their pupils, even if they were serial troublemakers. It was a crucial fact that I intended to exploit to my maximum advantage. I couldn't wait for the first day of school.

When the big day finally arrived, I woke up with a mixture of dread and delight. I was excited to start this new chapter of my life, but equally apprehensive about walking into the unknown. I meticulously combed my hair and put on my trendiest clothes. I was eager to leave a good impression. I had learned the word "cool" on television from a certain Arthur Fonzarelli in an addictive series called *Happy Days*. I wasn't sure exactly what it meant, but I was sure that I wanted to be cool. In my quest for instant popularity, I had brought a small American football as a bargaining chip. It was a major cultural concession, because balls were meant to be round. I couldn't understand why it was shaped like an eggplant. With these preparations, I embarked on my anthropological expedition. I was finally ready to meet Canadian children in their natural habitat.

Upon arriving at Harrison Public School, I noticed that I was one of only two brown children. I was visibly different. The Canada of the 1970s was not yet a multicultural society, at least as we understand that idea today. There were very few non-Europeans in those days. The mass exodus of Iranians, the emergence of "Tehranto," was still some time away. In those days, I was genuinely exotic!

My first day at school had been awkward. After my mother dropped me off, I couldn't find anyone that was willing to talk with me. I was ready to deliver my English phrases in pellucid prose, but first I needed an audience. Later, I sat in the classroom attentively. I could barely understand what the teacher was saying, but I nodded my head knowingly to impress my classmates. When I saw what the other children were wearing, I realized that my clothing and hairstyle were definitely not cool. Suddenly, the recess bell rang and the children rushed out to play in the schoolyard. I decided to seize the opportunity to win friends by strategically deploying my newly purchased football.

I looked around and saw a group of boys. I approached and anxiously introduced myself with halting English: "My name is Payam. Do you want to play with me?" Finally, my adventure was about to begin. But things didn't go according to plan. At first they looked at me with curiosity. Then they laughed at me, imitating my exaggerated accent and pointing at my clothing. They said things I couldn't understand, but I knew they were being mean. One of them took my football and started calling me names. With the few words I knew, I demanded that he return it. It was not a wise move. Soon the boys encircled me, yelling what sounded like profanities. They were itching for a fight. This was not the welcome I had expected. It sucked to be an immigrant!

I tried to leave the hostile circle that was closing in. I couldn't understand what I had done to deserve this. Suddenly, one of the boys blocked my exit. He had clenched fists, his stare full of hatred. Before

I could say anything, he punched me in the face, really hard. I held my mouth with both hands, in shock. A stream of blood flowed through my fingers onto my brand new shirt. They were laughing, taunting me with cries of "Paki, go home." I held back my tears, in defiance. My mind drifted to that beautiful mulberry tree back in Iran, dancing in the wind in our beautiful orchard. "Go home," the boys howled again and again. I wanted nothing more; but my home was gone.

THE PRISON OF IDENTITY

Exile is a longing to belong. It is an emotional space that we often confuse with a physical place. I was told that Canada is the promised land, but I pined for Iran. From the vantage point of schoolyard politics, I was a despised minority in Canada. I was not yet aware that I was a much more despised minority in Iran. There was seemingly no escape from this prison of identity. Confined by its oppressive walls, the best I could do was to retreat inside of myself and find comfort in romanticized memories, a stubborn clinging to an increasingly perfect past.

In the months that followed, I learned the art of feigning cultural assimilation in order to survive. It was like a ruse of war for a badly outnumbered army of one, facing daily brawls and racist slurs. I quickly learned that I must not only speak two different languages, but also assume two different identities — I was Iranian at home, Canadian at school — to the point where I no longer knew which of the two was my true self. Becoming Canadian was not a magic moment. It was a work in progress.

My exoticization as the oriental "other" was not always ill-intentioned. Children of that generation had a more limited cultural horizon for making sense of difference. Some imagined me as a curious creature out of *One Thousand and One Nights*. Thanks to bedtime stories and television, some could relate to these ancient tales from the Golden Age of Islamic civilization: "Aladdin's Wonderful Lamp," "Ali Baba and the Forty Thieves," "The Seven Voyages of Sinbad the Sailor." These were the images I had to play with to please an otherwise hostile audience. I willingly played the role of storyteller to entertain them, like a precocious Scheherazade fighting for her life. It was annoying to explain that we had no camels in our garage or harem in the basement, but I took great pleasure in almost convincing a gullible classmate that we had a real flying carpet at home. I would learn in later years that such stereotyping was not "politically correct." But making friends by pretending to be a Disney cartoon character was far better than apologizing for hostage-taking and suicide bombing.

As my school years came to a close, the all-purpose pejorative "Paki" label was giving way to a more sophisticated taxonomy of bigotry. Thanks to the simplistic sound bites and sensational images that passed as the evening news, Arabs and Iranians were emerging in the popular imagination as a barbaric race of crazed terrorists. Instead of getting better, the ordeal of guilt by association was getting worse. It didn't matter that we were actually the biggest victims of those same bearded fanatics appearing on their television screens, or that Western leaders had sabotaged secular democracy in our countries. Our story was irrelevant. We were merely a blank screen on which others projected their psychological needs, of either scorn or of pity.

Whether in the schoolyard or in global politics, the clash of civilizations is a convenient escape from the visceral fear of embracing others. The bully and the bigot, the tyrant and the terrorist, need to inflict pain on others to escape their own pain. Connecting with others renders us vulnerable; accepting differences challenges our way of life. The cowardly way out is to make enemies rather than doing the hard work of learning and growing. Why struggle to discover a deeper identity when hatred is within easy reach?

For much of history, Islamic civilization has been the enduring "other" of the Western world, and Western civilization the enduring "other" of the Islamic world. But the reality today is that the irresistible forces of globalization, the inexorable expansion of our collective consciousness, is infusing diverse peoples with an ever broader sense of belonging. That is exactly why the extremists are panicking. In these times of accelerating change, they need each other more than ever. The white crusaders and the wicked jihadists are inseparable dancing partners, entangled in an awkward tango of mutual disgust. Whether they like it or not, identities are not fossils in a museum. They are inherently dynamic, constantly shaping and being shaped by others, in a never-ending exchange of perspectives. Amidst intensifying interdependence, parochial identities will invariably give way to a wider loyalty. Then better to negotiate the inevitable by dialogue rather than violence. The xenophobic hissy fit of identity warriors is futile avoidance of a shared future.

Multiculturalism, though, is a messy affair. It is much more than a celebration of colourful costumes and culinary pleasures. Transcending prejudice requires something more than superficial familiarity with those on whom we bestow condescending tolerance. Understanding the multi-layered identities that shape us requires openness to other realms of experience, a willingness to genuinely listen to the stories of those who are foreign to us. We each have a unique path, but when our journeys occasionally converge, we may discover that we also have a shared humanity; that we all suffer, whatever our identity may be. The universality of human rights means that despite our differences, we all deserve to be treated with the same dignity. We should not project demeaning stereotypes on others, portraying them as savages to justify our bigotry. But in celebrating diversity, we should also not become apologists for those that abuse others in the name of tradition.

There is no doubt that human rights are conditioned by cultural context. But claims of cultural relativism as challenges to universality are a different matter. Should we respect torture, intolerance, and misogyny as expressions of diversity? That depends very much on whether we ask the victim or the perpetrator. There may be genuine differences of opinion among and within cultures, but when claims of religious exceptionalism are invoked by authoritarian rulers, they must be treated with great suspicion.

In 1983, as tens of thousands were executed to consolidate Khomeini's totalitarian theocracy, an Iranian diplomat had rebuked condemnation by the UN Human Rights Commission on the grounds that the Islamic Republic "recognized no authority or power but that of Almighty God and no legal tradition apart from Islamic law." It was a cynical sleight of hand, casually conflating Almighty God with the Almighty State. "The Universal Declaration of Human Rights," he claimed, "represented a secular understanding of the Judeo-Christian tradition [that] could not be implemented by Muslims and did not accord with the system of values recognized by the Islamic Republic of Iran." His government, therefore, would "not hesitate to violate its provisions, since it had to choose between violating the divine law of the country and violating secular conventions."

These philosophical musings were hardly about the subordination of the secular to the sacred. The hostility to human rights, justified by allegedly incontestable interpretations of the Sharia, was sectarian subterfuge, a hijacking of the divine for diabolical ends. The Sharia was whatever Iran's rulers wanted it to be so they could stay in power. The toxic fusion of theological obscurantism and populist hatred was modern tyranny dressed in traditional clothes. But growing up as the immigrant child, I couldn't easily deconstruct the intricacies of political Islam for an audience that was at best indifferent, and at worst openly hostile. Being the godless infidel in the East and the camel-driving terrorist in the West, I learned, was quite a predicament.

This prison of identity was particularly ironic because the most important Bahá'í principle I had learned from my parents was the oneness of humankind. Our prophetic figure, Bahá'u'lláh, called for "beholding the entire human race as one soul and one body." One of the first quotes that we memorized in Sunday school was: "The earth is but one country and mankind its citizens."

Another thing we learned was to abandon blind imitation of traditions and to investigate reality on our own unique spiritual journey. In place of obsolete dogma and obscure rituals, our relationship with the mystical universe was defined as a longing for reunion: "Whither can a lover go but to the land of his beloved?" Bahá'u'lláh wrote. "And what seeker findeth rest away from his heart's desire?" We also learned that the ayatollahs should be replaced by elected leaders; that nobody has a monopoly on the truth. Such freedom of transcendent self-discovery, without theological control by clerical intermediaries, was an existential threat to the *ulama*'s business model. Democratization of religious knowledge would make their sophistry redundant; it would undermine their privileged role as meddling mystical middlemen. "Knowledge is a single point," an Islamic tradition said, "but the ignorant have multiplied it."

The Bahá'í view on gender equality was a source of particular anger for clerics like Khomeini. As children we learned that humankind has two wings: the male and the female. The teaching of one of our central figures, Abdu'l-Bahá, was that "so long as these two wings are not equivalent in strength, the bird will not fly." In 1963, when the shah gave Iranian women the right to vote, Khomeini had indignantly warned: "Equality of women and men is Abdu'l-Bahá's choice, and the shah without understanding steps up and declares the equality of women and men . . . compulsory education for all women is Abdu'l-Bahá's vote...our country, our religion is in jeopardy!" Misogyny was integral to the conservative clerics' oppressive cult of control. Calls for gender equality by the Bahá'ís was an intolerable heresy within a heresy.

During the nineteenth century, the rapid spread of revolutionary Bahá'í ideals was alarming for both the Qajar monarchy and the *ulama*. It undermined the political absolutism founded on Iran's core Shia Islamic identity. The British statesman George Curzon wrote in 1892 that what he described as "a creed of charity" and "common humanity" that espoused "freedom from bigotry" and "friendliness even to Christians" now had nearly a million followers. He observed that "they are to be found in every walk of life, from the ministers and nobles of the Court to the scavenger or the groom, not the least arena of their activity being the [Muslim] priesthood itself."

It was in the same year that the profligate Persian king Nasir al-din Shah was forced to cancel a British tobacco concession that undermined local producers, following a nationalist revolt by the *ulama* and bazaari merchants. Under these circumstances, the monarchy and Islamic clerics found common cause in scapegoating Bahá'ís as subversive foreign apostates. Popular rage and mob violence was unleashed by portraying them as a combination Anglo-Russian conspiracy and religious heresy — a fusion of every conceivable evil that must be destroyed by all means.

That was the other thing that we learned as Bahá'í children growing up in Iran; that our immediate ancestors were survivors of terrible pogroms. One historical episode that was etched into our minds was the so-called martyrs of Yazd, though at our tender age, we were spared the gruesome details. In the late nineteenth century, when the declining Persian Empire was mired in conflict and chaos, political opportunists used anti-Bahá'í hatred to increase their power and influence. One of these was Sheikh Najafi, an ambitious religious leader who was known as "son of the wolf" for his treachery. Whenever it suited his purposes, he accused his opponents in the constitutionalist movement of being Bahá'í heretics. He flaunted his religious zeal by inflammatory sermons, telling his followers that killing Bahá'í apostates was a religious duty that would bring divine blessings.

In the summer of 1903, violent mobs attacked Bahá'ís in the city of Yazd, killing countless people with what can only be described as savage cruelty.

A contemporaneous account provided a vivid glimpse of the horrors of this genocide:

> A great multitude, armed with swords and daggers, invaded the house of a believer, a tinsmith by trade, beat his wife and babes, broke their household utensils, smashed the furniture and demolished their home. Then, arresting the helpless father, they paraded him through the streets until they arrived at a butcher's shop, where they set on him with meat axes . . . [H]e lay bleeding and motionless.

Not even the children were spared:

> During this time, his little son, eleven years old, was at school. His school fellows, being urged by their teacher, attacked this innocent lad . . . [and] tortured that dear boy, beating him with sticks, stabbing him with penknives, picking him with needles and awls in such a manner that the pen is unable to portray it, tongue and lips cannot utter it, nor can heart or mind imagine it.

The mourning mother too was treated with appalling cruelty:

The mother of that dearly loved boy, seeing her martyred son, her slain husband and her brother, all covered with blood and dust, began to weep and lament over their condition, and especially that of the child ... [S]he was beaten into insensibility by the human vultures surrounding her.

In 1903, my great-grandmother Jamaliye lived in this same city of Yazd. She came from a Muslim background, but her family had become Bahá'ís. At the time, she was pregnant with her first child. A mob ransacked her home and threw her off the balcony from a great height. She was taken for dead, but miraculously survived. At night, under cover of dark, her husband spirited her away to exile in tsarist Russia, where they could enjoy religious freedom. Because of her grave injuries, she had a miscarriage. But she was meant to live. In 1910, she gave birth to my maternal grandmother, Zuhuriye, in Ashgabat, the "City of Love," on the Russian frontier with Persia.

These astonishing stories from my childhood were part of a remote heroic past, seemingly unconnected with the comfortable lives we enjoyed in modern, prosperous Tehran. They were things we would memorize in Sunday school to keep our

parents happy. History was a series of facts, inci-
dents, and personalities placed in a clear sequential
order, with obvious moral lessons: the tribulation
of ancestors from a distant past. History was not
yet a lived experience.

REVOLUTIONARY ILLUSIONS

As I tried to fit into Canadian society as an adolescent immigrant, religious persecution was the
last thing on my mind. My human rights concerns
revolved around the twin scourges of facial acne
and dental braces, and trying to forget that awkward slow song at my first school dance, hanging
off a much taller girl named Leanne on my tippy
toes. I had come to learn the hard way that recit-
ing mystical poetry was not a suitable pickup line.
So I decided to dump the nerdish Rumi in favour
of AC/DC; it was the patriotic Canadian thing to
do, I thought at the time. Despite my natural talent
at playing air guitar, my career as a heavy metal
enthusiast was short-lived. When asked about my
refusal to embellish the back of my jean jacket
with a stylish marijuana leaf, I had to admit it was
because my parents would permanently disown

me. My credibility as a rebellious bad boy was forever destroyed. I had no choice but to assume the
default ethnic disco look. What followed were heinous fashion crimes, an aesthetic atrocity in the
sight of all decent people.

In those days, disco music was morphing into
house music, presaging the days of hip hop and
rap. Angry songs full of obscene words were especially the rage. Fortunately, our elders didn't speak
enough English to understand the expletives. We
would play these songs at family gatherings and
laugh hysterically as they merrily clapped to the
wicked rhythm. Some of them would even sing
along, parroting the vulgar words with a strong
Persian accent! We were truly awful. But one of
the advantages of being a semi-assimilated immigrant was that you could poke fun at those who
were even less assimilated.

My quest to become a full-fledged Canadian was
progressing in fits and starts. But 1980 was a year
of momentous significance. It was in that year that
I found myself standing before a judge, in my best
suit and tie, with a room full of strangers. In one
voice, but diverse accents, we pledged allegiance to
the British queen and to the laws of Canada. We
were now officially citizens. The ceremony filled

IN SEARCH OF A BETTER WORLD

me with patriotic sentiments. But just as I celebrated my new status, the home that I once knew was about to be destroyed.

On February 1, 1979, an Air France 747 landed in Tehran's Mehrabad International Airport. It was carrying Khomeini on his triumphant return after fifteen years of exile in Iraq. For the religious masses, it was a messianic return. As the ayatollah emerged from the airplane, millions of jubilant Iranians celebrated in the streets. They imagined his arrival as their long-awaited deliverance: the advent of a just and democratic future. Amidst revolutionary frenzy, the people voted for an Islamic Constitution. Dispensing with the "quietist" Shia tradition that for centuries separated state and religion, it embraced Khomeini's vision of political salvation through absolutist Islamic rule: the totalitarian theocracy that he had promoted throughout his years of exile.

In those days, the Islamic revolutionaries were the darlings of the political left. After meeting Khomeini in Paris, where he spent his last days of exile, the renowned French intellectual Michel Foucault enthusiastically described the ayatollah's utopian ideology as "This thing whose possibility we have forgotten since the Renaissance and the great crisis of Christianity, a political spirituality." Amidst the feverish *tiers-mondisme* of the time, the charismatic cleric had become the Iranian incarnation of Mahatma Gandhi — a fashionable image quickly abandoned once he assumed power and began his campaign of mass murder. The flirtation of radical Western intellectuals with Khomeinism would soon become a drunken one-night stand that was best forgotten. The Iranian people didn't have the same luxury; they couldn't just press the delete button and move on to the next intellectual project. Consumed by revolutionary euphoria, they hadn't quite understood the kind of "liberation" they had endorsed in the referendum that anointed Khomeini as the "Supreme Leader."

Aside from the oracles of the academy, Western statesmen were equally misguided in their appreciation of the situation. While still in Paris, Khomeini feared American support for a military takeover in Iran. On January 27, 1979, just a few days before his return to Tehran, he sent a secret message to reassure Washington: "You will see we are not in any particular animosity with the Americans," he said. The Islamic Republic will be "a humanitarian one, which will benefit the cause of peace and tranquility for all mankind." In those days, Islamic populism had a certain appeal among American policy-makers; it was after all a grass-roots anti-communist ideology. In fact, unleashing jihadist fury against the Soviets in the Islamic "arc of crisis" surrounding Central Asia was endorsed as a brilliant strategy. "That we but teach bloody instructions," Shakespeare wrote in *Macbeth*, "which, being taught, return to plague the inventor."

At first, the understanding among the broad revolutionary movement was that an inclusive political coalition would rule the Islamic Republic, while Khomeini would be a religious figurehead, a spiritual guide for the masses. But Khomeini had a different idea in mind. Within days of his return, he began the first of what would become many thousands of summary executions before the notorious Islamic Revolutionary Courts. The findings of guilt were based on vague Sharia law charges, such as "warring against God," "sowing corruption on earth," or "insulting Islam." The executions were promptly carried out by his sadistic chief executioner, Sadegh Khalkhali, otherwise known as the "hanging judge." In his memoirs, Khalkhali stated his only regret: "There were many more that deserved to be killed but I could not get my hands on them." Khomeini dismissed fair trials as a

"Western absurdity." He famously said, "Criminals should not be tried; they should be killed." In fact, the first executions were carried out on the roof-top of his temporary home in central Tehran, the Refah School for girls.

The early victims of this killing spree were the senior officials of the imperial government. But as Khomeini's totalitarian vision of political Islam was translated into reality, the executions quickly ensnared an ever-widening circle of political groups that stood in his way. In time, the same national-ist and leftist forces that had been his erstwhile revolutionary allies would also become the object of his murderous wrath. He would even persecute eminent orthodox Islamic clerics who opposed the merger of state and religion, consistent with the Shia tradition. This revolution, like others, would devour its own children.

As terrible as things were, they would soon take a dramatic turn for the worse. On September 22, 1980, Iraqi president Saddam Hussein invaded Iran, starting a catastrophic eight-year war that would claim an estimated one million lives. What followed was a long and ugly campaign of trench warfare, with waves of soldiers slaughtered for triv-ial territorial gains. The conflict was reminiscent of the horrors of the First World War, complete with excruciating deaths by chemical weapons and poison gas. It would eventually escalate into a "War of Cities," with air raids and ballistic missiles targeting urban centres like Tehran and Baghdad. The Iran-Iraq war would only come to an end when the so-called Tanker War in the Persian Gulf threatened Western oil supplies.

By 1982, the unexpectedly strong Iranian resistance had reversed Iraq's military fortunes. Iranian territory was liberated, and Saddam called for a ceasefire. But it served Khomeini's purposes to continue what he now portrayed as a "Holy War" to galvanize his radical ideology and export the revolution. Just as Saddam appealed to Arab nationalism against the "Aryan" Persians, Khomeini invoked Shia fury against the "godless" secular Baathists. Meanwhile, just as Khomeini equated Zionism with a "cancerous tumour," the Islamic Republic bought weapons from Israel, with whom it shared Saddam as a common enemy. This Faustian pact gave new meaning to the expression "politics makes strange bedfellows." But things would get even more complicated.

By 1983, fearful of an Iranian victory, President Ronald Reagan dispatched a special envoy to meet

Saddam in Baghdad. His mission was to offer American support in the war. That emissary was a man named Donald Rumsfeld. Twenty years later, in 2003, he would play a central role as the U.S. secretary of defence in the ill-conceived invasion that would overthrow Saddam Hussein, give Iran its long-sought Shia stronghold in Iraq, fuel sectarian warfare with the Sunni, and help create the monstrous Islamic State in Iraq and Syria (ISIS). It was a notable instance of geopolitical calculations gone wrong, a strategy of playing with matches in a room full of explosives and hoping for the best.

One of the enduring images of the Iran-Iraq war that shocked me most was that of child soldiers my own age. Thousands were recruited in "martyr's brigades" and sent to the front lines as cannon fodder and human minesweepers. In order to attract more volunteers, those killed were glorified as war heroes who had gone to paradise. Khomeini celebrated their sacrifice to help recruit more children. "Our leader," he said, "is that thirteen-year-old child who threw himself with his little heart against the enemy." He didn't mind sacrificing children, so long as they weren't his own.

By 1988, the once-thriving Iranian nation was devastated and traumatized; the war had become too costly to continue. Khomeini was forced to accept UN Security Council Resolution 598, which imposed a ceasefire on the parties. Ending the war, he said, was "worse than drinking poison." Having failed to defeat Saddam, he unleashed his fury against his domestic opponents. He issued a fatwa calling for the mass execution of leftist political prisoners with "revolutionary rage and rancour." Within a few days, an estimated five thousand people were put to death. They were secretly dumped in mass graves in the Khavaran cemetery, on the outskirts of southern Tehran.

The mothers that spontaneously gathered in that desolate spot to mourn their children became known as the Mothers of Khavaran. Like the Mothers of the Plaza de Mayo who defied the Argentinian military junta, they would become heroic symbols of the human rights movement. A mother who has lost her child has nothing else to lose. She will stop at nothing to demand justice. Instead of being punished, the members of the so-called death commissions that sent their children to the gallows were rewarded with promotions as ministers of justice and judges of the Supreme Court. Amidst these horrors, the legendary Persian diva Hayedeh sang a song of lament: "Sunny days,

farewell." A dark cloud of gloom had encircled Iran;
it would cast a long shadow, both on world history
and on our personal lives.

LIFE AFTER DEATH

My family's worst fears about the fate of our vulnerable community were beginning to come true.
Khomeini had an obsessive hatred for Bahá'ís. In
the early days of the revolution, he had declared
that this religious minority was in fact a treasonous "political party" created by the British and
Americans to destroy Islam. He condemned Bahá'ís
as heretical "spies" and called for their elimination.
The chief justice of the Revolutionary Courts had
made clear that the punishment for apostasy was
death. The religiously sanctioned murder of our
loved ones was about to begin.

On November 11, 1979, my friend Marjan's
father, Alimorad Davoodi, a respected professor
of philosophy at the University of Tehran, went for
his habitual afternoon walk in Laleh Park, a green
oasis in an urban jungle, not unlike New York's
Central Park. When he failed to return, Marjan
went to that beautiful park, where she had enjoyed

strolls with her adoring father, to search for him. Her efforts were in vain. She would never see him again. Like other prominent Bahá'ís in those early days of the revolution, he had disappeared without a trace.

In the months that followed, as the Islamic Republic's sinister agenda gained momentum, it would no longer hide its plan to exterminate prominent Bahá'ís. One of them was Kamran Samimi, a respected linguist, a fun-loving, gregarious man, and everybody's favourite uncle. He was arrested, along with seven other members of the elected Bahá'í national assembly. After a sham secret trial before a Revolutionary Court, they were all convicted of espionage and sentenced to death. Many years later, we would receive the shocking video of the kangaroo court hearing, which had been smuggled out of prison by a sympathizer. We would finally see in that grainy footage what had transpired in his final hours.

The trial began with an angry mob chanting, "Death to the enemies of Islam." It was a strong hint that this would hardly be a fair trial. What followed was a travesty of justice that would be comical if it weren't so tragic in outcome. With no evidence whatsoever, the prosecutor, seething with hatred, fabricated paranoid conspiracy theories through exceptional leaps in logic. In one remarkable scene, Kamran Samimi was accused of espionage for Israel because he had informed people outside Iran about the mass expulsion of Bahá'í children from schools. His supposed "crime" was reporting the obvious truth of the Islamic Republic's policy of religious persecution, a policy openly proclaimed in Iran through hate propaganda but hidden from the eyes of the international community. When the defendant calmly explained that he was simply relaying what the distressed children had told their parents, the enraged prosecutor silenced him by accusing the children too of being spies.

Shortly after, on December 27, 1981, Kamran Samimi was executed by firing squad. The Iranian officials justified the killings through the usual revolutionary polemics: "These colonial, more specifically Zionist assistants and spies, have fought for years with the rule of Islamic Sharia in our country . . . It is binding upon religious judges and courts to punish them accordingly." When we viewed the video of his trial years later, we assumed that it was filmed in anticipation of a forced confession that would be broadcast on national television. Presumably, it was never shown because it had no propaganda value: the innocent men went to their deaths but never gave in to their torturers.

This is how the world looked in 1980, when I had just become a Canadian citizen. These heartbreaking events ripped me back to my country of origin, shattering innocent childhood memories of what was once an idyllic emotional space called Iran. But the Canadian response was something I will never forget. It was in July of that same year that the House of Commons became the first legislature in the world to adopt a resolution condemning Iran's persecution of the Bahá'ís. Canada also became the first Western country to open its doors to Bahá'í refugees. What was a trickle when we first arrived became a flood as thousands were forced to flee. Amidst the despair and helplessness, this outpouring of sympathy meant so much to our bereaved community. In the years that followed, whenever new waves of refugees would arrive from some conflict halfway around the world, I would always imagine what it felt for them to lose their country, how important it was for them to feel welcome in their new home.

Canada would also go on to play an important role at the UN, sponsoring General Assembly resolutions to expose Iran's appalling human rights record. By 1985, a UN report by Benjamin Whitaker, a British member of the UN Commission on Human Rights, referred to the systematic killing of Iranian Bahá'ís as "genocide," a word I was hearing for the first time, but one that I would revisit many times in my future human rights career. For us, this was a time of intense despair; we felt powerless to save our loved ones, but we had to do what little we could. In pursuit of justice, we appealed to that court of last resort called public opinion. I would later learn from survivors of Iran's prisons that according to some of the hanging judges, many more Bahá'ís would have been killed had it not been for this global outcry. I would grow up understanding that speaking truth to power could be a matter of life and death; that bearing witness and shining the light on injustice, even in the darkest moments, was fundamental to fighting tyranny against overwhelming odds. But that realization was little comfort as news reached us that those near and dear to us had been killed in the torture chambers of Iran.

Firuz Naïmi touched the lives of all who had the good fortune of crossing his path. He was a malaria specialist, a compassionate physician who paid for the medicine of his poor rural clients out of his own pocket. My parents loved him and his spouse dearly. We would always hear stories about their adventures together. Such was their friendship that my parents' courtship had been under their watchful eye. They were surreptitious matchmakers, and thus thrilled at my parents' marriage. The two young couples went on vacations together. I remembered their trip to Europe very well, because they had brought back the best of all gifts: the Märklin model railroad set from Germany, the toy that made me forget all other toys.

Sometime after June 14, 1981, the phone rang at our home in Toronto. It was a long-distance call. It was a habit among Iranians to yell into the speaker during overseas conversations, to ensure that their voice would carry across the ocean. But this was not just any call. I could tell something was wrong. My father listened intensely. He would say "yes" in between long silences as the muffled voice from the other side spoke. When he put the phone down, he was visibly stunned. Our life would never be the same again.

The devastating news was that Dr. Naïmi's mutilated body had been found dumped in the street. A nurse had discovered him in the early morning, in front of the same hospital in Hamadan where he had cured so many patients. His bones were shattered; in places, his body had been ripped open. We surmised from the horrible injuries that he probably died of torture and was shot afterwards just to create the impression of an execution. The last image I had of my beloved uncle was a photograph of his lifeless body on the prison floor, drenched in blood, his sparkling eyes forever shut. I would try to un-see that image for many years. I preferred to remember him by the photographs in my parents' album, from their vacation in Europe, when they laughed without a care in the world.

His fellow prisoners would later recount that on the night of his execution, he and the other Bahá'ís had shaved and put on their best clothes. They stood with defiance and dignity, knowing what awaited them. Some of the inmates had wanted to alert their families, but the courageous men did not want to wake up their loved ones with news of their impending execution. "Let them sleep tonight," they said. "They face heavy burdens tomorrow." In his last will and testament, hastily written on a scrap of paper, Dr. Naïmi said his final farewell to his beloved wife, Akhtar:

My dear companion,
With greetings and affection and gratitude for
our shared life, because they will execute us
tonight and they adamantly refuse to show us
the judgement sentencing us to death, I bid you
and the family farewell and ask that you take
care of my mother...please don't be too troubled when I am gone.

Until the very end, this selfless soul put the welfare of others before his own.

An ambulance had taken the victims to the
mortuary in a procession through the streets of
Hamadan. The many bystanders who saw their
mutilated bodies wept and wailed at the grim sight.
Defying the hate-mongering of the government
and a prohibition on mourning the victims, thousands of Muslims and Bahá'ís joined hands in
bereavement at a moving burial ceremony. They
commemorated these honourable men in a unified
gathering full of transcendent humanity that was
itself the greatest tribute to what they had stood for.
We heard later that the prison guard who tortured
Dr. Naïmi had gone mad and committed suicide
in the holy city of Mashhad. Watching these horrors unfold, being helpless to do anything, was

intensely painful. But the worst was yet to come.

On the surface, Mona was no different than any of my other friends from Sunday school back in Iran. We were of the same age, in the same community, in the same country. But there was a consequential difference between us: one of us moved to Canada, the other remained in Iran; one of us would live, the other would die.

All those who knew Mona were enchanted by her beautiful presence. She was intensely thoughtful and immensely kind. Her remarkable character mingled with her striking appearance: long black hair, glowing olive skin, penetrating green eyes, and a radiant smile. The images of Mona's outwardly conventional life show her doing the things one would expect of any teenager. In one photo, she is holding a guitar; in another she is dancing in a colourful traditional dress; in yet another she is on the shores of that same sea where we spent vacations as children. There is a photo of her father, Yad'u'llah, looking at the youngest of his two daughters in adoration. In another Mona is with her loving mother, Farkhundeh, beside a birthday cake and a bouquet of red and white flowers; and there is yet another photo, this one of her funeral, her grave full of flowers, her grief-stricken family mourning her loss.

Mona lived in Shiraz, a fabled city of beautiful gardens and legendary poets. The most renowned of these was Hafez, who spoke of the transcendent joys of love in a rebuke to religious hypocrisy:

Love is
The funeral pyre
Where I have laid my living body.

All the false notions of myself
That once caused fear, pain,

Have turned to ash
As I neared God.

Alas, in Mona's time, the religious leaders equated divine transcendence with death of the innocent, not the death of the ego that Hafez spoke of.

Mona was a diligent and idealistic high school student. She volunteered her time at the local orphanage. After the expulsion of Bahá'í pupils from elementary schools, she took it upon herself to teach the children at home. But there was also a fearless and fiery side to this otherwise gentle and caring soul. Mona was an outspoken defender of human rights, this in a country where speaking the truth carried grave consequences.

On one occasion, her religious studies teacher had assigned a class essay. The topic was: "The fruit of Islam is freedom of conscience and liberty." Like the other students, she was expected to deferentially repeat revolutionary polemics, glorifying Iran's rulers as just and wise. Instead, she had written a provocative essay on their treachery and hypocrisy.

"Freedom," Mona wrote, "is the most brilliant word," but there have always been "powerful and unjust" men who have resorted to "oppression and tyranny...Why don't you let me be free...to say who I am and what I want? Why don't you give me freedom of speech so that I may write for publications or talk on radio and television about my ideas?...Yes, liberty is a Divine gift, and this gift is for us also, but you don't let us have it...Why don't you push aside that thick veil from your eyes?"

In a Canadian high school, such words from a sixteen-year-old rebel with a cause would have won the praise of her teachers. In Iran, it would cost Mona her life.

On October 23, 1982, at 7:30 p.m., while she was sitting on the couch, studying for her English exam, the Revolutionary Guards raided Mona's home.

Everything was ransacked in search of a pretext to incriminate her in imaginary crimes. They did not find anything, but that hardly mattered. They grabbed her and her father and took them to prison. Her mother recounted begging them to stop: "She's just a child, where are you taking her? Please don't take her." They produced Mona's essay and retorted: "The person who wrote this isn't a child."

For the next eight months, Mona was confined to a filthy prison cell. She endured repeated interrogations and brutal torture. Her tormentors did what they could to extract a confession for fabricated offences such as "misleading children" and "espionage for Israel." But they failed. My dear friend Ruhi Jahanpour was in prison with Mona and the other Bahá'í women in Shiraz. She was among the very few that survived.

Ruhi described the horrible pain of *bastinado*, the whipping of the soles of the feet with cables: "They blindfolded me and tied me to a kind of bed, and then they put my feet there . . . After a few lashes they would pause for a little bit, because they knew our feet were getting numb and they wanted us to feel the pain. They would continuously say things like, 'If you deny your faith, I'll let you go.'"

Following these vicious beatings, the women would be dumped in their cell with swollen bleeding feet, unable to walk. Ruhi explained that the prison guards had been told that this brutality would hasten the apocalyptic return of the messianic Hidden Twelfth Imam awaited by the Shia Muslims: "We have to get rid of all of you to prepare the way for him to come. The only reason that he hasn't come yet is because of you dirty people."

Having failed to break Mona's will through torture, the prison officials used her father to make her more compliant with their demands. When they threatened to flog her in front of him, she calmly said: "I am ready." But her father beseeched her to give them whatever information they wanted. She agreed on the condition that she could embrace her father. In his arms, both full of tears, she confessed: "I was a children's class teacher."

Mona's only "crime" was that the Islamic Republic did not approve of her beliefs. The religious judge who interrogated the prisoners had given the Bahá'ís a stark choice: "Islam or execution." It was an ultimatum to convert or face death. In a final attempt to force Mona to change her mind, the authorities arrested her mother. The judge gave her a blunt warning: "We will kill your husband...

we will kill your daughter . . . and you can go home and mourn their loss." But the more they tortured Mona, and the more they used her parents against her, the more she refused to budge. Having endured so much pain, she was no longer afraid of death.

On March 12, 1983, Mona's father was hanged with several other Bahá'ís in a polo field in Shiraz, their lives extinguished where the Game of Kings was once played. Mona wept in her prison cell, remembering her final farewell, when she had kissed his eyes, knowing that the end had come. It was now her time to say farewell. She knew what awaited her, but she was determined to live her last hours with courage and dignity. Her mother recounted the few minutes they were given to say their final goodbyes:

We walked a little way and then she stopped . . . She looked into my eyes and said, "Mom, you do know that they are going to execute me?"

Suddenly my whole being seemed to be on fire. I didn't want to believe her. I said, "No, my dear daughter, they are going to let you go. You will get married and have children. My greatest wish is to see your children. No, don't even think that."

Mona's mother was in desperate denial; but she could no longer escape the reality of her daughter's impending execution. She recounted how Mona comforted her as they bid farewell for the last time: "I felt so small before the greatness of her soul, as if she were the mother and I the child."

On the evening of June 18, 1983, the head of Adelabad prison called out the name of Mona and nine other Bahá'í women. Under cover of darkness, they were driven in a minibus to the same polo field where her father had been executed. The driver, devastated by what he saw, would later recount what transpired on that terrible, infamous night. The ten women were hanged one by one. Mona was the last to be brought onto the scaffold. She had been forced to watch the agonizing deaths of all her friends. She had endured months of ruthless torture. She had suffered unspeakably at the loss of her father. And now, in her last moments, the merciless men that were about to snuff out her precious life were subjecting her to vicious insults. As Mona stood on the gallows, in a final act of defiance, she smiled at her executioner.

In the early hours of June 19, 1983, sometime between 4 a.m. and 5 a.m., the lifeless bodies of the ten women were brought to the prison morgue.

Later that day, Mrs. Mahmudnizhad came to iden-
tify her daughter. As she stared at Mona's beautiful
face, she hoped that her daughter's eyes would open,
that she would smile at her one last time. As she
stood there, lost in her grief, one of the prison
guards approached her. She braced herself for yet
more vicious insults. But instead, the mighty-
bearded revolutionary broke down in tears: "Please
forgive us. We...have no authority.... Please forgive me. Please." She embraced the prison guard,
calming him like a child.

When the story of Mona's ordeal reached me,
I became dazed and devastated. It took some time
for the reality of her execution to sink in. Here I
was, a Canadian teenager, worried about popularity among my high school friends, while back in
Iran, the youth were being killed for writing an
essay. It became increasingly difficult to reconcile
my mundane concerns with the enormity of what
had transpired. This was not a passing sound bite
in the television news, an unfortunate event in a
distant place, an abstract victim soon to be forgotten. This was an intimate, lived experience; it sliced
through my complacency like a knife.

I had arrived in Canada, dreaming in the clouds.
Now I found myself in the dark abyss of a recurring

nightmare. I was a spectator watching helplessly as our loved ones were killed, as the innocent world I once knew was irretrievably shattered. Looking back from my place of exile, I felt an overwhelming surge of rage and sorrow. I became numb with inextinguishable pain. Mona's death changed everything. I would never be the same person again.

THE PURSUIT OF JUSTICE

The horrors of the Islamic revolution stirred within me an all-consuming search for answers. I was desperate to understand why the lives of our loved ones had been extinguished, why their tormenters couldn't be brought to justice, why the UN didn't stop this from happening. Above all, I wanted to understand how I could reconcile such suffering with my life of ease and comfort in the West. My search for answers took me from the classrooms of Harrison Public School to the lecture halls of Harvard Law School. As a child of Iranian parents, I had three professional choices: law, medicine, or social disgrace. But beyond bourgeois respectability, or even intellectual curiosity, I came to the academy in pursuit of justice. Studying international human rights law was a philosophical balm for my wounds.

At Harvard, I discovered great minds but little empathy. I encountered venerable mentors, brilliant intellects, and ambitious students, including this tall, skinny guy called Barack Obama. But there was little knowledge of suffering to infuse brilliant ideas with a deeper meaning. I grappled with the idea of "cutting-edge" scholarship. There was a certain hubris, I thought, in assuming that a new theory renders ancient wisdom irrelevant. I tried to make sense of the epic theoretical warfare among some faculty, wondering about the impact of footnotes on the future of humankind. I was doing my best to learn, but my head was overflowing with obtuse impenetrable jargon; I was diagnosed with chronic syllable fatigue.

In one seminar, I simply couldn't understand the dense postmodern text we were studying. I felt stupid until I realized that the author too didn't quite understand what he had written. The conceptual combat among the scholars, the competition to outdo rivals, was somehow familiar. It reminded me of the contending exegeses and interpretations of Quranic text among the *ulama*; of obscure metaphors and grammatical constructions giving rise to schisms and heresies. There was, I thought, a difference between pursuit of knowledge and pursuit of power.

I had once struggled to write a sentence in English. Now I found myself at one of the most prestigious universities, among the chosen few, on the path of professional success. But as impressive as it was, I couldn't connect this self-contained world of overachievers with the grim reality of the oppressed. I knew it was important to sharpen the intellect, but reason was powerless against the enormity of felt experience. The knowledge that mattered most, I realized, could only be found on the ground, in the intimate trenches of human struggle, not by observing the world at thirty thousand feet. We set out in pursuit of justice not because of some great intellectual idea but because we are deeply touched by human suffering.

In 1990, in the closing months of my university studies, my beloved grandmother Zuhuriye passed away in her sleep in Toronto. Born in 1910 in exile in tsarist Russia, her mother, Jamaliye, having miraculously survived the 1903 pogroms in Yazd, Zuhuriye was exiled back to Iran during the Stalinist purges of the 1930s, and finally exiled to Canada by Khomeini's revolution in 1979. As I stood by her grave in the cemetery, mourning her loss on a bitterly cold winter day, I thought about the silent power of her resilience, her serenity, her unconditional love. On her gravestone, a prayer was inscribed that we learned as children back in Iran: "Behold the candle... It weeps its life away drop by drop... to give forth its flame of light."

Now, faced with the inevitability of death, I pondered my life choices and what I would one day look back at as I drew my last breath. I reflected on the meaning of those words — that like a candle, our light shines in the darkness only if we are willing to burn. We had come to Canada in search of freedom, but at that moment I wondered what purpose it would serve if I wasted my life on selfish mediocrity, defining success by the trappings of status and wealth, ignoring the fire that was raging within. I remembered Mona's last wish, that the youth should arise in service to humanity, that they should move the world.

I had a stark choice: to exercise my freedom to become a bystander, or to commit my life to struggling for justice. At that moment, I realized that there was no turning back. I was too far from home, from the innocence I once knew; I couldn't un-see what I had seen. When someone touches us, their soul finds a new home, long after they are gone. Mona had become a part of me. Deep in the recess of my being, the humbling immensity of her soul had become my silent guide from beyond. For me, fighting for human rights was not a career choice. It was my only path of redemption.

To this day, the Islamic Republic of Iran persecutes the Bahá'ís for their religious beliefs, just as it goes on a diplomatic charm offensive to end its international isolation. In 2014, the historic cemetery in which the remains of Mona and 950 other Bahá'ís rested was excavated by the Revolutionary Guards to remove any trace of this heinous crime. The mighty Revolutionary Guards are afraid even of her bones.

"When setting out on a journey, do not seek advice from someone who never left home." I left home a long time ago, against my will. I didn't want the journey until I realized that I had no choice. I wandered, wounded and confused, on a wondrous path that would take me to extraordinary places and spaces, from the lofty summits of selfless love to the dark abyss of searing sorrow. If there is any advice I would humbly dispense, it is that the fountain of all knowledge is felt experience. If our heart is broken often enough, if we are patient in our times of loss, we will discover the astonishing resilience of the human spirit. Without embracing pain, without breaking open, we will never start our journey to a better world.

"I speak a little English." I had rehearsed those words carefully on that fateful journey from Tehran to Toronto, before the innocent world I once knew was forever destroyed. I speak better English now. But I also know that if we listen carefully, we will hear a voice that is not in need of words:

I know you are tired, but come. This is the Way.

TWO

THE PURSUIT OF GLOBAL JUSTICE

TRIALS AND TRIBULATIONS

"YOUR HONOUR, I HAD TO DO IT." An intense silence fell upon the courtroom. All eyes were fixed on the defendant, in anticipation of his next words. "If I had refused, I would have been killed together with the victims." There was a two-second delay as I listened to the English translation of his testimony on my headset. I could not understand his Serbo-Croatian mother tongue, but once the tears began to stream from his eyes, he spoke the transcendent language of irredeemable loss: "I am not sorry for myself but for my family, my wife and son who was then nine months old."

The historic trial at The Hague had taken an

unexpected turn. I was unprepared for his weeping. His confession, his contrition, had confused my Manichean conception of right and wrong. It introduced an unsettling moral ambiguity where none should exist. The accused, Dražen Erdemović, was on trial for the mass murder of 1,200 innocent men in Bosnia after the fall of Srebrenica in July 1995. I stood across the courtroom, a young, idealistic UN prosecutor, charging him with crimes against humanity; but instead of righteous rage, I felt sorry for him.

In 1946, following the postwar Nazi trials, the Nuremberg judgement recognized that "crimes against international law are committed by men, not by abstract entities, and only by punishing individuals who commit such crimes can the provisions of international law be enforced." The idea of human rights, the idea of the rule of law, cannot be reconciled with impunity for atrocities. It is elementary that mass murder cannot go unpunished. Yet for much of modern history, global justice has been a distant dream, either totally ignored, or applied selectively within the constraints of power realities. The zero-sum politics of the Cold War ensured that the Nuremberg precedent would go no further. Atrocities were tolerated, even encouraged, so long as the perpetrator was on the right side of the ideological divide.

In 1991, amidst the post–Cold War euphoria following the collapse of the Soviet Union, the Yugoslav Wars haunted Europe with the spectre of "ethnic cleansing" and genocide. This was a unique window of opportunity to resume the long-delayed pursuit of global justice. In 1993, the UN Security Council established the ad hoc International Criminal Tribunal for the former Yugoslavia (ICTY) to prosecute the perpetrators of war crimes and crimes against humanity. It was the first time in UN history that leaders of a sovereign nation were called to account for atrocities. In 1994, after the horrific extermination of almost a million people in Rwanda, the UN established a second ad hoc court, the International Criminal Tribunal for Rwanda (ICTR), to prosecute the *génocidaires*. By 1998, this momentum had opened the way for adoption of the Rome Statute for the International Criminal Court (ICC). After half a century, it marked the long-awaited realization of the post-Nuremberg ideal of individual accountability. It was the beginning of the end for the culture of impunity that had tolerated genocide for so long. But like all other historic journeys, there was a great distance between the romance and the reality of pursuing global justice.

I had graduated from law school in 1990, shortly before the outbreak of the Yugoslav Wars. Struggling to cope with the wounds inflicted on my family by the murderous Iranian regime, I had grappled with how international law could help those who suffer injustice. There was a desperate naïveté to my graduate thesis on enforcement of human rights law by international courts. While my classmates were poised to make a fortune on Wall Street, I was fantasizing about bringing the "bad guys" to justice, at a time when war crimes trials were a remote dream. But this far-fetched fantasy would come to pass, against all expectations. I would become one of the first UN prosecutors at The Hague in a historical experiment that revolutionized international law. It was a case of being in the right place at the right time, or perhaps in the wrong place at the wrong time, depending on how you look at the toll of dealing with mass graves for a decade of your early professional life.

In those days, the triumphant narrative of doing justice, of righting wrongs in the courtroom, had captivated everyone's imagination. I was very much in demand on the lecture circuit, a rising star in jurisprudential hairsplitting. Yet, as I discussed the methodical rituals of legal process on prestigious panels at five-star hotels, I felt a profound disconnect between the idea of global justice and the grim realities that it conveyed. What exactly did it mean to punish someone for genocide?

Erdemović's encounter with radical evil began in the late afternoon of July 11, 1995. On that day, the notorious Bosnian Serb general Ratko Mladić walked triumphantly on the streets of Srebrenica. After days of relentless artillery bombardment, the besieged town had fallen to his military forces. The murderous assault against civilians made a mockery of what the UN had declared a "safe area" for thousands of fearful Bosnian Muslim refugees that had sheltered there. They were the victims of "ethnic cleansing," a grotesque euphemism for atavistic atrocities amidst the violent disintegration of multi-ethnic Yugoslavia.

The Bosnian Serb president, Radovan Karadžić, had directed his army to "create an unbearable situation of total insecurity with no hope of further survival or life for the inhabitants of Srebrenica." He had succeeded. The ruthless bombardment, the prolonged starvation, had pushed the refugees beyond the limits of human endurance. The small hospital was crowded with the dead and the injured, screaming and crying in agony. Bloodied children with horrific shrapnel wounds and missing limbs mixed with exhausted mothers delivering babies on the filthy floor. Without any facilities or medicine, the few doctors did what they could to help the victims. At one point, an artillery projectile shattered the windows of the hospital. News came that the soldiers were entering the town.

In frantic desperation, several thousand fled to the UN compound in the village of Potočari. The small Dutch peacekeeping force was their last refuge. Having endured several days in the suffocating summer heat with no food or water, even those fortunate enough to escape the bombardment were listless from dehydration and malnutrition. The panic-stricken crowd pressed into the perimeter; those too weak to stand were trampled underfoot. Some handed their babies to the UN soldiers, begging them to save their precious lives. There were rumours circulating that a world away, in the UN peace negotiations in Geneva, diplomats had decided their fate: Srebrenica would be sacrificed to secure a peace agreement, and now these hapless people had to suffer the consequences of abandonment by the distant arbiters of human affairs.

The following day, General Mladić appeared

in Potočari, accompanied by television crews. He was filmed smiling, handing out sweets to children, reassuring the world that there was no cause for concern. Later that day, soldiers started picking people out of the terrified crowds. Throughout the night, the survivors heard screams and gunshots. A witness testified that three brothers were taken away — two teenagers and a child. Some time later, their mother found them with slit throats. In the days that followed, the sporadic revenge killings became systematic. On July 16, 1995, Erdemović's military unit, the Tenth Sabotage Detachment of the Bosnian Serb Army, was sent on an unspecified mission to the Branjevo collective farm, near Pilica, to the north of Srebrenica. There, they were told to await instructions. In the hours that followed, busloads of Muslim prisoners began to arrive, blindfolded with their hands tied behind their backs. They were taken in groups to a meadow and shot.

At first, Erdemović had refused orders to execute the prisoners. His military commander gave him a blunt choice: "If you are sorry for them...line up with them and we will kill you too." The young father of an infant child, an ethnic Croat married to an ethnic Serb, he wanted no part in this vicious ethnic war. He was simply in the wrong place at the wrong time.

An estimated seven thousand men were executed after the fall of Srebrenica, in July 1995. It was the first genocide on European soil since the Second World War. In its judgement, the Trial Chamber of the UN tribunal described "scenes of unimaginable savagery," of men buried alive, of children killed before their mothers' eyes, of mass graves where bodies were unceremoniously dumped; these were, in the words of the Egyptian judge Fouad Riad, "truly scenes from hell, written on the darkest pages of human history." Looking at Erdemović on the stand, I wondered whether this historic trial — the first war crimes trial since the Nuremberg Tribunal — was a moral triumph or a futile ritual.

The evil was so extreme, so unfathomable, that it defied diminution to the antiseptic confines of legal procedure. Is it ever possible to achieve justice after genocide? Or is its enormity such that no punishment is enough? And if someone should be held accountable, is it only the conspirators like Karadžić and Mladić who issue the orders to kill, or also the "small fish" like Erdemović who become the executioners?

We have the privilege of asking such questions today because holding leaders accountable for mass atrocities, however limited and selective in practice, is no longer a utopian fantasy. The Yugoslav Wars provided a unique opportunity to transform the ideal of global justice into a reality. It opened the way for the ICC, a weak institution at the margin of power realities, yet nonetheless an unprecedented challenge to the culture of impunity that has prevailed for so long. The early glimmering of this new conception of international legitimacy stands in sharp contrast to the casual acceptance of atrocities throughout much of history. For too long, the extermination and enslavement of vanquished nations was deemed the natural right of the victor. The transformation of ritual barbarity into an international crime cannot be taken for granted. It was, and remains, an epic story of defending humanity in the darkness of despair.

HUMANITARIAN LAW

The modern encounter between war and humanity began unexpectedly on June 24, 1859. On that evening, a Swiss businessman named Henri Dunant arrived in the town of Solferino, in the Italian Kingdom of Lombardy. He intended to meet the French emperor, Napoleon III, to discuss his commercial interests in the French colony of Algeria. Nearby, Napoleon had just concluded a major battle with the army of the Austrian emperor, Franz Joseph I. Amidst the scenes of massive carnage, Dunant witnessed thousands of wounded soldiers scattered across the battlefield, abandoned without medical care, dying slow agonizing deaths. Shocked at this horrible sight, he took it upon himself to organize the local women to treat the wounded in a makeshift hospital. The moral sensibility of the Swiss gentleman was a product of nineteenth-century European bourgeois society. Had he lived in pre-modern Europe, the reality of daily life — nasty, brutish, and short as it was — would have moderated his sympathy for suffering soldiers. But now, the moment was ripe for a humanitarian movement. By 1863, the efforts of this businessman turned humanitarian entrepreneur had led to the establishment of the International Committee of the Red Cross to protect the victims of war.

In that same year, during the American Civil War, President Lincoln had issued the Lieber Code on the laws of war. Its author was the

German-American émigré Franz Lieber, a former Prussian soldier who had been wounded in the Battle of Waterloo. A resident of South Carolina, he had seen the horrors of African slavery first-hand. When the Civil War broke out, instead of siding with the South, he joined the (anti-slavery) Union army with two of his sons; his other son fought, and died, on the Confederate side. Having witnessed the same Napoleonic Wars that had moved Dunant to establish the Red Cross, Lieber, the philosopher-soldier, understood the importance of minimum humanitarian standards. In 1861, he delivered a series of seminal lectures on "The Laws and Usages of War" at Columbia University in New York. In 1863, these became the basis for the *Instructions for the Government of Armies of the United States in the Field*. The unprecedented scale of the Napoleonic Wars and the humanitarian sentiments of modern society had coalesced to produce legal constraints on warfare.

Humanitarian law, as it became known, was intended to humanize the inherent inhumanity of organized violence. In 1899, as the tempestuous nineteenth century drew to a close, this fledgling movement reached a turning point. Tsar Nicholas II of Russia, concerned with the impact of the Napoleonic Wars on his realm, convened a peace conference in The Hague, hosted by his cousin, Queen Wilhelmina of the Netherlands. His idealistic call for disarmament was interpreted cynically by the European powers as a ploy to reduce the crippling financial burdens of the arms race on the House of Romanov. The German emperor, Kaiser Wilhelm II, remarked derisively that he would go along with "the conference comedy" but keep "my dagger at my side during the waltz."

The unprecedented gathering of world leaders did not succeed in legislating peace. But drawing on the Lieber Code, the plenipotentiaries unanimously adopted the Hague Convention on the Laws and Customs of War on Land, the first comprehensive humanitarian law treaty presaging the Geneva Conventions of 1949. A separate declaration was adopted Prohibiting the Discharge of Projectiles and Explosives from Balloons. It would be rejected in the coming years, when the enormous military potential of air warfare became apparent.

By the standards of the time, the emergence of these principles of humanity represented revolutionary progress for the rule of international law. But it was not accompanied by any means for their judicial enforcement. It would take yet further calamities for the idea of an international criminal tribunal to emerge.

On June 28, 1914, the fortunes of humankind took a dramatic turn for the worse. On that day, just before 10 a.m., the archduke of Austria, Franz Ferdinand, and his wife, Duchess Sophie, arrived in Sarajevo by train. Bosnia and Herzegovina was then a province of the Habsburg Empire, having been wrested from the Ottoman Empire in 1878. It remained a cauldron of conflict. Yugoslav nationalists like Gavrilo Princip were waging a violent campaign for independence. They wanted to unite all southern Slavs with the neighbouring Kingdom of Serbia. June 28 was an especially poignant day for Serb nationalists: it was St. Vitus Day, commemorating the killing of Saint Prince Lazar and other Serbian martyrs at the hands of the Ottomans in 1389. Within an hour of their arrival in Sarajevo, upon leaving a reception at the spectacular City Hall, the royal couple had been assassinated by Princip, setting into motion a chain of events that would soon lead to the First World War, a global conflict even more catastrophic than the Napoleonic Wars.

Kaiser Wilhelm II, who had ridiculed the 1899 Hague Peace Conference, was a central protagonist in the war, fighting on the side of the Central Powers, together with the Austrian Empire. The cataclysm that followed would not end well for him. On November 9, 1918, after four years of disastrous conflict, he found himself in the Belgian resort town of Spa, facing military defeat at the hands of the Allied powers and revolutionary unrest at home. He was forced to abdicate and escaped into exile in the Netherlands, which had remained neutral during the war. But the nations that had waged war against him still had unfinished business.

The 1919 Treaty of Versailles, ending the war with Germany, called for the emperor to be tried before an international tribunal for "a supreme offence against international morality and the sanctity of treaties." It was an unprecedented demand for victor's justice in a peace agreement: the idea that the vanquished should be brought to criminal justice had now entered the political imagination of the international community. But it never came to pass. The Dutch Queen Wilhelmina, invoking the right of political asylum, refused to extradite him. Having been spared the humiliation of a trial, Wilhelm hoped that the Nazi party would restore the House of Hohenzollern to the throne. But Adolf Hitler, who had served in the vanquished German Army during the First World

War, felt nothing but scorn for the deposed emperor. Kaiser Wilhelm died in exile on June 4, 1941, in the Netherlands, under Nazi occupation, ashamed that his own children had supported the anti-Semitic pogroms in Germany. Queen Wilhelmina, who had refused to extradite him, was now herself in exile in London, with her children yet further away in Ottawa. The still-unfolding unparalleled savagery of the Second World War would soon lead to a turning point in the history of international justice.

JUSTICE AT NUREMBERG

On November 29, 1943, as the Allied powers advanced on Nazi forces, the Soviet leader, Joseph Stalin, hosted a dinner in Tehran for the British prime minister, Winston Churchill, and the U.S. president, Franklin D. Roosevelt. As the powerful leaders shared a sumptuous meal, the conversation turned to how they should deal with Germany after the war. True to form, Stalin proposed that the top 50,000 German military officers should be killed. Churchill was somewhat less ambitious: he favoured only the summary execution of Hitler and the top Nazi leaders. By 1945, U.S. president

Harry Truman had persuaded the Allied powers that instead of summary executions, the Nazi leadership should be prosecuted before an International Military Tribunal in the city of Nuremberg.

The Nuremberg trials were held without the most notorious Nazi leaders. Adolf Hitler, Heinrich Himmler, and Joseph Goebbels had all committed suicide before the indictment was signed. Falling from hubris to humiliation, they escaped justice, but only by self-inflicted punishment. At trial, the most significant of the defendants was Hermann Goering, who had been second in line to Hitler. He was known as Prisoner Number One. As the most senior German official, he had assumed that he could negotiate with the occupying Allied powers. But now he was a prisoner, standing trial for his monstrous crimes. Goering was charismatic and confident, expressing no contrition for his acts. He defiantly invoked German patriotism to justify his conduct, defending Hitler and the Reich. On October 1, 1946, the tribunal sentenced him to death. Back in his prison cell, the once-nonchalant defendant was trembling with fear as he grappled with the reality of what awaited him. On October 14, 1946, the night before his execution, he took his own life by swallowing cyanide.

At the opposite end of the spectrum was the remorseful Albert Speer, minister of armaments and war production, who willingly confessed to his guilt. "Hitler and the collapse of his system," he testified, "have brought a time of tremendous suffering upon the German people." Upon being sentenced to twenty years' imprisonment, he remarked that having admitted to his share of the guilt, "It would be ridiculous if I complained about the punishment." Upon his release from Berlin's Spandau Prison in 1966, he wrote in his memoirs that for the horrors of the concentration camps and slave factories, "no apologies are possible."

In 1946, another international military tribunal, this one for the Far East, was established in Tokyo by the Allied powers. Twenty-eight of the most senior Japanese officials were put on trial, but Emperor Hirohito and the imperial family were spared to facilitate the postwar transition to democracy. Like Nuremberg, the Tokyo trials were aimed at delegitimizing fascism. In the words of the American prosecutor Joseph Keenan, war criminals "should be stripped of the glamour of national heroes and exposed as what they really are — plain, ordinary murderers."

The Nuremberg and Tokyo trials were of course

an instance of victor's justice. The crimes of the Allied powers against German and Japanese civilians were beyond the jurisdiction of the tribunals. The annihilation of entire cities, the massacre of hundreds of thousands by aerial "terror bombing" — Berlin, Dresden, and Hamburg in the West, and Tokyo, Hiroshima, and Nagasaki in the East — these were all ignored. But still, the decision to give the vanquished a trial in place of summary executions was revolutionary by the standards of the time. In the words of the U.S. prosecutor Robert Jackson:

> That four great nations, flushed with victory and stung with injury, stay the hand of vengeance and voluntarily submit their captive enemies to the judgment of the law is one of the most significant tributes that Power has ever paid to Reason.

The Nuremberg and Tokyo trials disaggregated the legal abstraction called the sovereign "state." The imposition of criminal liability on leaders embodied the truth that institutions and bureaucracies were merely an instrument by which such individuals could commit diabolical crimes on a vast and unprecedented scale; it reflected the reality that international law could only be enforced if they were brought to justice. It did not matter that the perpetrators were heads of state or public officials; they would be punished on an equal footing with any other criminal. If anything, their high rank and position of responsibility aggravated their culpability.

There was a certain logic to the individualization of guilt. For one thing, it transformed inexorable primordial hatred into a rational moral choice. The mystification of radical evil as an expression of intrinsic human cruelty could not be reconciled with a post-Enlightenment European civilization founded on reasoned conceptions of right and wrong. In a more instrumental way, an objective historical record of such crimes would help with postwar Germany's "de-Nazification" by educating the public about the shocking truths obfuscated by years of propaganda. In the words of Robert Jackson, the Nuremberg Tribunal established "incredible events by credible evidence." Beyond individual punishment, justice in this context was about cleansing society from the inverted morality of the Nazi death cult.

Several of the Nazi leaders were sentenced to death by hanging. But even the death penalty seemed incongruent with the extermination of six million Jews. The renowned philosopher Hannah Arendt wrote to Karl Jaspers, her mentor at Heidelberg University, that the Nazi crimes "explode the limits of law; and that is precisely what constitutes their monstrousness. For these crimes, no punishment is severe enough." Perhaps there was a deceptive appeal to reducing such overwhelming inhumanity to the confines of legal procedure; a war crimes trial was like an exorcism ritual, casting evil out of European civilization and reaffirming modernity's myth of progress.

One of the lasting contributions of the Nuremberg trials was the concept of "crimes against humanity." During the drafting of the charter of the tribunal, it became apparent that the laws of war applied only if the victims were foreign nationals of states at war with Germany. Atrocities against German civilians or the nationals of the Axis powers did not qualify as war crimes. Of course, simple murder was a crime recognized by all civilized nations. But without an exceptional scale, such atrocities didn't justify the intrusion of international law into the domestic jurisdiction of states.

"Crimes against humanity" thus covered this

jurisdictional gap by imposing liability for all mass
atrocities irrespective of the victim's nationality,
ensuring that the persecution of Jews would not go
unpunished. The idea that international law con-
strains a state's treatment of its own nationals was a
revolutionary development by the standards of the
time, an unprecedented encroachment on state sovereignty, presaging the 1948 Universal Declaration
of Human Rights.

But there was yet another crime, even more
heinous, that emerged in the crucible of Nazi
transgressions. Winston Churchill had referred
to the extermination of European Jews as a
"crime without a name." The French prosecutor
at Nuremberg, Auguste Champetier de Ribes,
remarked that the Holocaust was "a crime so monstrous, so undreamt of in history throughout the
Christian era up to the birth of Hitlerism, that
the term 'genocide' has had to be coined to define
it." It was the Polish jurist Raphael Lemkin who
had taken it upon himself to introduce that grave
term into our vocabulary. "Genocide" denoted a
species of crime against humanity aimed at the
intentional destruction of human groups because
of their identity; a type of collective homicide.
Lemkin wrote about the horrors of the Nazi gas

chambers with scholarly detachment. Yet his was an intimate encounter with the Holocaust: a Polish Jew, he had lost forty-nine members of his family, including his parents. His insurmountable grief spurred a passionate one-man campaign leading to the adoption of the Genocide Convention by the UN General Assembly in 1948. It was, he wrote in his memoirs, "an epitaph on my mother's grave," the transformation of his anguish into a "moral striking force." Behind every new chapter in the progress of international law, there were countless personal tragedies.

The immediate postwar period witnessed exceptional ferment in the development of global justice. The novel principles of the 1946 Nuremberg judgement, including crimes against humanity and the irrelevance of official capacity to criminal liability, were codified and entrenched in international law. In 1948, the UN General Assembly called on the International Law Commission "to study the desirability and possibility of establishing an international judicial organ for the trial of persons charged with genocide." A draft statute was proposed in 1951. But it didn't go any further. The world was now in the grips of the Cold War, and ideological divisions took priority over global justice. The Americans and Soviets were willing to support tyrannical regimes committing mass murder so long as it served their narrow interests. Genocide was condemned in the abstract as the "ultimate crime," but tolerated in practice as millions were slaughtered with impunity, always in the name of a greater good. The Nuremberg legacy became a distant past and the punishment of genocide a distant dream.

Throughout the twentieth century, international justice had followed a predictable pattern: at opportune moments, unconscionable atrocities would lead to ever more lofty principles and institutions. This dialectic, of disaster begetting progress, would emerge once again in the post–Cold War era with the Yugoslav Wars. Some fifty years after the Nuremberg judgement, it would finally set the scene for the establishment of a permanent international criminal court.

GROUND ZERO

"I call to witness time, the beginning and end of all things — to witness that every man always suffers loss." When it was published in 1966, Meša

Selimović's *Death and the Dervish* was widely acclaimed as a masterpiece of Yugoslav literature. The story, set in eighteenth-century Ottoman Bosnia, reflected Selimović's despondence at the seeming futility of resistance against injustice. When he died in Sarajevo in 1982, he was hailed not as a Bosnian Muslim, but as a Yugoslav. His Sarajevo was a multi-ethnic city where most marriages were mixed. In fact, it had even been a place of refuge for victims of religious persecution. In 1492, Sephardic Jews fleeing the Spanish Inquisition had come to Bosnia because of the relative tolerance of the Ottomans. Baščaršija, the enchanting Sarajevo bazaar that inspired Selimović, still boasts a fusion of mosques, churches, and synagogues standing together in eclectic harmony. Befitting a city that was a crossroads of civilizations, Sarajevo's main thoroughfare was named Meša Selimović Boulevard.

The 1984 Winter Olympics cemented the cosmopolitan reputation of the city. It was a glorious celebration for Sarajevans, even if the ghastly mustard-coloured Holiday Inn built for the occasion was a monument of brutal socialist architecture, a blemish on the famous Selimović Boulevard. But in later years, during a vicious ethnic war in what we called ex-Yugoslavia, that expansive thoroughfare bearing the literary giant's name became known as Sniper's Alley. There, from the surrounding rooftops and hills, amidst the abandoned streetcars and scorched buildings, hundreds of civilians — many of them children — were mercilessly killed by sharpshooters.

The siege of Sarajevo began on April 7, 1992. It would last almost 1,400 horrible days. A recent law school graduate, I had been dispatched by the UN to investigate human rights abuses in Bosnia. My boss was the former Polish prime minister Tadeusz Mazowiecki, one of the leaders of the anti-communist "Solidarity" movement, who had been appointed as the UN human rights envoy for the former Yugoslavia. Brimming with idealistic human rights fantasies, I was about to get a rude awakening as my expectant eyes opened to the grim realities of war. I would enter Sarajevo aspiring to save the world; I would leave struggling to save my own soul.

The journey into the besieged city from the outside world began with the legendary UN airlift from Zagreb in neighbouring Croatia. At the check-in counter, a makeshift sign advertised "Maybe Airlines" (maybe you'll get there, maybe you

won't). The sign was decorated with random stick-
ers, souvenirs from its loyal customers: Médecins
du Monde and Médecins Sans Frontières, CNN and
ITN, the Canadian and Swedish flags. Above the
sign, the only destination indicated was "Heaven."
It promised to be an eventful flight.

The Maybe Airlines schedule was notoriously
unreliable, and there was always the prospect of
anti-aircraft fire at lower altitudes, requiring an
abrupt nosedive landing into Sarajevo airport. To
add insult to injury, passengers were herded into
the white propeller aircraft together with the cargo
containers: it was truly cattle-class, without even
the peanuts or frequent flyer miles. But once the
roar of the engines began, we were reminded that
the airlift was a vital lifeline of food and medicine for besieged Sarajevo. These were flights of
mercy that helped keep the city alive. In that horrible place, the sight of the white metal doves flying
in the blue sky inspired hope and humanity.

Upon landing at Sarajevo International Airport,
we entered a different dimension. Once the cargo
bay opened at the back, we were greeted by a welcoming party of French blue helmets protecting
the airport *"Dépêche-toi!* Hurry up!" they shouted
aggressively as we disembarked. On the tarmac,

the aircraft was a sitting duck for snipers and artillery fire; it had to be unloaded and reloaded within a matter of minutes. The battered terminal building into which we ran was a sorry sight for a gateway to the world. With illuminated blue letters proclaiming "Aerodrom Sarajevo," it had once welcomed throngs of tourists to the fabled city. Now the missing letters made for fractured words adorning a broken structure, precariously sheltered by crude fortifications made from cargo containers and piles of dirt. The journey into the city was filled with debris and roadblocks on eerily abandoned streets. The graffiti on one bullet-riddled wall read: "Welcome to Hell."

The struggle for survival in Sarajevo was a quotidian heroism. The Bosnian Serb Army did its best to terrorize the civilian population, and the Sarajevans — Serbs, Croats, and Muslims alike — did what they could to salvage their humanity. Back on Selimović Boulevard, as we peered out the small window in the back of the UN armoured vehicle that took us to and from meetings, the sight of dead bodies had become disturbingly normalized. In Sniper's Alley, crossing the street was a potentially fatal hazard for pedestrians. Many had no choice but to walk through this central artery in their daily search for food and water. There was, in particular, an open stretch of the boulevard that was exposed to sniper fire from the surrounding rooftops and hills. Once the pedestrians reached that crossing, they would run as fast as they could, resigned to their possible fate. There was even a road sign warning, "Beware of Snipers."

Some pedestrians were young and ran fast. Others, the elderly and children, were slower and more vulnerable. The snipers spared no one. They killed hundreds, leaving the bodies in the street in pools of their own blood until a blue helmet, a loved one, or a good Samaritan could safely retrieve them for burial at one of Sarajevo's rapidly expanding cemeteries. An image seared into my mind is that of a woman, probably in her sixties, with stylish dress and fashionable boots, lying motionless on the sidewalk with her neatly coiffed hair. The groceries she was carrying were spread around her, and blood flowed from her head. I wondered what her name was and who was waiting for her at home to share a meal.

The intention of the siege was to make life unbearable by crushing both body and soul. In their delusional pursuit of an ethnically "pure" state, the warmongers saw multi-ethnic Sarajevo as a symbol of everything they despised. Integral to this atavistic ideology was cultural vandalism to eradicate the symbols of a common identity. On August 25, 1992, the Bosnian Serb Army bombarded the magnificent National Library, known as the Vijećnica. The stunning Moorish structure, with graceful arches and coloured glass, was built in the nineteenth century by the Habsburgs to house the City Hall. In 1914, it was the last place the royal couple visited before their assassination. On August 25, 1992, after having survived two world wars, the exquisite monument to a shared past finally succumbed to the all-consuming flames of blind hatred. Some three million rare books and artifacts, including both Ottoman and Habsburg archives, were irretrievably lost. The fire surged out of the windows, casting a diabolical glow in the night sky, and the people watched helplessly as their cultural treasures went up in the billowing smoke. Some raised their hands in supplication, begging the heavens for deliverance.

As these horrors unfolded and some voices clamoured for intervention, the British statesman and peace mediator Lord David Owen famously told the besieged Sarajevo residents: "Don't live under the dream that the West is going to come and sort this problem out." For the Sarajevans, there was no dream to be had; just a recurring nightmare of daily survival, without hope of either peace or justice. The only proposal on the table was appeasement of the same hate-mongers who were ripping multi-ethnic Bosnia apart, as if giving them what they wanted would solve the problem.

Abandoned by the world, those who had lost everything fought back the only way they could: with the indomitable resilience of the human spirit. The iconic musician Vedran Smailović became an embodiment of this epic struggle for dignity in the dark abyss of despair. Defying the guns of war, he went to the destroyed Vijećnica and played the cello in its ruins. His rendition of Albinoni's Adagio in G Minor captured the desperate sorrow of this forsaken place. It inspired the maestro Zubin Mehta to conduct, in the same ruins, an unforgettable performance of Mozart's Requiem by the Sarajevo Philharmonic Orchestra, several members of which had been killed. The transcendent beauty of art had become a visceral resistance against dehumanization.

In contrast to the elegant National Library, the hideous Holiday Inn on Selimović Boulevard had withstood the shelling and was still in use. The only exception was the side facing the mountains, which had been badly damaged by Serbian artillery. The journalists frequenting the hotel would wryly advise newcomers not to ask for a room with a view. The television crews knew the best places to position themselves on the boulevard to catch that coveted footage of someone getting shot. At best, these shocking images were a way to awaken the sleeping conscience of bystanders a world away; at worst, they were a sick form of war pornography, an extreme version of reality TV for distant audiences numbed by mindless entertainment.

As the war unfolded, Bosnia became a gruesome media spectacle. The news cycle was flooded with commentary by savvy pundits and erudite experts, casually interspersed with hellish images trivialized by constant repetition against the "breaking news" background loop. For those of us watching the broadcasts from ground zero, the televised depiction of human suffering seemed like a spectator sport of superficial sentimentality. There was no meaningful engagement with the context that had created the misery. The mass exodus of refugees was treated as a humanitarian crisis, a natural disaster rather than the consequence of the actions of ruthless men emboldened by the world's indifference. There was also the ever-present danger of compassion fatigue as the fleeting attention of audiences moved on to the next tragedy. Fortunately for the victims, they were white Europeans and not the easily forgotten masses of Africa and Asia. As their harrowing stories came to the surface of public consciousness, the comforts of denial were gradually surpassed by a mounting outcry for intervention; it brought together political leaders and journalists, human rights activists and academics, some motivated by empathy, others just eager to get a piece of the action. There was admittedly a pressing need to give a voice to the victims, to expose the truth to the world, but Bosnia had also become an industry, the making of many careers at the expense of other people's misfortune.

One lesson I learned in Bosnia was that in war, death is not the worst thing that can happen to people. Having your life instantaneously extinguished by a sniper's bullet was less painful than the lasting wounds of torture. Amidst this gallery of horrors, the use of rape as a weapon of war was particularly appalling. Unlike the carnage on the streets, sexual violence was invisible, beyond the reach of the television cameras, confined to detention camps and makeshift brothels, where anguished women had become the trophies of war. Those that suffered this humiliation were doubly victimized, once by suffering the rape, and twice by suffering shame and silence in their own communities. For too long, sexual violence was dismissed as an unfortunate by-product of war. In Bosnia, it emerged as a deliberate instrument of "ethnic cleansing." Listening to the victim testimony was heartbreaking. The story of a fourteen-year-old who took her own life after being repeatedly raped was devastating. Many became pregnant. Some had abortions, while others were forced by their captors to give birth, a vicious occupation of their wombs that became known as the new war crime of "forced pregnancy." Yet others contracted STDS and HIV infections from their rapists. Unlike those that fell in Sniper's Alley, the traumatized survivors of these abominations died a slow, agonizing death every day.

Sexual violence, for so long a blind spot of humanitarian law, thankfully received unprecedented attention during the Yugoslav Wars. It became the subject of myriad media stories, NGO reports, academic publications, and panel discussions. But the victims languishing in the refugee camps experienced this *cause célèbre* differently. In desperate need of help for healing, some felt their suffering was being exploited for the benefit of others. They were repeatedly re-traumatized by outside saviours eager to tell their stories, but they were given few resources for rehabilitation. Some refused any further interviews. From their vantage point, there was even a dark side to virtue.

I increasingly noticed a profound disconnect between the reality of human suffering and the discourse of elites. One notable instance was the debate over statistical data. In 1993, a European Community commission of inquiry, headed by Dame Anne Warburton, estimated the number of rape victims at twenty thousand. By contrast, our UN investigation, with the assistance of medical experts using more scientific methodology, estimated a lower number of a few thousand rapes. There was disappointment and controversy in activist circles, as if the lower figure undermined the gravity of these heinous acts. There was something profoundly perverse about privileging numeric abstractions over the intimate experience of survivors. Perhaps, given the fleeting attention span of the public, sensational statistics is what it took to prevent the atrocities from falling into oblivion. But on the ground it was blindingly obvious that behind every victim there was a name, a story, a universe of relations forever lost, unspeakable tragedy that no statistic could ever capture. The magnitude of the injustice, and the imperative necessity of humanitarian intervention, was manifest. With every new atrocity that came to light, we hoped the UN would finally find the political will to put an end to these horrors. But it would not come to pass.

On February 5, 1994, Sarajevans took advantage of a respite from fighting to shop for food at the Markale open-air market. Around noon, when the market was at its busiest, an artillery projectile landed in the midst of the crowd, killing and injuring hundreds. The scenes of carnage that followed were shocking. Once again, war crimes were captured on film and broadcast for the world to watch. We hoped this atrocity would finally result in decisive action by the UN to break the siege. Instead, a month later, diplomats convened an emergency meeting at the UN in Geneva. There they expressed their displeasure with the ruthless killers by adopting an indignant resolution. The text noted that the UN Human Rights Commission was "moved by the horrible massacre" and that it "strongly condemns the policy of genocide and 'ethnic cleansing.'"

It was a surreal experience to witness this pretense of meaningful action, as if these murderous monsters would somehow be deterred by the haughty admonitions of diplomats. After the vote, I sat bewildered in the delegates' lounge of the Palais des Nations, the UN Headquarters in Geneva where the defunct League of Nations once stood. I had a panoramic view of the majestic Swiss Alps, but all I saw was the artillery on the mountains of Sarajevo. Instead of the friendly chatter, I heard the echo of sniper fire and the sound of screams. As the diplomats celebrated their moral triumph with some drinks, I sipped my bitter coffee with trembling hands, wondering how many more people had been killed on Selimović Boulevard that same day.

The absurdity of the situation, of the delusional, empty words, was unbearable. It was even more preposterous, I thought to myself at the time, that the victims in urban Sarajevo were fortunate compared to those in rural Bosnia. They were visible, close to television cameras, so at least they had the privilege of ritualistic UN reprimands against their aggressors. As in most wars, the poor and dispossessed in the periphery suffered the most, but they were out of sight and out of mind. Alerting the world to their woes was one of our challenges.

On April 30, 1993, I arrived in Ahmići village. Some days earlier, its rural Muslim inhabitants had been slaughtered at the hands of a Bosnian Croat militia. We had come from Sarajevo to investigate the atrocity on behalf of the UN. There was suspicion at the time that the Bosnian Croats had joined the Bosnian Serbs to affect a two-way ethnic partition of Bosnia, at the expense of the Muslims. It was a new and disturbing front in the war, and it complicated the already remote prospect of UN intervention.

We arrived at the village in the relative safety of the UN British battalion's Scimitar armoured vehicles. The scene was one of utter devastation. The minaret of the local mosque had been blown up. It had collapsed on an adjacent roof, its silver needle-like cone-tip ominously pointing to the sky like a missile. The Muslim homes were all destroyed by fire; some were still smouldering. The Croatian homes were untouched. The militia knew exactly who to target. They had gone door to door, systematically killing and burning, not even sparing the cows and dogs. There was a stench of death in the village. Some bodies had been retrieved, but others were still under the rubble. Each told a tragic tale. In one instance, a young man had been shot at the front entrance of his home. He was apparently trying to defend his family. His wife and small children, who had been hiding in the basement, had apparently been burnt alive, their charred remains a tormented contortion of limbs. One of the UN soldiers was sobbing at the sight.

We walked the desolate streets in our blue helmets, trying to find an eyewitness. In the distance, we saw an elderly woman with two small children. As we approached her to ask questions, we suddenly heard the unmistakable sound of sniper fire. Somebody didn't want us snooping around the village — somebody didn't want the world to know the truth. We were sitting ducks in the middle of an open field. The split second when a bullet passed close to my head lasted an eternity; animal fear had transformed everything into slow motion. There is a brutal clarity once the survival instinct takes over. The only question at that moment was how to return to the armoured vehicle without getting shot. I noticed a camera crew that had been trailing us some distance away. They were eagerly filming my perilous predicament. This time, it was me who was the unwitting star in the macabre action thriller, like those hapless souls running every day through Sniper's Alley. I wondered if my family would watch my last moments on the evening news.

Meandering through the village, hiding as best as I could from the sniper's scope, I somehow made it back to the armoured vehicle unscathed. My fury overwhelmed my fear. Instead of relief at my narrow escape from the clutches of death, I was exploding with anger. I was disgusted with the cruelty and cowardice of the perpetrators. I was overcome with grief at the immensity of the injustice; what kind of people, I thought to myself, could kill a mother and her children in cold blood? In my confused frenzy, I demanded to see the militia commander. I wanted to, I needed to, give him a piece of my mind. The utter suicidal stupidity of what I was about to do eluded me at that moment of reckless rage.

Some time later, not far from Ahmići, I burst into the office of General Tihomir Blaškić. I had assumed that his militia must have been responsible for the attack. Consumed by what I had seen, I was undeterred by the menacing soldiers flanking him, brandishing assault rifles. Dispensing with the usual formalities, I placed my UN blue helmet on his desk, calmly sat down, stared him in the eyes with fury, and gave him a graphic account of what I had witnessed. My impulsive impudence could have cost me dearly; yet somehow he listened, unable to meet my gaze. He had a wife and children, I thought to myself. How could he fail to understand the enormity of what his soldiers had done? Having exhausted all that I could say, I stood up, told them they should all be ashamed, and walked out of the room.

I passed many sleepless nights pondering in the silence of my conscience if I could have done more. The images of the burnt bodies of the children haunted me for a long time. But I could not unsee what I had seen; I had to cope with the reality as best as I could. The only thing I knew for certain was that silence was not a choice. Even against overwhelming odds, the beginning of justice was to bear witness to the truth.

RIGHTS, WRONGS, AND REALISM

Blaškić was hardly the worst of the war criminals I encountered. The pangs of guilt that I saw in his demeanour actually gave me a glimmer of hope that perhaps he realized the moral gravity of what had transpired. Far from the confines of formal deliberations at UN Headquarters in Geneva, I had

the luxury of confronting him without the diplomatic euphemisms that sanitized the stark reality
of mass murder so powerful men could go on con-
ducting business as usual. In the halls and corridors
of the Palais des Nations in Geneva, there were different rules of decorum. Here, the teachers would
tell children in the classroom to play fair but treat
the schoolyard bullies with deference.

My encounter with the masterminds of genocide
occurred in Geneva, during one of the meetings of
the Yugoslav Peace Conference, co-chaired by former U.S. secretary of state Cyrus Vance and former
British foreign secretary Lord David Owen. There,
walking down the stairs, amidst the bodyguards
and camera crews, I saw for the first time in real
life the familiar face of a man I already knew very
well. A few steps in front of me, with his charming
smile and convincing demeanour, was the dema-
gogic Serbian president, Slobodan Milošević, the
arch-villain of the horrors that I had witnessed
first-hand. For one moment, I felt the instinctive
excitement of encountering a celebrity; but that
thought was quickly dissipated by the dark reality behind the pomp and circumstance on display.

A graduate of the University of Belgrade's law
school, Milošević was a charismatic and ambitious

leader, rising quickly through the ranks of the Communist Party. His father, Svetozar, a Serbian Orthodox priest, had committed suicide in 1962, and his mother, Stanislava, a schoolteacher, had also taken her own life in 1972. In the waning days of socialist Yugoslavia, as suppressed nationalist sentiments were coming to the surface in the fragile multi-ethnic federation, Milošević the socialist had refashioned himself as a populist ethnic entrepreneur. Amidst a turbulent post-communist transition, he gave his adulating followers a strong sense of identity and purpose. That resurgent self-image, built on fear and hatred, would not end well.

On June 28, 1989, in a famous speech on the occasion of St. Vitus Day, Milošević had commemorated the six hundredth anniversary of the Battle of Kosovo in 1389. It was a day of mourning and memory, arousing nationalist passions; it was no surprise, perhaps, that Princip had assassinated Archduke Ferdinand on this same day in 1914. Speaking from a podium elevated on the Gazimestan monument in that historical battlefield, Milošević brought the vivid past back to life. "Six centuries later," he told the massive, restive crowd, "we are engaged again in battles" that "cannot be won without resolve, bravery, and sacrifice, without the noble qualities that were present here in the field of Kosovo in the days past." At a time of mounting tensions between Albanians and Serbs, in that symbolically potent battlefield, he proclaimed to frenzied chants of "Slobo, Slobo" that Serbia's destiny was to heroically defend European civilization against Muslim invaders.

With those words, Milošević's historical mythology transformed the angry crowds into anti-Muslim warriors, as if the battle of 1389 had occurred yesterday. Serbian pride was restored through a narrative of perpetual victimization, justifying the atrocities that followed as a legitimate act of self-defence. Ensuring that all Serbs lived in a single ethnically pure State, he claimed, was the only way to protect the nation against a new genocide at the hands of the "Turks." This selective incendiary surfeit of memory would have catastrophic consequences.

The early beginning of the atrocities in Bosnia in 1992 and their subsequent spread to Kosovo were not surprising. In 1991, the world had already witnessed the first stage of "ethnic cleansing" in Croatia as Milošević implemented his vision of a "Greater Serbia" by eliminating ethnic Croats in the Krajina and Slavonia regions. I had previously visited the devastated baroque town of Vukovar, on the Danube River, the flashpoint where nationalist tensions between Milošević and Croatian president Franjo Tuđman first transformed a manageable political conflict into a brutal war. From the UN helicopter, the once thriving city appeared as a pile of rubble, its landmark water tower punctured with holes like a wounded giant. Many in Serbia had opposed the Yugoslav army's brutal siege of Vukovar, described by one anti-war leader as the Hiroshima of nationalist madness.

But just as Milošević fanned the flames of fear among Serbs, Tuđman obliged him with inflammatory historical revisionism, like his notorious minimization of atrocities at the Jasenovac concentration camp during the Second World War, where thousands of Serbs perished under the pro-Nazi Ustaše puppet state in Croatia. On an earlier visit to the Presidential Palace, in the picturesque Vila Zagorje outside Zagreb, our delegation had been treated first-hand to one of Tuđman's romanticized lectures on the imaginary past. Listening to his words, I could see how the delusional comfort of demonizing others had ripped Yugoslavia apart.

Back at the UN peace conference in Geneva, walking just behind Milošević in the Serbian delegation, were the strongman's executioners, Radovan Karadžić and Ratko Mladić. Karadžić, a smug and self-satisfied man with a signature bouffant hairstyle, was a psychiatrist and self-styled poet turned nationalist politician. In 1985, he and his partner in crime, Momčilo Krajišnik, had been convicted for embezzlement of public funds to build vacation homes in the ski resort of Pale, outside of Sarajevo, from which he now commanded the brutal siege as the president of the newly created Bosnian Serb Republic. Karadžić had studied at Sarajevo's Medical School. He had specialized in the treatment of depression at Koševo hospital, where Bosnian doctors now performed surgery on his bleeding victims by candlelight. His poetic rumination entitled "Sarajevo" provided a glimpse into the mind of an evidently disturbed man: "The city burns like a piece of incense," he wrote. "In the smoke rumbles our consciousness."

In 1992, as the country disintegrated in slow motion under the pressure of centrifugal nationalist forces, the tensions in Bosnia had reached a climax. The secession of Slovenia and Croatia had upset the delicate ethnic equilibrium in the Yugoslav federation. Without the coercive glue of communist ideology to keep the different nations together, the ethnic balance of power could no longer be sustained: the majority Muslims and Croats now wanted a separate Bosnian state, but the Serbs refused to become a national minority. Karadžić did not mince words about what awaited the non-Serbs: "You will take Bosnia and Herzegovina to hell and the Muslim people into extinction," he warned, "because if there is a war, the Muslim people will not be able to defend themselves." That ominous warning had now become a reality.

Walking next to Karadžić was Ratko Mladić, the Bosnian Serb military commander known as the Butcher of Bosnia. Seemingly mindful of the unstoppable onslaught of his forces against the defenceless Muslims, he had the self-assured smirk of a ruthless conqueror; some called him a "charismatic murderer." Mladić was a tribal warrior who had no compunctions telling journalists concerned with human rights: "Borders have always been drawn with blood." He had lost his father during the Second World War, when he was just three years old — an event that shaped his view of the world. His father, Neđa, a fighter with the Yugoslav communist partisans under the legendary marshal Josip Broz Tito, had been killed by the infamous Ustaše fascist Croatian militia. The atrocities of the Četnik fascist Serbian militia had been equally notorious. But for Mladić there was only a single narrative: that of absolute Serbian victimhood. He firmly believed that the war he had unleashed against the Muslims had, in fact, been thrust upon the Serbian people. As is often the case, self-depiction as the victim was the prerequisite to victimizing others. Defending his nation, he proclaimed, was "a holy duty." Upon entering Srebrenica in the summer of 1995, he had reportedly declared: "In this place, we will have our vengeance against the Turks."

But Mladić, the pitiless killer, had a soft spot. While he had no compunction in slaughtering the children of Muslims, he was the adoring father of his own daughter, Ana. The promising medical student at Belgrade University was the apple of his eye. He would shower her with affection and smother her with kisses. Mladić even expressed his fatherly love with guns. His prized possession was a pistol he had received as an award upon his successful graduation from the military academy. Ana meant so much to him that he swore to fire his pistol for the first time only on hearing the news that she had given birth to his first grandchild. Among his many weapons, this one was reserved for celebratory gunfire, for joy rather than genocide.

The sight of men whom I regarded as monsters being treated as dignitaries at the UN was repugnant. It was obscene, I thought to myself, that a bicycle thief in Geneva was more likely to be punished than a war criminal. It was not just that they enjoyed impunity for mass murder, but that they were actually rewarded for it, by making themselves indispensable to a peace agreement. The conversation between the diplomats and activists reflected the tensions between peace and justice. The diplomats would remind us that politics is "the art of the possible," whereas the idealists dreamed the impossible. What incentive, they pointed out, would there be for the men who could stop the killing to conclude a ceasefire if they would be prosecuted after they put down their weapons? Political realism, we were told, must prevail over utopian fantasies. But realism seemed to be confused with cynicism. Somehow, the burden of proof was on human rights defenders to justify their cause, based on the dubious presumption that appeasement of ethnic hate-mongers was a viable solution to ethnic war. In fact, the opposite was true: it wasn't that justice stood in the way of peace; it was that peace was not realistic without justice.

The peace-versus-justice debate reflected the

diametrically opposed views on the origins of the Yugoslav catastrophe. The view that ethnic partition and impunity for genocide was the only realistic political solution assumed that ethnic war was an inescapable outburst of primordial hatred, as if people with different identities were doomed to destroy each other and thus must live separately. With the collapse of the Soviet Union in 1991, the "clash of civilizations" had been proffered as the new post–Cold War dividing line. It was appealing to thinkers whose simplistic binary vision could not fathom the alternative vision of an inextricably interdependent world. In a famous lecture delivered in 1992, the eminent Harvard professor Samuel Huntington had explained the Bosnian war by noting matter-of-factly, "The fault lines between civilizations will be the battle lines of the future." How, I wondered, could the interethnic fabric of Bosnia be reconciled with a clash of civilizations? Was there something the great intellectual saw from the ivory tower that I couldn't see on the streets of cosmopolitan Sarajevo?

While the simplistic clash-of-civilizations theory became fashionable among intellectuals and politicians, those of us on the ground had a different perception of reality. The former U.S. ambassador to Belgrade Warren Zimmermann had astutely observed that although "there was plenty of racial and historical tinder available in Yugoslavia...the conflagrations didn't break out through spontaneous combustion. Pyromaniacs were required." Far from inevitable, incitement of hatred and war was a political choice, an instrument by which ruthless demagogues elevated themselves to power. By individualizing guilt, it seemed, justice demystified the cynical and false view that people of differing identities will invariably slaughter each other. The simple testimony of Erdemović captured the artificiality of ethnic war that somehow evaded the pundits and experts: "Honourable Judges...I feel sorry for all the victims in the former Bosnia and Herzegovina regardless of their nationality," he had told the tribunal. "I have lost many very good friends of all nationalities only because of that war, and I am convinced that all of them, all of my friends, were not in favour of a war...But they simply had no other choice. This war came and there was no way out." But these voices didn't matter to the worldly-wise; from a safe distance, they had already made up their minds about the causes of the war through an exotic narrative of inexorable tribal hatred.

JOURNEY TO JUSTICE

My unexpected journey to global justice began on September 30, 1992, when I arrived in war-torn Yugoslavia for the first time. Just one month earlier, the notorious Omarska and Trnopolje concentration camps near Prijedor, in northwestern Bosnia, had been discovered. A camera crew with ITN had captured shocking images of emaciated civilians behind barbed wire, reminiscent of a dark past that Europe had seemingly put behind. One of the Muslim prisoners, Fikret Alić, with gaunt face and hollowed eyes, protruding ribs and shrivelled stomach, his pants hanging from his skeletal waist, had become the iconic image of the horrors unfolding in Bosnia. Staring at the world from the cover of *Time* magazine, he was the anguished face of thousands of faceless victims. Amidst the public outcry, political leaders had dispatched a European diplomatic mission to report on the atrocities, and I accompanied the distinguished emissaries as a junior advisor. Still in my twenties, my strongest asset was my political naïveté; it led me to the obvious conclusion that the enforcement of humanitarian law required prosecutions before an international criminal tribunal.

The idea of war crimes trials found resonance with the Swedish diplomat and jurist Hans Corell, a senior figure in our mission who would go on to become the UN legal counsel under the secretary-general, Kofi Annan. A refined and erudite man, impeccably dressed and proficient in several languages, Corell was a conspicuous anomaly among the thugs we encountered in the war zone. A memorable occasion was his meeting in the stronghold of Knin with the so-called minister of justice of the self-styled Republic of Serbian Krajina, an unwashed man with an unkempt beard, sporting the uniform of the extremist Četnik militia. He had been directly implicated in atrocities against Croatian civilians. Blissfully oblivious to the limitations of his thuggish audience, Ambassador Corell lectured the menacing warlord about human rights law, like a stern schoolmaster scolding a delinquent student. Some complained that the straitlaced bureaucrat was too puritanical, too caught up in notions of right and wrong, in disregard of political realities. To me, it was a highly commendable flaw under the circumstances. During our whirlwind tour of Croatia, Ambassador Corell and I engaged in existential conversations about our profession as jurists, about the purpose of the mission, about the fundamental moral challenge that Yugoslavia posed to the credibility of humanitarian law. It was to us not a clash of civilizations that was at issue but a clash between civilization and barbarity, with justice as the dividing line between the two.

After an exhaustive few days of meetings and investigations, our delegation retreated to Vienna to draft a report. In an Austrian Foreign Ministry building not far from the impressive Hofburg palace of Habsburg times, we deliberated on a suitable response to "ethnic cleansing." We felt that at this stage of the war, reaffirming the obvious fact that systematic atrocities had been committed or registering condemnations with righteous platitudes was not particularly useful. Instead, we resolved to stretch our mandate and made what we considered to be a meaningful response: a recommendation that an international criminal tribunal be established to prosecute those most responsible for war crimes. Far from being an impediment to peace, individualization of guilt, we felt, was essential for deterrence of further atrocities; it was also a vital ingredient of postwar inter-ethnic reconciliation, absolving groups of the collective guilt that would feed the nationalist narratives of the next war.

As morally correct as it was, the idea of war crimes trials was, at the time, an absurd proposal that was met by some with political ridicule. After all, throughout the UN era, a culture of impunity had prevailed, and it seemed natural to some that powerful leaders were beyond the pale of justice. It took some imagination to conceive the world differently, and with our concrete and detailed proposal, the idea of prosecutions was now on the table. It showed that justice was indeed an option. Despite the cynical scorn of some, the growing tide of outrage at inaction against the atrocities made it difficult to ignore the proposal. It was, in effect, an attempt at the construction of a different political reality, one in which accountability was part of the cost-benefit calculus of power. The momentum was such that by May 25, 1993, the UN Security Council had taken the unprecedented step of establishing the ICTY. It was, after a half-century hiatus, a sudden resurrection of the Nuremberg legacy.

A few months later, on April 3, 1994, I arrived in The Hague as the first legal advisor to the prosecutor of the newly established UN tribunal. Having specialized in international criminal law in law school shortly before, at a time when there was no prospect of an international criminal tribunal, I

had kicked myself for the folly of ensuring my prolonged unemployment notwithstanding Ivy League
credentials. The pressures were many to jump ship
and move on to another career. But the temptation
to throw myself into the Yugoslav cauldron was
irresistible. Perhaps, when we experience loss in
our own lives, we take a greater interest in the loss
of others. As I entered my bleak new office with its
hideous blue carpet and plastic furniture, I felt so
grateful. It was as if the heavens had opened and
landed this historic opportunity in my lap. But I
was ambivalent about the intersection of professional accomplishment with human suffering; I felt
both hubris and humility.

A young lawyer brimming with intellectual
excitement and moral purpose, I was ready to
make history as a UN prosecutor. The only problem was that there was still no chief prosecutor, just
an empty building with a handful of administra-
tive staff in isolated cubicles. The tribunal was still
an imaginary institution. Some time earlier, the
judges had attended a swearing-in ceremony with
some fanfare. It created the impression of justice
in motion, but that was far from the truth. I busied
myself laying the foundation for the future court
with pithy research papers on the law of genocide.

In the following months, more staff was recruited to begin the cumbersome work of criminal investigations, but there was still no foreseeable prospect of arresting defendants.

Some smugly celebrated the fact that, unlike Nuremberg, the tribunal would not be an instance of victor's justice. But holding war crimes trials while acquiescing in the ethnic partition of Bosnia was like prosecuting Hitler while accepting the annexation of Poland. Without an occupying army to arrest the accused, we could only hope for symbolic justice by issuing arrest warrants that would go unexecuted. The tribunal, we felt, was a paper tiger, made to appease the conscience of the world, and not a genuine commitment to accountability. But it was all we had, and it was our responsibility to do our work and hope for the best. The stories of victims were horrendous and difficult to digest, not least because listening to them reminded me of watching helplessly from exile as our loved ones were tortured and murdered by extremists in my native Iran. But the slide into the dark abyss had begun. I logged an insane number of hours, consumed by my work, with round-the-clock stress and a deepening depression, and no prospect that anybody would ever be arrested. This slow destruction of my physical and psychological health was either an act of stupidity or an act of love.

A small but growing band of lawyers and investigators, we spent our days drafting rules of procedure, legal opinions, witness statements, and indictments, and our nights talking obsessively about work and incessantly watching the news, trying to predict the outcome of the war and its implications for our success. Our professional and personal lives became indistinguishable, much to the chagrin of our spouses. The tribunal's humble and affable president, the renowned Italian international law professor Antonio Cassese, had adorned his office with black-and-white photos of the victims, a constant reminder of our purpose as a motley crew of legal warriors besieged by political indifference. We would share bland meals in the dingy cafeteria, and Professor Cassese would conduct spontaneous seminars on our unpredictable adventure, gesticulating passionately in his characteristic Neapolitan style, wondering out loud whether our experiment would end in a fiasco.

Within the first months of my arrival, we had drafted a rudimentary indictment against Karadžić and Mladić, charging them with war crimes and crimes against humanity. There was now an arrest

warrant against them and a sense of satisfaction that at the very least, even if they were still
in power, they were now stigmatized as accused
criminals and wanted persons rather than dignitaries. Since there was an obligation to arrest them,
they could not travel abroad and became politically isolated. It was all that we could hope for
at the time, aware that even this symbolic justice
could be undermined if they used their position
of power to exchange a ceasefire for amnesty in a
future peace agreement. The reality was that we
had a lofty mandate to enforce humanitarian law
but nobody whom we could prosecute. As the tribunal recruited staff with want ads, we surmised
that we should also advertise for a defendant, in the
hope that a suitable candidate would apply.

Some observers had assumed that the indictments could at least deter further atrocities,
warning the warlords that the world was watching
and that their crimes would one day be prosecuted.
But after the fall of Srebrenica in July 1995, that
illusion was shattered. It became clear that mere
threats would not prevent ruthless killers from executing their designs. Wishful thinking would not
bring about justice. By August 1995, however, the
military tide was turning in favour of the Croats

and Muslims. In November, as Serb forces were pushed back, the American diplomat Richard Holbrooke brought the Serbian president, Slobodan Milošević, together with the Croatian president, Franjo Tuđman, and the Bosnian president, Alija Izetbegović, to the Wright-Patterson Air Force Base, near Dayton, Ohio. Seizing the moment, he put them under intense pressure to conclude a peace agreement. Back in The Hague, we feared that the chief culprits would use the conclusion of hostilities as a bargaining chip to extract an amnesty. It was promising nonetheless that Karadžić and Mladić were not invited to the talks, on account of their status as fugitives. On December 14, 1995, the General Framework Agreement for Peace in Bosnia and Herzegovina was signed in Paris, bringing to an end the vicious Bosnian war. Instead of providing an amnesty, it required the cooperation of the parties with the tribunal and provided that indicted leaders could not continue to hold public office. Justice had survived the peace deal, at least in theory. But without the accused in The Hague, the tribunal was still not a credible court.

A TRIBUNAL WITH TEETH

Under the Dayton Peace Accords, a sixty-thousand-strong NATO force was deployed in Bosnia. This appeared to be the tribunal's long-awaited means of executing its arrest warrants. The peacekeeping mandate, however, did not extend to arresting accused war criminals. In fact, policy-makers were adamantly opposed to undermining the neutrality of the force. Some feared a repeat of the 1992 Mogadishu debacle, when U.S. soldiers had become entangled in the disastrous attempt to arrest the Somali warlord Mohamed Farrah Aidid. Furthermore, bringing perpetrators to justice was deemed irrelevant to military disengagement and post-conflict stability. It was a repeat of the debate between political realism and human rights idealism, as if they were mutually exclusive.

It wasn't long before it became clear that there was, in fact, a symbiotic relation between peace and justice. It should have come as no surprise that the costly peace-building process was being sabotaged by ethnic extremists. Their ideological platform of fear and hatred was diametrically opposed to the reconstitution of Bosnia as a single multi-ethnic state. A convergence between political realism and human rights idealism was gradually emerging: lasting peace required justice, not because of some lofty moral aspiration, but because of the realities on the ground. The toothless tribunal was about to become a credible court.

On July 10, 1997, a Chinook helicopter belonging to the Seventh Squadron of the British Royal Air Force landed in a remote site in Prijedor. This was the same region where in 1992 the world had first witnessed the notorious concentration camps in Omarska, Trnopolje, Keraterm, and Manjača, where thousands were tortured and killed. The helicopter carried two five-man teams of the Special Air Service (SAS), armed with nine-millimetre pistols and arrest warrants. Their mission, code-named Operation Tango, was to arrest Milan Kovačević and Simo Drljača, the Prijedor mayor and police chief respectively in 1992. Both were charged with genocide, and covert surveillance had confirmed their exact location. The first special forces team entered Prijedor hospital, where Kovačević was the director. They arrested him without incident and flew him to The Hague, where he was put on trial. The following year, prior to the judgement of the tribunal, Kovačević died of a heart attack in the UN detention unit.

The second special forces team was responsible for arresting Drljača. They found him at the Prijedor reservoir, fishing with friends. He was armed and opened fire on the British soldiers. They returned fire in self-defence, killing him on the spot. Operation Tango had changed everything. As news of the incident spread throughout Bosnia, the suspected war criminals were no longer laughing at the Hague Tribunal. They understood the language of force very well. Fearful of meeting Drljača's fate, some even surrendered voluntarily to NATO troops.

In the months that followed, the peacekeeping forces became increasingly engaged in executing the arrest warrants. A notable occasion was the arrest of Momčilo Krajišnik, a "big fish" who was among the most senior Bosnian Serb political leaders and Karadžić's partner in crime. On April 3, 2000, in the middle of the night, French soldiers broke down the door at his home in Pale and wrested him from his bed. The photo of the once-untouchable politician captured in his pajamas was a memorable image of his sudden fall from grace.

The successful transformation of the Yugoslav Tribunal into a credible judicial institution provided a precedent and impetus for the long-awaited establishment of a permanent penal court. It was a laboratory demonstrating both the viability of UN prosecutions and the importance of eradicating impunity for sustainable peace. In 1994, the UN Security Council had established a second ad hoc court for Rwanda, this one based in Arusha, Tanzania. After the establishment of a tribunal for Yugoslavia, it was unthinkable not to do the same for Rwanda, where almost a million people had perished. Elsewhere, in Sierra Leone and Cambodia, "mixed" or "hybrid" tribunals were established, combining the benefits of international expertise and impartiality with the legitimacy of national participation and ownership. After decades of impunity, there was now a contagion of accountability, shifting the boundaries of power and principle in international affairs. The burgeoning field of "transitional justice" grappled with the need for wounded nations to reckon with the past in order to build a better future. There was now a widespread consciousness that instead of imposed amnesia, atrocities must be addressed, whether through punitive justice like the Yugoslav Tribunal or restorative justice like the South African Truth and Reconciliation Commission; sweeping them under the carpet was not a viable option. It was the coming of age of global justice.

On July 17, 1998, amidst this exceptional ferment of the ICTY and ICTR, delegates at a diplomatic
conference in Rome adopted the Statute of the
International Criminal Court. It was the consummation, some fifty years later, of the universal
institutionalization of the Nuremberg legacy —
its transformation from a historical artifact into
a contemporary reality. In practice, however, the
universality of justice was still a work in progress.
Though potentially global, the court's jurisdiction
was limited to those nations that were signato-
ries to its statute. It was predictable that certain
powerful nations with military might, as well as
the nations with the worst human rights records,
would not accept the court's competence. For tyrannical leaders, inviting such scrutiny would be like
signing their own arrest warrants. The only rem-
edy for this jurisdictional gap was compulsory
referrals by the UN Security Council. The ICTY
and ICTR were both enforcement measures that
were not dependent on the consent of the affected
nations. But Security Council action too was subject to political selectivity, and the veto power of its
Permanent Members, in particular the Americans,
Chinese, and Russians, each with their own geopolitical agenda. The failure in later years to refer

the atrocities in Syria to the ICC was a case in point, as the mass murder of half a million people went unpunished. Nonetheless, unlike its ad hoc predecessors for the former Yugoslavia and Rwanda, the ICC's mandate was much broader in scope, and its reach would extend to countries as diverse as Uganda and Congo, Sudan and Libya.

This exclusive focus on Africa would lead to accusations by some political leaders that the court was a Western instrument dispensing neocolonial justice. When the Yugoslav Tribunal was first established, however, the complaint was the opposite: the victims had the benefit of justice only because they were Europeans. Caught between the short-sighted selective justice pursued by political realists and the exaggerated expectations hoisted upon it by idealists, the fledgling ICC would invariably encounter resistance by those who thought it was going too far and reproach by those who thought it wasn't going far enough. But for those of us who remembered the dark days of complete impunity, the court was a beautiful sight to behold, despite its flaws and blemishes.

RECKONING AT THE HAGUE

By 1998, the Yugoslav Tribunal had already succeeded beyond what most imagined. It had become the catalyst for a revolution in global justice. But it still had unfinished business. Although many prominent suspects had been arrested, those most responsible were still at large. Karadžić and Mladić had gone into hiding, and Milošević was still the head of state in Serbia, beyond the reach of the NATO forces, whose mandate was limited to neighbouring Bosnia. For the tribunal, there was no choice but to wait until the opportunity was ripe for apprehending the suspects. Justice delayed was better than justice denied. Holding powerful men accountable, we would come to learn, was a long-term game.

In 1998, the ethnic war had spread from Bosnia to Kosovo, the majority-Albanian province where Milošević had first fanned the flames of hatred a decade earlier. The conflict between Serb forces and Albanian rebels quickly escalated into large-scale ethnic cleansing. It resulted in a mass exodus of refugees and destabilization of neighbouring States. On March 24, 1999, NATO began a campaign of aerial bombardment against Serb forces.

On May 27, 1999, the tribunal's Canadian prosecutor, Louise Arbour, charged Milošević for crimes against humanity for the persecution of Kosovo's Albanian population (having worked in record time to prepare the indictment). It was the beginning of the end for the Serbian leader. Plagued by his own hubris, he had finally overplayed his hand.

Following military defeat in Kosovo and the mounting cost of successive wars, Milošević was confronted by widespread political unrest. In a popular rebuke to authoritarian nationalism, the Otpor! student movement organized mass protests calling for democracy and human rights. The magic spell of populist hysteria had broken. Following accusations of fraud in the presidential election of September 24, 2000, popular rage reached a boiling point. By October 5, 2000, hundreds of thousands of people had descended on Belgrade from all parts of Serbia. This time, instead of "Slobo, Slobo," which they had chanted on St. Vitus Day in 1989, their slogan was "He is finished, he is finished." Upon hearing the news that he had resigned, they broke out in jubilant celebrations in the streets of Belgrade. Just as he had risen to power riding a wave of popular anger, the erstwhile nationalist saviour was now forced to step down by the disillusionment of the same Serbian people. They had finally woken up to the grim reality of his delusional demagoguery. His spectacular downfall at the hands of Serbs exploded the myth of the war as a "clash of civilizations." It vindicated those of us who saw it as a conflict between despotism and democracy.

On June 28, 2001, coinciding with St. Vitus Day, the exact same day that Milošević's inflammatory 1989 speech had unleashed the demonic forces that would rip Yugoslavia apart, he was extradited to The Hague to stand trial for crimes against humanity. It was the consummation of the dramatic demise of a once-invincible leader who now had to answer for his crimes. Seeing him finally in the defendant's dock was unbelievable: the first ever UN trial against a former head of state. Milošević was unrepentant. He did his utmost to turn the hearing into a platform for propaganda, to peddle his nationalist diatribe one last time, portraying himself as the victim of an anti-Serb conspiracy. But the trial rendered his theatrics redundant. Justice revolved around the simple question of guilt or innocence for atrocities, not disputed historical mythologies. After an exhaustive four-year trial, the tribunal adjourned to render its historic judgement. But the hand of fate intervened to cut the path of justice short. On March 11, 2006, shortly before the decision was to be delivered, Milošević died of a heart attack in his prison cell. It was an inglorious end to a grim chapter of history.

The victims of Milošević were denied the satisfaction of a final verdict. However, for those in Bosnia, the former Serbian president was a distant villain, whereas the duo of Karadžić and Mladić had had a more direct hand in the tragedy that had befallen them. But shortly after the Dayton Peace Accords, both of them had seemingly vanished into thin air. For more than a decade, their whereabouts remained a complete mystery.

JUSTICE DELAYED NOT DENIED

"We are energetic beings . . . Disruption in energetic flow leads to the loss of vital energy and tiredness which constitutes the beginning of all problems with health." With this introduction, the Human Quantum Energy website advertised the benefits of alternative medicine, including acupuncture, homeopathy, macrobiotic diet, and ancient Indian Ayurvedic treatments. These holistic healing techniques were administered by the eccentric Dr. Dragan Dabić, living at 267 Yuri Gagarin Street, named after the famous Soviet cosmonaut who first travelled to outer space in 1961. Instead of an intrepid space explorer, the friendly recluse was known as a "spiritual explorer." With a striking mane of white hair complemented by a long white beard, the popular healer had a mysterious, otherworldly air about him, as if he were the repository of magical powers from another planet. A soothing and skilled practitioner, master of the seven chakras, he published and lectured widely, appeared on television, and was sought after by those suffering from disease, depression, and distress. On July 21, 2008, the world discovered that the mysterious Dr. Dabić was none other than the psychiatrist Dr. Radovan Karadžić.

Once the news of his arrest spread, Sarajevo erupted in euphoric celebrations. Jubilant crowds waving Bosnian flags poured onto the streets as hundreds of cars honked approvingly. This time, Sarajevo was besieged by a sense of justice. Elsewhere, one of the Srebrenica survivors, Nura Begić, was so overcome with excitement that she could not eat or sleep. One of the Omarska camp survivors, Edin Ramulić, said in disbelief: "I am happy that I survived until this day to hear the news that Karadžić is arrested and he will be taken to The Hague." His capture, his encounter with justice, redeemed the humanity of those that had suffered so terribly at his hands.

The historic trial at The Hague was a tantalizing twist of fate for Dražen Erdemović. Having served his five-year sentence, he had now returned to the tribunal as a witness for the prosecution. When he had confessed to his crimes in 1996, he explained it was "because of the peace of my mind, my soul, my honesty." Now, having redeemed his own humanity through contrition, he was about to come face to face with the once-powerful man who had so fundamentally changed the course of his life. Karadžić had refused legal counsel and conducted his own cross-examination of Erdemović, once his subordinate in the Bosnian Serb Army and now a crucial witness against him.

"Why did you decide to tell the prosecution this story?" Karadžić asked Erdemović in reference to the Srebrenica mass executions.

"Why did I decide that, Mr. Karadžić?" he responded. "I decided that because I realized that my life had been ruined on that day. It's because of that and because of all the persons who were victims on that day."

On March 24, 2016, following an exhaustive trial with hundreds of witnesses and myriad exhibits lasting five years, the Trial Chamber convened a hearing to read the final judgement. As presiding judge O-Gon Kwon of South Korea read the verdict, Karadžić stood impassively with his arms stiff by his side, listening to the long list of crimes he had committed. He avoided looking at the public gallery packed with survivors, many of them grieving widows and mothers who had lost their husbands and sons, like the Mothers of Srebrenica. He was now at the end of the same road to hell that he had created for so many innocent people.

"The Chamber," Judge Kwon declared, "hereby sentences you to forty — four-zero — years of imprisonment."

At seventy years of age, Karadžić would spend his remaining years behind bars. But outside the tribunal, one of the Mothers of Srebrenica was seething with anger that he had not received a sentence of life imprisonment. For some, no punishment could atone for the magnitude of their loss.

Ratko Mladić, the Butcher of Bosnia, had also been at large, but for him too, time was running out. On May 26, 2011, after sixteen years on the run, he was arrested in the village of Lazarevo, north of Belgrade, where he had been hiding in his nephew's modest shack. I remembered him as a menacing killer, but now, back in public view, he was a shadow of his former self, a frail old man with one arm paralyzed by a stroke. By choosing the path of perdition, Mladić had become a war hero to some, but in a cruel twist of fate, he had robbed himself of his greatest love. Back in 1994, his daughter, Ana, whom he adored with all his being, had fallen in love. Just twenty-four years old, her whole life ahead of her, she had met a classmate at medical school by the name of Goran, a handsome and charming man who had stolen her heart. They were lost in the blissful oblivion of young love, but their worlds were about to collide: Goran came from a family of human rights activists for whom Ana's doting father was a hideous monster.

There was no discussion of politics in the Mladić household, and the state-controlled Serbian media shielded Ana from knowing the truth. But now her boyfriend, Goran, with whom she wanted to have children and raise a family, told her about her father's heinous crimes. At a conference in Moscow, they had spent some romantic days together away from home, dreaming about their future. But everywhere they went on their Russian getaway, they were surrounded by hellish images of Sarajevo on television. Somewhere on Selimović Boulevard, a pedestrian lay in a pool of blood, her life snuffed out by a sniper's bullet, and now Mladić's precious girl had to witness her father's abominations broadcast around the world.

Goran told Ana that she must confront Mladić or they could have no future together. She was forced to choose between her father and her future husband. Under pressure from Goran but fearful of destroying her family's harmony, Ana attempted to broach the subject gently. She told her father she was volunteering to work as a nurse on the front lines, that she wanted to see the reality of the war through her own eyes. But Mladić dismissed her suggestion with a patronizing "Come on, my angel." She couldn't bring herself to say more. Goran scolded her for refusing to accept that she had been raised by a monster, saying that he could not live with her.

Finally, overcome with grief, the gentle, loving Ana decided to teach her father a lesson he would never forget. On March 25, 1994, she went to his cabinet and took out his prized pistol. In another world, he would have fired it in celebration when Ana and Goran gave him his first grandchild. But now, all was lost; her dream was shattered. Ana shot herself in the head. She had died of shame.

Mladić's comrades said that after losing Ana, he became a broken man. He never recovered. Some said that he lost his mind, unleashing his fury on the hapless victims of Srebrenica. He was vicious and victorious in war, but the sight of Ana in the morgue finally brought him to his knees. He tearfully removed a lock of her hair, looking at her beautiful face one last time. Years later, on May 31, 2011, his last wish before his extradition from Belgrade to The Hague was to visit her grave, where he laid flowers and shed more tears at her loss. There he was, sixteen years after I last saw him in Geneva: Mladić the mighty warrior, now Mladić the grieving father.

On July 2, 2013, Erdemović made his last appearance at the tribunal. He testified to Mladić's role in Srebrenica, closing a horrible chapter of his life. After that, I would never see the man I had prosecuted again. Just as Mladić reappeared after many years, Erdemović disappeared under an assumed identity at an undisclosed location. He could finally put the past behind him and start a new life with his now-eighteen-year-old child.

THE ROAD TO REDEMPTION

On May 9, 2014, the restored National Library reopened in Sarajevo. Selimović Boulevard once again bustled with traffic, and the hideous mustard-coloured Holiday Inn was still standing. The mosques in both Ahmići and Srebrenica were rebuilt. Over time, the physical destruction was erased, and life went on, but the wounds on the inside remained. The trials at The Hague gave the victims some measure of justice, but that could not bring back the dead.

The Mothers of Srebrenica have mostly laid to rest the bones of their loved ones, painstakingly retrieved by forensic experts from the mass graves and identified with DNA analysis. Some, like Nura Mustafić, still haven't found the remains of their children. They still live in the hope that their sons will one day show up at their door. Others have to be content with holding on to familiar objects that were discovered among the bodies: a pair of glasses, a watch, a comb, a toothbrush, or a trinket. A memento of their loved ones, just as the man who put their sons in that grave held on to a lock of his daughter's hair.

The tribunal had become a success beyond

anything I had imagined. I had spent a good part of what remained of my youth witnessing horrors, cheating death, fighting for justice, making history; and now that it had all come to pass, I felt that it was so vital, yet so inadequate. Exhausted by the toll of those years, I was overcome by a sense of futility. The rules of power had to change; humankind desperately needed a moral compass, a division between right and wrong. But to reduce the enormity of the pain to the punishment of this or that villain was to indulge in the illusion that through rituals of judicial closure we had learned the deeper lessons of confronting the radical evil in our midst.

Justice is, above all, a redemption of our shared humanity. It restores not only the dignity of the victim but also that of the perpetrator, and it is also a reminder to the bystander that our true vocation is to demand justice for all, because we are but one in essence. Walking out of the tribunal for the last time, leaving behind my years as a UN prosecutor, I stood in front of that wretched building in The Hague where I had seen so much misery, and there, on the front lawn, beside a large fountain, my tearful eyes fell upon a bereaved mother from Srebrenica. Not knowing each other's language, we both smiled knowingly, despair embracing hope, speaking silently the wisdom that in a cruel world, the sharing of wounds opens us to the inextinguishable light within.

THREE

THE WILL TO INTERVENE

NEVER AGAIN?

"A COCKROACH CANNOT GIVE BIRTH to a butterfly." That is what they were told. You cannot change someone who is inherently evil. In a complicated world, it was an appealing message in its simplicity; a convenient explanation for impoverished people whose children went to bed hungry. The daily humiliation, the desperation, the rage, the scapegoating — all the ingredients of an imminent explosion were there. What followed should have come as no surprise. It could have been stopped, but nobody cared. The world simply stood by and watched.

Cockroaches and butterflies; these thoughts raced through my mind as Samuel grabbed my nose with his chubby hands, a twinkle of mischief in his beautiful brown eyes, fluttering his long eyelashes. Éloge Butera was visibly proud to see his adorable toddler sitting on his mentor's lap. I was equally proud to see my former student, now a successful lawyer, with a beautiful, thriving family. I had taken a liking to him from our very first encounter, when he walked into my office seeking guidance for his studies. The law students at McGill University were all impressive overachievers, survivors of a highly competitive selection process. But Éloge was a different kind of survivor. He had literally cheated death. In a bewildering twist of fate, he had made it to law school because, in childhood, he had been denied entry to another school, in Kigali, during the 1994 Rwandan genocide.

On December 9, 1948, the UN General Assembly adopted the Genocide Convention. In the shadow of the Holocaust, amidst solemn vows of "never again," nations declared their commitment to the prevention and punishment of this odious scourge. But in the years that followed, "never again" became "ever again." Throughout the UN era, countless millions were slaughtered while the world stood by and watched. Having worked as a UN prosecutor on the Yugoslav Tribunal, I found myself in

Rwanda in 1995, helping set up the newly established International Criminal Tribunal for Rwanda (ICTR). There was no doubt about the imperative of punishing the *génocidaires*. But the shocking scenes of carnage in the streets of Kigali, the Rwandan capital, were a stark reminder that justice cannot bring back the dead. The more fundamental question in my mind was: Did this need to happen? Could it have been stopped? Was genocide an inescapable historical reality, an unavoidable expression of intrinsic predatory aggression? Or was it a premeditated political choice that was foreseeable and thus preventable? And above all, if it was possible to stop genocide, was there a will to intervene among those with the means?

The conception of mass murder as rooted in human nature is often a convenient absolution from our shared responsibility to confront injustice. It is true that even if war has declined historically, there is still plenty of organized violence in the world. Looking at our brutish past, we may well conclude that despite some improvements, we are merely territorial mammals with an insatiable appetite for agression. Indeed, humankind is unique in mastering the destruction of its own kind. Our species makes the fiercest of beasts look tame in comparison.

We cannot simply wish radical evil away with the magic wand of noble sentiments. But the view of human beings as incorrigibly murderous creatures does not withstand scrutiny, not least when experienced from the vantage point of the trenches rather than distant philosophical speculation. In fact, a more intimate engagement with the realities of these tragic situations teaches us in unexpected ways that mindless cruelty is not necessarily our true vocation. Let us imagine for one moment that mass murder is, in fact, a deliberate decision, a calculated calamity, a hateful but artificial construction of identity as an instrument of power. If that were the working assumption, how would we encounter radical evil differently?

Familiarity with the anatomy of genocide may well suggest that often the great evils of our time are predictable; and if they are predictable, the case could be made that they are also potentially preventable. This conception of the challenge before us liberates us from cowardly surrender to those cynical impulses that perpetuate the myth of inexorable doom — an effortless despair that leads to our disengagement from unpleasant realities. There is, in fact, much that we can learn from the artificiality of such catastrophes. It takes tremendous effort to bring dormant aggression to the surface and to give it a coherent collective expression. This is as true of mass atrocities in distant lands as it is in the ominous rise of populist hatred and terrorism in our own midst. There is nothing random or spontaneous about radical evil; it is a conspiracy of prodigious proportions. Rarely does it just creep up on us without warning. The real question is not whether we can stop genocide; it is whether we have the will to intervene.

Long before the horrors of 1994, Éloge was already the victim of the virulent disease of hatred that, left unchecked, would lead to the genocide. He was in the second grade when he first realized that he was different from his Rwandan classmates.

"The first time that my teacher asked all the Tutsis to stand in my class, I didn't stand up. I didn't know what a Tutsi was, or that I was one."

Amidst the rising tide of populist hatred, his parents had attempted in vain to shield him from the humiliation of ethnic labelling by the Hutu majority.

"My teacher screamed at me and told me to stand up like the other cockroaches," he recalled. "From that day, I understood: being a Tutsi was something very terrible, and I should be ashamed of myself and my family."

For the next four years of elementary school, Éloge and the few other Tutsis in his class had to endure the ritual of standing up in class and being shamed for who they were. The bullying they witnessed within the confines of their school would soon spill over to the streets of Kigali, forever destroying the life they once knew.

PLEASE DON'T ABANDON US

On the evening of April 6, 1994, shortly before 8:20 p.m., the Rwandan presidential jet circled around Kigali Airport in preparation for landing. President Juvénal Habyarimana was returning from a regional summit in Dar es Salaam, Tanzania, accompanied by the president of Burundi, Cyprien Ntaryamira. Earlier, he had met with the president of neighbouring Zaïre, Mobutu Sese Seko, in Gbadolite, Mobutu's humble ancestral village, which had been transformed into the "African Versailles," with opulent palaces built in the style of kleptocratic kitsch. Amidst the controversy surrounding the UN-brokered Arusha Peace Agreement, Mobutu had warned Habyarimana against further travel. The agreement, signed on

August 4, 1993, envisaged power-sharing between the Rwandan Patriotic Front (RPF) — Tutsi insurgents based in Uganda — and the government of Rwanda, representing the Hutu majority.

The process of demilitarization and the establishment of a broad-based Government of National Unity were to be facilitated by the UN Assistance Mission in Rwanda (UNAMIR). The 2,500 peacekeepers — including soldiers from the former colonial power Belgium as well as Bangladesh and Ghana — were under the command of Canadian general Roméo Dallaire. The Arusha Accords were a promising end to a conflict dating back to the 1959–61 Hutu Peasant Revolution against the Tutsi establishment. By the time of Rwanda's independence in 1962, the revolution had resulted in a flood of 120,000 Tutsi refugees into Uganda and other neighbouring countries. But extremists of the Hutu Power movement, supported by Rwandan military forces and the notorious Interahamwe youth militia, were opposed to the infiltration of Tutsi "cockroaches" in Rwanda. For them, the "Tutsi problem" could only be eliminated by eliminating the Tutsi.

The arrival of President Habyarimana's sleek Falcon 50 aircraft — a gift from French president

François Mitterrand — was broadcast live on the popular Radio Télévision Libre des Mille Collines (RTLM), the mouthpiece of Hutu Power. Suddenly, a loud explosion was heard throughout Kigali. The announcer stopped and an interlude of classical music followed. Then the news bulletin came: "President Habyarimana's plane has been shot down ... The president is dead." On final approach, the aircraft had been struck by two surface-to-air missiles in rapid succession. It had crashed in a great ball of fire, its wreckage strewn across the Kanombe neighbourhood, on the perimeter of the presidential mansion. There were no survivors.

RTLM was quick to blame the Tutsis. For the extremists, the time had finally come to exterminate the cockroaches. In the hundred days that followed, up to one million people were killed, a rate of mass murder far more efficient than the Nazi concentration camps. An estimated three-quarters of Rwanda's Tutsi population was slaughtered before RPF forces defeated the *génocidaires*. It was an archetypal genocide, even by the appalling standards of the twentieth century.

On that fateful evening, Éloge and his family left their home in the same Kanombe neighbourhood where the presidential jet had crashed. They were running to save their lives: "We had learned that groups of soldiers were walking into Tutsi homes and killing everybody in them. My father's brother was already killed. We hid in the bushes all day that first day without any food or water. We could hear gunshots being fired and people yelling as they were being killed in their homes. My sister was still a baby, but she didn't cry."

As I listened to him over dinner at an Indian restaurant in Montreal, I remembered visiting the Hindu temple in Kigali, some twenty years earlier, when I was on the ground with the UN. It was close to the Amgar Garage, owned by Georges Rutaganda, the notorious vice-president of the Interahamwe. The militia had conducted house-to-house searches and set up roadblocks to weed out the Tutsi among the terrified crowds in the streets. Their task was made easy because Rwandan identity cards indicated the bearer as either Hutu or Tutsi. Some were killed on the spot with machetes and clubs. Others were detained in the Hindu temple before being slaughtered in a nearby valley. Many women and girls were subject to horrific sexual violence before their death. Nobody was spared; not even the children. In the Kinyarwanda language, "Interahamwe" meant "those who work together."

The "work" was the extermination of the *inyenzi* —
the Tutsi cockroaches.

Rwanda was *le pays des mille collines*, the land
of a thousand hills, a stunningly beautiful country of carefully cultivated micro-farms, verdant
pastures with grazing cattle, snow-capped vol-
canoes, and the famous gorillas in the mist. As
my flight landed in Kigali for the first time, the
view from above resembled a giant manicured
garden. The bucolic image was difficult to reconcile with the grim sights that I would witness
on the ground. Behind the Amgar garage, amidst
bright flowers and eucalyptus trees, we found an
open pit. It had been filled with mutilated corpses
like the many others strewn across the streets of
Kigali. A million victims was an inscrutable statistical abstraction, but the intertwined bodies piled
on top of each other told a more intimate story.
Their faces stared back from the grave, silently
screaming, "Why?" Each had a name, I thought,
a universe of thoughts, emotions, and relations,
unrealized dreams and ambitions. Now they lay
there, motionless, their lives extinguished by the
ravages of blind hatred.

I didn't know eleven-year-old Éloge then, but
he too had been there with his family, not far from

that site of horror where I stood. It would be more than a decade before the hand of fate would bring us together, from the dirt floor of that school where he was humiliated for being a Tutsi to my office at the university where he would shine for who he was. But the journey was long and tortuous, and first he had to be denied entry to the École Technique Officielle (ETO) in Kicukiro.

On April 7, 1994, after spending the night hiding in the bushes, Éloge and his family arrived at the entrance of the ETO. Run by the Salesian Catholic fathers, the school was considered a safe haven because a contingent of ninety Belgian peacekeepers had been stationed there. Code-named Beverly Hills by the UN soldiers, it was anything but a glamorous location. Thousands of terrified Tutsis had overwhelmed its classrooms and grounds seeking protection, as they had done at churches and schools and hospitals throughout the country. They came bleeding and limping, with deep gashes and open wounds, in stunned silence, like the walking dead. Outside the school gates, the Interahamwe roamed menacingly, brandishing machetes and clubs, guns and grenades, drinking beer and chanting hateful slogans. They made clear their murderous intentions, as the crowd of some two thousand cowered in fear. All that stood between them and a grim end was the UN presence.

By the time Éloge and his family arrived in the evening, there was no more room in the UN compound. The schoolhouse and surrounding playing fields were packed to the hilt. Despite their desperate pleas, his family was turned away: "That night, we tried to go to a school that was protected by the United Nations for shelter. We were not allowed in because they had too many people there already. We slept in a dairy farm that night, and then we walked through a long, rainy day, trying to leave the city of Kigali." Being refused admission at the ETO was the best thing to happen to Éloge. Had his family been allowed to stay, they would all have been killed.

It is a horrifying thought that my adoptive brother could have been one of the mangled bodies in that gruesome pit. I imagine that had it not been for a random twist of fate, I would have never known Éloge, and Samuel would not now be sitting on my lap, playing with me. In fact, Éloge had been saved by a chain of events of which he had no knowledge at the time.

In the early morning of April 7, 1994, the same day that he was turned away from the ETO,

Rwanda's prime minister, Agathe Uwilingiyimana, had prepared to leave her home. The moderate Hutu leader, known as Madame Agathe, intended to address the nation on Radio Rwanda, to urge calm, to demand an end to the violence, and to call for a full investigation of the president's assassination the night before. She was accompanied by ten Belgian and five Ghanaian peacekeepers. Before they could leave, the Rwandan Presidential Guard surrounded them, disarmed the UN soldiers, and murdered the prime minister and her husband. By noon that day, most of the moderate Hutu leadership had been killed, removing any political obstacles to Hutu Power's diabolical plan. Some time later, the ten Belgian soldiers were tortured and killed, their mutilated bodies put on public display. The Ghanaians were spared. The intention of the extremists was clear: they wanted to frighten the UN into leaving so that they could exterminate the Tutsis with a free hand.

In the following days, the force commander, General Dallaire, sent an urgent request to the UN in New York to double the peacekeeping force to five thousand troops. The additional forces, he thought, could protect civilians against the murderous mobs, as they were doing at the ETO. But there would be no reinforcements. To the contrary, even the UN force already on the ground would be withdrawn, abandoning the Tutsis to the onslaught of the *génocidaires*. Between April 9 and 11, 1994, French and Belgian soldiers arrived on military aircraft to evacuate Western expatriates from Rwanda. The abandonment of the victims had begun.

In those fateful days, as people were running panic-stricken through the streets of Kigali, my dear friend Esther Mujawayo was hiding with her three small girls in the Lycée Notre Dame de Cîteaux, where her husband was the school principal. She knew that the UN withdrawal was a death sentence for the Tutsi. The soldiers were evacuating the white people. The Rwandans called them *umuzungu*, a Swahili word meaning "one who moves around," inspired by the itinerant eighteenth-century European traders who made their fortunes in East Africa. Now the Europeans were on the move once more, boarding army trucks, some with their dogs and cats, seeking to escape the hellish nightmare engulfing Rwanda.

Esther explained what happened at the school where she was hiding: "I saw the UN soldiers coming to pick up one mixed [race] girl, white mother, Rwandan father...I begged them to take my five- and three-year-old daughters to my friend in Belgium. The youngest, six months old, was to stay with me." It was, she thought, the best way to save the life of at least two of her little girls. But the soldiers explained that while they could take a mixed-race girl, and even the white expatriates' pets, there was no room for Rwandan children.

"The life of a European dog," she told me tearfully, "was more important than the life of my daughters." In the days that followed, her husband and some two hundred extended family members were killed. Esther had to find another way of saving her children.

Éloge recounts the horrors of those days: "That week was a nightmare for me. I saw people being killed. I saw hundreds of dead bodies floating in the river. We were literally running for our lives. We also had nothing to eat, which made us weak and terrified." It was a holocaust, but not one concealed behind the walls of a concentration camp. It was unfolding in plain sight, and the world watched, and did nothing.

By April 21, 1994, the UN Security Council had all but abandoned the Rwandan Tutsis. Exactly one year earlier, on April 21, 1993, at the opening of the United States Holocaust Memorial Museum in Washington, President Clinton had bemoaned "the death of millions whom our nations did not, or would not, or could not save." But Holocaust remembrance was a fetishistic incantation for distant events, its historical lessons divorced from present realities. For pragmatic decision-makers, it was now time to pull out from Rwanda, before political fallout from another Mogadishu-type quagmire for Western troops. No politician would lose votes for forsaking an obscure country in Africa, even at the cost of a million lives. Thus it was that exactly a year after the solemn pledges of "never again," Security Council Resolution 912 abandoned Rwanda to its fate while absolving bystanders through the euphemistic jargon of diplomacy. The catastrophic failure of political will, the callous indifference to the plight of the victims, was sanitized as an "adjustment" of UNAMIR's mandate. It was a green light for the *génocidaires*.

Dismissing the genocide as an unfortunate outburst of tribal hatred rationalized the decision to abandon Rwanda in its hour of need. There was no geopolitical imperative, no strategic interest or oil or minerals that could justify intervention. At most, the suffering of others was inconvenient for our collective conscience, but even that would

quickly pass. There was a momentary expression
of distress as the images of bloated bodies littering
the streets of Kigali, or floating in Rwanda's rivers
and lakes, were broadcast on television. But soon it
was overtaken by other breaking news and entertaining spectacles, like the O.J. Simpson trial. For
those still interested in Africa, the newly released
Lion King provided an alternative reality: a happy
ending, courtesy of Simba, the heroic exile who
returned the light of justice to a darkened realm.

Back at the ETO, amidst the escalating violence,
Lieutenant Luc Lemaire, the commander of the
Belgian contingent, had ordered his soldiers to
assume defensive positions at the perimeter of the
compound to protect the civilians. Food and medical supplies were running out, but he assured them
that so long as the UN flag was flying over "Beverly
Hills," they would be safe from the murderous
mob outside the gates. But now the unthinkable
had happened: he had received orders to withdraw.
Knowing that he had no say in the matter, he was
searching his conscience to see how he could break
the terrible news to those that looked to him for
protection against a horrible death. He gathered
the crowd and announced that soon they would
have to disperse and save themselves. Shocked and

panic-stricken, the Rwandans begged the soldiers not to leave.

On April 10, the arrival of French troops at the school was celebrated with applause and cheers. The Tutsi crowd at ETO was in denial: the French troops had come to help the UN withdrawal, not to save the Rwandans. The following day, on April 11, the UN vehicles began to leave the compound one by one. The world's betrayal had begun. The men and women, children, and elderly chased the soldiers, begging them, "Please don't abandon us." Others tried in vain to hang on to the trucks as they drove away. Soon the convoy was gone, and with it, their last hope for survival. Devastated and defenceless, those left behind could see Rutaganda standing menacingly at the school gates with a gun. The frenzied Interahamwe militia were just behind him with their crude weapons, eager to start the "work." The people knew what awaited them. They began to cry.

IS PREVENTION POSSIBLE?

The dead speak no more, and survivors, like Éloge and Esther, try to heal their wounds, living the outward semblance of a normal life. We express grief and sympathy for their suffering; we register outrage at the injustice; we indulge in the familiar refrain of "never again"; and sometime later, we find ourselves recycling the same indignation for some other calamity, a Darfur, an Aleppo, a South Sudan, or some other exotic place that momentarily captures our attention, until it is forgotten in the oblivion of past tragedies that have befallen nameless others. Perhaps we open our hearts to some refugees, messengers of a nightmarish world that we can scarcely imagine, but amidst the flood of misery drowning the multitude, we can only help the fortunate few. In lamenting human suffering, we often labour under the misconception that atrocities are somehow inevitable, like a tsunami that comes out of nowhere to destroy everything in its path, a natural rather than man-made disaster.

The prevention of genocide isn't about waking up at the eleventh hour when the armed robbers have already broken into our home. There is no UN 911 emergency number to call. By the time the Interahamwe were outside the gates of the ETO school, the options had already been narrowed to the use of military force, and whether we like it or not, intervention was too politically costly to be feasible. When doom is imminent, time is of the essence, and it is usually too late to act without a prohibitive cost. The reality is that unless powerful nations have the will to intervene in pursuit of their own narrow interests, humanitarian intervention is unlikely to happen. But even if there is a will to intervene, mobilizing troops is a time-consuming process in a situation that requires rapid intervention before violent escalation is beyond control. We must therefore find solutions that aren't dependent on a messianic saviour arriving just in time to rescue victims from the clutches of death.

The continuing failure to establish a UN rapid-reaction force reflects a narrow conception of national self-interest in global politics. When the first UN secretary-general, Trygve Lie, proposed the creation of a UN Guard in 1948, both the Americans and Soviets thought it was a "terrible idea." Locked in the myopic logic of the Cold War, neither superpower wanted a UN force that it could not control. Zero-sum politics could not entertain a transcendent common interest. With the collapse of the Soviet Union in 1991, deliberations on the role of the Security Council in maintaining peace emerged once more. A UN Standby Arrangements System, whereby nations would provide troops as required, was promising at first, but a chronic problem of slow deployment, poor training, and inadequate equipment persisted.

Following the Rwandan genocide, the need for a standing force was raised once more by the UN secretary-general, Boutros Boutros-Ghali. In the 1995 Agenda for Peace, he proposed a UN "rapid reaction force" at a "high state of readiness." This would become the Security Council's "strategic reserve for deployment where there was an emergency need for peace-keeping troops." But even in the wake of the Rwandan genocide, the Security Council preferred to maintain the inadequate Standby Arrangements System.

The opportunity to adopt more robust peace enforcement mandates would arise with the spillover of the Rwandan genocide. Following the RPF victory in July 1994, there was a mass exodus of some two million Hutu refugees throughout the Great Lakes region. The most significant concentration was in the immediately adjacent Kivu region of neighbouring Zaïre. Sizeable refugee camps were established, under control of the *génocidaires*. They allied themselves with Mobutu, who had enjoyed close relations with Habyarimana. In fact, following his assassination, Habyarimana's remains had

been interred at a mausoleum in Mobutu's ancestral home, Gbadolite, where they had met just
days before the Rwandan presidential jet had been
shot down. With Mobutu's blessing, the *génocidaires* began massacring the Tutsi population of the
Kivu region and prepared to retake Kigali from the
RPF. The conflict quickly escalated, and by 1996
the RPF and Ugandan forces, together with allied
militias, had marched on Kinshasa, overthrown
Mobutu, and installed the Congolese rebel leader
Laurent-Désiré Kabila as the new president. Zaïre
was renamed Democratic Republic of Congo (DRC).
The First Congo War was over.

But soon Kabila fell out with his erstwhile allies
and sought help from yet others. He invited Angola,
Namibia, Zambia, and Zimbabwe to intervene
against the Rwandan and Ugandan forces, in what
became known as the Second Congo War, though
some called it Africa's First World War. By the
time Rwanda and Congo signed the Pretoria Peace
Agreement in 2002, the spillover of the Rwandan
genocide had caused the death of an estimated six
million people through a combination of massacres,
starvation, and disease. It went largely unnoticed.
Whatever response the suffering of the Congolese
people elicited, the chaos was also an opportunity

for mining interests to amass fortunes from conflict minerals in collusion with the marauding militia wreaking havoc on civilians. The UN Mission in the Democratic Republic of Congo (MONUC) was mandated by the Security Council to stabilize the situation in the Kivus, where extremist militia were still massacring and raping at will. With a mandate to protect civilians, and with the shame of the Rwandan genocide hanging over the UN, MONUC was gradually given the means of fighting the predatory militia with combat troops and helicopter gunships. UN peacekeeping had turned a corner; now there was a new concept of "peace enforcement" with some teeth.

But these interventions after the fact, as important as they were, did not address the problem of preventing mass atrocities before they occur. There have been some isolated success stories, such as the UN Preventive Deployment Force in Macedonia. The small but timely force helped prevent the escalation of tensions between Macedonian Slavs and Albanians amidst the violent disintegration of the former Yugoslavia during the 1990s. Macedonia did not go the way of Croatia, Bosnia, and Kosovo. It was the conflict that didn't happen. But that was the result of an exceptional confluence of favourable circumstances and political will to prevent the devastating spread of the Balkan wars in southern Europe. Notwithstanding some success stories, for the most part we have to live with the unfortunate reality that in a world of competing priorities, UN peace enforcement is a costly tool of last resort, dependent on political whims and often unavailable at the right time.

Confronting radical evil requires political imagination, an understanding of the anatomy of mass murder. The early warning signs of genocidal violence provide cost-effective opportunities for intervention that may not be available once an otherwise manageable conflict has escalated to the point where UN troops become the only viable option. We must appreciate that once a situation has become headline news, once it has become an item on the UN Security Council's agenda, the window of opportunity to take feasible preventive measures may already have passed. Even if we cannot foresee genocide with mathematical exactitude, the vital ingredients of such political catastrophes are often manifest well in advance. Reinforcing UNAMIR at the eleventh hour could have saved many lives. But a much easier and surprising solution was available, had the UN acted earlier, before malignant forces metastasized into genocidal violence. In genocide prevention, the measure of success is what does not happen; and what does not happen requires early intervention, before the virulent disease of hatred spreads.

THE ART OF DEMONIZING OTHERS

"Getting rid of lice is not a question of ideology. It is a matter of cleanliness." The words are seemingly innocuous, until we appreciate the context. Nobody likes lice. They are a cause of infestation and disease. We wouldn't think twice about eradicating the filthy insects, irritating and insignificant as they are. But Heinrich Himmler's use of that metaphor on April 24, 1943, in Kharkov, occupied Soviet Ukraine, was far from innocent. The notorious Reichsführer of the Nazi SS was motivating his foot soldiers with a passionate speech so that they would dutifully obey orders to exterminate Jews on the eastern front. The Einsatzgruppen death squads, not unlike the Interahamwe, were instrumental to implementing the Final Solution. But the soldiers needed encouragement to kill. The reluctance to murder the innocent had to be overcome by transforming appalling cruelty into glorious heroism. "Anti-Semitism," Himmler explained, "is exactly the same as delousing."

"The Holocaust," it has been said, "did not begin in the gas chambers. It began with words." Cockroaches and lice, snakes and rats — the dehumanization of others is always a precondition for their destruction. We cannot harm those for whom we have empathy. The killer, the torturer, must first convince himself of the righteousness of his cause in order to reconcile callousness and cruelty with a caring and compassionate self-image. Hatred is a bifurcated delusion, a carefully constructed disconnect between disparate and contradictory aspects of human identity. That is why radical evil is always committed in the name of a greater good, glorified as an act of cleansing and purification. In fact, the inverted morality of the perpetrator is such that he sees himself as the victim of those he victimizes.

The wrongs justifying violence may be real or imaginary. But the demonization of others as the inherent source of evil is less about the reality of the victim, and more about the needs of the perpetrator. The group identified as the enemy becomes a blank screen on which the hate-monger projects all the fears and fantasies of his own making,

all the negative qualities that threaten his fragile self-image. As Jean-Paul Sartre famously said:
"If the Jew did not exist, the anti-Semite would
invent him." Scapegoating begins with a myth that,
repeated enough times, becomes the incontestable
truth. But translating imaginary hatred into real
violence, motivating the executioners of genocide,
brings with it the problem of visceral identification
with human suffering.

"I must say that our men who took part in these
executions suffered more from nervous exhaus-
tion than those who had to be shot." Paul Blobel
was a commander of Einsatzgruppe C. This was
the notorious unit responsible for the mass execution of some thirty-four thousand Jews in Babi Yar
ravine near Kiev — the largest single massacre of
the war. Now a defendant before the United States
military tribunal at Nuremberg, he complained
that while the victims were resigned to their fate,
their executioners "experienced a lot psychologically." His co-defendant, Otto Ohlendorf, a former
commander of Einsatzgruppe D, also felt sorry for
perpetrators who suffered from emotional distress. He testified that the mobile gas-vans were
introduced for the psychological well-being of the
SS troops, to make things easier for them; but it

turned out that shooting the victims next to mass graves was better after all, because unloading the asphyxiated corpses from the vans resulted in "unnecessary mental strain."

It was understandably difficult for those SS troops who were devoted family men at home to murder women and children in cold blood at work, even if it was for the greater good of the "master race." Alcohol consumption could ease the pain, but the reality was that the men of the Einsatzgruppen were severely traumatized and many had nervous breakdowns. Faced with their overwhelming cognitive dissonance, they needed Himmler's comforting reassurance that they were decent, honourable men doing the dirty work of exterminating lice and thus contributing to human betterment.

Hate propaganda is an integral element of extreme violence. Violent words set the stage for violent acts. Such hatred is best understood as instrumental rather than impulsive. We may feel deep-seated resentment and loathing towards others, whether because of real or imaginary wrongs. But the transformation of such impulses into an instrument of systemic violence, far from being a spontaneous crime of passion, requires careful premeditation and planning. In fact, collective demonization requires considerable skill and effort. It needs to be inspired, learned, expressed, and perfected, like a perverse art form. More so than anywhere else, Rwanda's demonologists showcased their talents on RTLM radio, skillfully exploiting historical tensions to mobilize the Hutu masses.

The origin of the Hutu-Tutsi fault line in contemporary Rwanda is intertwined with the European racialist theories of the nineteenth century. The Kingdom of Rwanda emerged in the fifteenth century in the Great Lakes region of Africa. Like its sister realm of Burundi, it was a highly centralized and stratified monarchy, equal in sophistication to the European monarchies of the time. There was a single Tutsi king — the *mwami* — ruling both Tutsi and Hutu subjects through local chiefs, though the pastoralist Tutsi clans had a privileged position over the agrarian Hutu. The lines between the two social castes, however, were blurred through intermarriage and ownership of cattle. The nobility included Hutu as well as Tutsi among its ranks. This relatively fluid identity would become rigidly fixed under colonial rule. The resulting dualism in the Rwandan imagination would have catastrophic consequences.

Rwanda and Burundi were among the last African territories to be colonized. Situated between Belgian Congo to the west and British East Africa to the northeast, both kingdoms were annexed in 1894 as part of German East Africa, together with Tanganyika to the east. The rapid expansion of European colonization in the nineteenth century was preceded by the Atlantic slave trade of the eighteenth century. The ruthless exploitation of African peoples had to be reconciled with the liberal human rights ideals of the Enlightenment. Thus colonial domination came to be rationalized by substituting the biological fact of a single human species with the supremacist myth of racial hierarchy. These pseudo-scientific theories involved a considerable degree of intellectual cherry-picking.

By the nineteenth century, Charles Darwin had coined the term "natural selection," feeding the intellectual imagination of the time. It was another contemporary Englishman, the biologist, anthropologist, and political theorist Herbert Spencer, who introduced the concept of "survival of the fittest" to the scientific lexicon. Social Darwinism was the curious application of this theory to social relations. It applied the survivalist logic of the animal kingdom to contrive a pseudo-scientific theory of racial hierarchy, in which imperial domination of an "inferior" black race by a "superior" white race was deemed a natural expression of human evolutionary progress.

The "civilizing" mission of the Europeans depended on the depiction of Africans as "primitive savages." The eighteenth-century Scottish philosopher David Hume expressed this prevalent sentiment by deeming "negroes and in general all other species of men...to be naturally inferior to the whites. There never was a civilized nation," he claimed, "of any other complexion than white." This presumed monopoly on cultural refinement could scarcely be reconciled with the sophisticated kingdoms of Rwanda and Burundi. The inconvenient fact of African civilization — whether in Axum, Benin, Ghana, Mali, Zimbabwe, or other ancient empires — required a conceptual solution consistent with the racialist ideologies of the time. The Hamitic hypothesis, as it became known, posited without any evidence whatsoever that African civilization could be attributed to a diluted subspecies of the Caucasian race that had migrated to the continent. In regard to the Tutsis, therefore, it could be concluded that although they were an inferior race compared to the Europeans, they were a superior

race compared to the Hutu, and racially predes-
tined to rule over them. The traditional Tutsi-Hutu
social class structure was thus transformed into a
rigid racial hierarchy. Consistent with the eugenic
pseudo-science of the time, anthropometric mea-
surements among Rwandans, such as the differing
height, nose, and skull size of Tutsis and Hutus,
became the basis for conflating outward physical
characteristics with hereditary differences in intellectual and moral capacity.

Following the defeat of the German Empire in
the First World War, Rwanda and Burundi became
Belgian mandates under the League of Nations. The
Belgians administered the colonies through the
Tutsi elites in a two-tier system that entrenched
the false racialist dichotomy and poisoned relations
with the humiliated Hutu. In 1926, colonial identification cards were introduced that designated the
bearer as either Tutsi or Hutu, a bureaucratic procedure that would in later years greatly facilitate the
genocide. Between 1959 and 1961, coinciding with
the decolonization period, Hutu nativist ideologies
called for liberation from both the white *umuzungu*
colonizers and their "foreign" Hamitic accomplices.
In the Hutu political imagination, the Tutsi had
become an alien race, a humiliating repository of

imperial domination. Upon independence in 1962, following the Hutu Peasant Revolution, the Tutsi kingdom was replaced by a Rwandan Republic ruled by the Hutu majority. Some thirty years later, on October 1, 1990, the Tutsi refugees in neighbouring Uganda, wanting to return to their ancestral home, had commenced the RPF insurgency, igniting the Rwandan Civil War.

THE TEN COMMANDMENTS

"And the LORD said unto Moses, Come up to me into the mount, and be there: and I will give thee tablets of stone, and a law, and commandments which I have written; that thou mayest teach them." Rwanda is a largely Catholic nation, and church-going Rwandans were familiar with this passage from the book of Exodus. The Ten Commandments, a cornerstone of Judeo-Christian belief, was the law of God; it was to be followed with unquestioning obedience. But in the days leading to the genocide, the Ten Commandments had assumed a different meaning in Rwanda.

The first issue of *Kangura* magazine was published in May 1990, coinciding with the early days of the RPF insurgency. Issue six, published in December 1990, contained an article entitled "Appeal to the Conscience of the Hutu." It warned that the attack by "bloodthirsty" Tutsi "extremists" was supported by "infiltrators within the country" who aimed to "conquer the country and establish a regime based on their feudal monarchy." It claimed that these infiltrators were using "money and the Tutsi woman" to once again place the Hutu under servitude. The Hutu were urged to wake up "now or never" and to "cease feeling pity for the Tutsi!" It was in this context that the "Ten Commandments" were introduced as a new Hutu ideology. They were to be propagated throughout society so that the Hutu would be "prepared to defend themselves against this scourge." By glorifying hatred in the language of biblical injunction, the propagandists appropriated the sacred to legitimize their insidious cause.

The commandments declared as a traitor any Hutu man who married a Tutsi woman, or who hired a Tutsi woman as a secretary or protege. It further declared that "all Tutsi are dishonest in their business dealings" and "only seeking ethnic supremacy"; any Hutu who did business with a Tutsi was thus a traitor. It also declared that educational institutions must be dominated by Hutus and that the Hutu ideology must be taught to pupils. Finally, it declared that the Rwandan Armed Forces "should be exclusively Hutu [and that] no soldier should marry a Tutsi woman." The message was simple: the Tutsis weren't fellow citizens; they were the enemy.

By February 1993, when issue forty of *Kangura* was published, the cumulative normalizing effect of hate propaganda had allowed the magazine to become even more extreme: "We have stated that a cockroach cannot give birth to a butterfly," one article declared. "A cockroach gives birth to another cockroach...Who can establish the difference between the *inyenzi* who attacked in October 1990 and those of the 1960s? They are all the same....The former are the offspring of the latter. Their wickedness is the same." That is what the Hutus were told. You cannot change someone who is inherently evil; you must crush them like an insect. It was the irrefutable logic of hatred that the evil of the other is manifest and not the product of the hater's perverse imagination: "The fact that in our language they are referred to as snakes is self-explanatory...A Tutsi is someone who has a sweet tongue but whose wickedness is indescribable. A Tutsi is someone whose desire for revenge is insatiable ... In our language a Tutsi is called cockroach because he takes advantage of the night to achieve his objectives. The word *inyenzi* is a reminder of the redoubtable snake whose venom is extremely poisonous." Thus it was that the collective consciousness was gradually poisoned, by attributing poison to others.

Kangura's hate propaganda was sophisticated and inflammatory. It was highly effective in pushing all the right psychological buttons. But its reach was limited. In 1990, the literacy rate in Rwanda was only 58 percent, and up to 95 percent of the population lived in rural areas. The publication could reach only the small urban educated classes. This was a significant obstacle to the Hutu Power conspiracy, because the efficient, industrialized extermination of the Nazi concentration camps was not possible in Rwanda. Killing a million people in every corner of the impoverished country using clubs and machetes required a highly organized grassroots army of enthusiastic executioners. Beyond publications targeting the literate urban elites, another, more accessible medium was needed to mobilize the masses for the "work" that lay ahead.

HATE RADIO

"Come and rejoice friends, God is merciful." It was a happy song, and radio was the voice of God. "Come and rejoice friends, cockroaches are no more." RTLM was established on July 8, 1993, just one month before the Arusha Peace Agreement was signed. It was the mouthpiece of Hutu Power, a toxic combination of entertainment and incitement that normalized vicious hatred among ordinary people. Everyone in Rwanda had a small radio. People listened all the time, everywhere, in offices and markets, cafés and bars, taxis and streets. With an appealing talk-show format that invited callers to participate — something new for Rwandans — the RTLM broadcasts became highly popular. They were a focus of social life, like a daily conversation among people sharing the latest gossip over a bottle of banana beer. The *génocidaires* understood well the tremendous potential of a popular radio program to brainwash the masses, to blur the lines between fact and fiction. The era of Internet false news had yet to arrive. The radio was still the best weapon of mass deception.

"There is no difference between the RPF and the *inyenzi* because the *inyenzi* are the refugees who fled Rwanda after the mass majority revolution of 1959, the fall of the monarchy and the establishment of a democratic republic." This was the constant theme of RTLM broadcasts: that all Tutsis were RPF terrorists and that all social problems must be reinterpreted through the prism of ethnic identity. The singular, obsessive historical narrative was one of radical opposition between Tutsi and Hutu, a relationship between the arrogant perpetrator and the humiliated victim: "The Tutsi had to be brought up knowing that he was the chief, that the Hutu child was under his authority." The broadcast went on to note that before 1959, "No Hutu would share his meal with a Tutsi; that was forbidden. It was inculcated in the Tutsis never to eat with Hutus... It was not because we did not want to eat with them, more so when they brought delicious food... How we wished to eat with them, but all in vain because it was forbidden." The year was 1993, and the escalating tone and incendiary content of the broadcasts was conditioning public opinion for what would soon follow.

A curious ten-year-old at the time, Éloge was full of mischief. "Despite my father's explicit prohibition to have the RTLM on in his home, we had learned to sneak around and listen to it because...

the message was entertaining," he explained. "At the same time that I was learning that there are some relatives serving in the RPF, it was kind of amusing to hear them described in the way this radio did." He paused, and continued: "Obviously it stopped to be funny when Hutus...took this message seriously and started to act upon it."

It was not apparent to ordinary people that this steadily rising tide would soon inundate the country in an unparalleled catastrophe; it was the story of the boiling frog, unknowingly cooked alive with the gradually rising temperature. Dire predictions of doom were either ignored or dismissed as exaggerations: *Surely it can't happen here.* As for the international community, Rwanda was simply not important. The resulting policy could be characterized as wishful thinking at best and willful blindness at worst. For the handful of human rights advocates and political analysts that cared to follow events in Rwanda in those months, the situation was alarming — RTLM was poisoning minds and inciting violence. An explosion was only a matter of time. Their warnings fell on deaf ears.

The hate broadcasts would soon take on an entirely different dimension: "Dawn is when the day breaks...When that day comes, we will be heading for a brighter future, for the day when we will be able to say, 'There isn't a single *inyenzi* left in the country.' The term *inyenzi* will then be forever forgotten, and disappear for good... That will only be possible if we continue exterminating them at the same pace."

The date was June 5, 1994. For two months, the slaughter had continued unabated. Dispensing with the subtle vilification prior to April 6, RTLM broadcasts now openly called for wiping out the Tutsi. In retrospect, the demonization had been a slippery slope. With the temperature rising steadily, the boundary between extreme hatred and extreme violence had suddenly collapsed. Just as they were the victims of genocide, the Tutsi were now blamed as the authors of their own misfortune, as a "suicidal" minority that was finally getting what it deserved.

"They have always considered themselves more intelligent and sharper compared to the Hutus," explained the announcer. "It's this arrogance and contempt which have caused so much suffering to the *inyenzi* and their fellow Tutsis, who have been decimated." Somehow, the perpetrators were not responsible for their actions. It was the victims who had brought this calamity upon themselves.

The pivotal role of the RTLM in orchestrating the genocide now went well beyond spreading the incendiary message that the Tutsi were the incarnation of evil. By this time, the radio broadcasts were naming and denouncing individuals, issuing specific instructions for murder throughout the country. Kantano Habimana was an especially popular and enthusiastic announcer with a wide following. In one instance, on May 28, 1994, news came that an Interahamwe militia had arrested a certain Yirirwahandi Eustache at a market. The issue was that although his identification card declared him a Hutu, he admitted that his mother was a Tutsi, and he was willing to pay a substantial sum of money to be spared. Habimana's exhortations were clear: "If you are an *inyenzi*, you must be killed. You cannot change anything. No one can say that he has captured an *inyenzi* and the latter gave him money as a price for his life. This cannot be accepted...He must be killed."

In yet another broadcast, Habimana encouraged those manning the roadblocks to take drugs to do the work even better: "I would like at this time to salute those young people near the slaughterhouse...The thing you gave me to smoke...it had a bad effect on me. I took three puffs. It is strong, very strong, but it appears to make you quite courageous. So guard the trench well to prevent any cockroach passing there tomorrow. Smoke that little thing and give them hell." As with the Nazi Einsatzgruppen, intoxicating substances helped ease the instinctive pain of murdering innocent human beings.

At every roadblock, the Interahamwe could be seen, machete in one hand and a radio in the other, minds poisoned, ready to kill. RTLM was Hutu Power's not-so-secret weapon of mass destruction. How else could the *génocidaires* have mobilized the multitude to extinguish so many lives in so little time? General Dallaire's last-minute call for reinforcements had fallen on deaf ears. There was no political will to jeopardize the lives of UN peacekeepers, even at the cost of a million African lives.

But there was a much simpler solution that had gone unexplored. Let us imagine that RTLM had been shut down: would the genocide have still happened? Would Hutu Power have successfully mobilized the masses to carry out the killings throughout the country? What if in the months before April 6, 1994, before Rwanda was saturated with hatred, ready for a spark to cause a conflagration, the world had heeded the early warning signs of the impending calamity and stopped the incite-ment that prepared the way for the horrors? How many lives would have been saved? How many des-tinies would have been changed?

The problem is not that radical evil is inevita-ble. The problem is that we don't really care about human suffering until it comes directly to our shores, or at least onto our television or computer screens. The solutions are there, but the politi-cal will is missing. There are plenty of innovative ideas and concepts and theories. In the UN jargon, we speak about the Responsibility to Protect civil-ians against atrocities — R2P, as it is called. There is now even a UN special advisor on prevention of genocide, a post established by Secretary-General Annan because of guilt over the UN's failure to stop Srebrenica and Rwanda. These are important concepts and institutions, but we often confuse the proliferation of terminology with genuine progress. New cutting-edge concepts, each more sophisti-cated than the previous; a plethora of studies and mandates and declarations; a procession of sol-emn regrets and expressions of sympathy; films and books bemoaning the past; awards and acco-lades celebrating the saviour's virtue — these are not a substitute for empathy and engagement, for meaningful action. This self-contained universe is often disconnected from the realities that it purports to address. When we fail to listen to the voices of survivors, to embrace the intimate reality of abandoning others in their hour of need, we fail to fathom the gravity of our failure to act. Without understanding the catastrophic consequences of indifference, we are wont to go about our lives as if nothing has happened, until we realize that it could also happen to us.

HEALING AFTER HELL

Gusaba is a colourful marriage ceremony, a revered ritual that signifies the union not just of husband and wife but also of two families and communities. As they have throughout the ages, the elders of the groom's family lead an entourage of aunts and uncles and eminent persons on behalf of their son to ask the bride's family for her hand in marriage. Like any decent girl from a good family, however, she will not easily surrender to these romantic overtures. Instead, the sizeable delegation must engage in a humorous exchange of wits and cunning, expressed in tongue twisters and playful bargaining, in which the bride's family must be charmed and persuaded to part with their precious daughter. If the team effort is successful and a suitable dowry is negotiated, then the celebration of the forthcoming nuptials may begin.

For the more affluent and notable Rwandan families, a performance by the famous Simon Bikindi at their wedding ceremony was a symbol of prosperity and prestige. Celebrated by some as Rwanda's Michael Jackson, he became famous with the 1990 release of a bestselling cassette of wedding songs. A talented performer, he combined elliptical rap-style lyrics with catchy folkloric tunes, mixing the modern with the traditional, English with French and Kinyarwanda — a fusion of diverse influences into a harmonious whole. But there was one kind of wedding he would not celebrate: that between a Hutu and a Tutsi.

Just as Bikindi wrote love songs, he also wrote war songs. His most troubling was deceptively titled "Nanga Abahutu" ("I Hate These Hutu"). "I hate these Hutus," he sang with a deep voice, "these de-Hutuized Hutus, who have disowned their identity, dear comrades." The *icyembe*, a music box with acoustic strings, accompanied his words with a hypnotic rhythm. "I hate these Hutus, these

Hutus who march blindly, like imbeciles." It was an inverted song of both Hutu self-hatred and pride, with an unmistakable subtext of hatred against the Tutsi. Its message was well understood among those who listened. Throughout the killings, RTLM broadcast Bikindi's popular songs, and megaphones mounted on vehicles blasted his musical message in the streets. Many cheerfully chanted his lyrics as they snuffed out the lives of their victims.

Some say there is a thin line between marriage and war, between love and hatred. It wasn't surprising that the prohibition of marriage between Hutus and Tutsis was one of the Ten Commandments, or that some people in mixed marriages even took the life of their own spouse. Without intimacy, there can be no extreme emotions, whether of compassion or contempt.

On April 6, 2014, on the twentieth anniversary of the genocide, I sat in a CBC recording studio in Montreal, to be interviewed together with the famous Rwandan musician, Jean-Paul Samputu.

"I lost my mind," he said as I listened in stunned silence. "Every day I drank to forget. It was like I was in hell. I wanted to kill Vincent, and since I couldn't kill [him], I started to kill myself." Listening to him brought back dark memories, reminding me of what it means to be a survivor of genocide. But there was also an ironic twist of fate. Just as RTLM had carried the hateful voice of Simon Bikindi, now CBC radio carried the healing voice of Jean-Paul Samputu so the world could hear his story — and an astonishing story it was. The Vincent he wanted to kill was his neighbour and best friend. Vincent Ntakirutimana was a Hutu and Jean-Paul a Tutsi. During the genocide, Vincent had killed Jean-Paul's family.

Jean-Paul had returned to his village on July 20, 1994, to find his family home empty. He learned that his father, mother, three brothers, and sister had all been killed. As if that wasn't devastating enough, he also learned that Vincent was one of the killers. Jean-Paul was overwhelmed with grief and bitterness. His seething anger soon consumed him. He began to destroy himself with drugs and alcohol. He was a rising star in the East African music scene, a singer and songwriter in six languages, but his musical career and personal life went on a downward spiral into a dark abyss.

"I was just waiting to die," he said.

In 2006, after several years of rehabilitation and spiritual healing, Jean-Paul won the International Songwriting Competition. He went on a world tour and performed with joy. He had turned his life around. His career was thriving, but he knew that he could only move on if he confronted Vincent. His opportunity came the following year, during the summer of 2007. Back at his village, he would meet Vincent once again, this time before a *gacaca* court. This traditional restorative "justice amongst the grass" brought the community together to acknowledge past wrongs and provide redress to victims. Together with the ICTR that tried the *génocidaire* leadership in Arusha, Tanzania, *gacaca* was a means of reckoning with the past and promoting reconciliation.

When Jean-Paul finally came face to face with Vincent, he stood up and said: "I forgive you." Some survivors became angry, and yet others called him a traitor. They thought he had lost his mind. But as Jean-Paul explained in the radio interview, "People often think that forgiveness is a gift to the offender. But forgiveness is for you, not for the offender... When I came to forgive him, it was like I won."

Later, while sharing a meal with Vincent, Jean-Paul asked him how he could have killed his best friend's father. Vincent answered: "Jean-Paul, do you know the rules of the genocide? Precisely because your father was my closest neighbour and my closest friend means that I was the one to go and kill him. Look, we went to the meeting to plan killings, and people wondered who would kill the old man Samputu. Everyone pointed a finger at me."

Like Simon Bikindi, Jean-Paul was a musician. But he had chosen a song with a different message: "We cannot continue hating each other. We have children who follow us, and if we don't give them a good education in love, another genocide will happen." As I heard those words, I was overwhelmed by the depth of his soul. The resilience of the human spirit and the capacity to survive the unthinkable were, I thought, astonishing. As I listened to Jean-Paul's voice in the recording studio, I wondered to myself how we who dispense liberal platitudes to others would deal with such suffering if it befell us. I pondered how much our superficial, self-satisfied societies have to learn from Jean-Paul's power of indomitable hope. If evil triumphs, it is because of the indifference of bystanders. It is because we choose not to feel the pain of others, to see them as our equals. Even if empathy doesn't figure in our utilitarian calculations, we should have no illusions that in an inextricably interdependent world, ignoring the suffering of others will not come back to haunt us one day.

THE BUTTERFLY EFFECT

In chaos theory, the "butterfly effect" describes how a small occurrence can change the course of the entire universe. This theory would have it that the flapping of a butterfly's wings somewhere in Rwanda could cause a storm in New York. But for those sipping coffee at a stylish café near Central Park in the early nineties, it seemed that the opposite was true: the small transactions in the global financial capital would wreak havoc a world away. "I made a killing on coffee futures," said one man clad in smart business attire to his friend across the table. And a killing it was, with catastrophic consequences for some.

Until 1989, the International Coffee Agreement had stabilized the price of coffee between $1 and $1.50 per pound. With increasing consumer tastes for higher-quality coffee and the shift to aggressive free-market policies, however, the quota system collapsed. By 1992, prices had plummeted to $0.50 per pound. Commodity traders and multinational corporations made huge profits, while coffee-exporting countries like Rwanda suffered an economic shock, losing almost half of foreign exchange revenues overnight. The impoverished farmers producing the coffee on the verdant hills of rural Rwanda suffered the most, sacrificed on the altar of the free market by invisible forces they could neither see nor understand. Their miserable fate was a glimpse of global capitalism conceived as the "survival of the fittest."

The situation would deteriorate further in 1990, when the World Bank and the International Monetary Fund pressured Rwanda to adopt free-market policies through "structural adjustment." The macroeconomic measures included devaluation of the Rwandan currency by 50 percent, combined with austerity measures to reduce public spending on health and education. The result was inflation, the collapse of purchasing power, a dramatic increase in external debt, and the implosion of public services. Without adequate medicine, there was a dramatic increase in malaria and other diseases. With tuition fees for primary schools, there was a massive decline in enrollment. The Rwandan peasantry was driven to desperation.

It wasn't difficult under these circumstances for extremists to channel the people's intense rage into violence. Beyond the failure to intervene, turning a blind eye to the global economy that pushed Rwanda over the edge was also an integral element of the calamity. Lulled by our complacent consumer culture, we may have smugly assumed in the recent past that our Western liberal societies are somehow immune from the scourge of hateful populism. Now imagine what would happen to the extremist currents in our midst if our economy plummeted overnight and our standard of living was suddenly cut in half. How far would we be from the abyss of violent scapegoating?

Without a profound consciousness of our shared humanity, with greed and hatred lurking just beneath, the outward semblance of civilization is but a fragile illusion. Perhaps the best antidote to our corrosive complacency is listening to the voice of survivors. Their stories are a powerful reminder of the best and the worst that is inherent in human nature, a reminder that our choices have grave consequences.

As I reflected on the profound disconnect between extreme suffering and the self-contained universe of elites, I wondered how I could contribute to bridging the wide gap between ideals and realities as an educator in the academy. A big part of the solution, I thought, was raising a new generation that defines leadership as empathy and engagement rather than cynical opportunism. If those with power are not touched by suffering, why would they bother to intervene against genocide in distant lands?

"When I was invited, I did not feel good, because talking of prevention, learning from the lessons of the past — 'let us be a lesson' — [is] like giving your body to science: 'take it, screen it, dissect it.'" I was filled with awe watching Esther Mujawayo on the stage, speaking to the captivated audience. The date was October 11, 2007. As chair of the Global Conference on Prevention of Genocide, I had asked her to be a keynote speaker before the impressive gathering of distinguished intellectuals and political leaders. *It is time*, I thought to myself, *that we in the ivory tower and corridors of power listen to these stories, so we can awaken from our moral slumber.*

"Of course I am mad," she said with palpable grief, "but ifs cannot bring back my family."

The what-ifs of a post-mortem examination. I wondered how it felt for Esther, having lost two hundred family members, to endure a dispassionate academic discussion about events that forever destroyed the life she once knew.

"I want to challenge you," she said, "to learn how genocide happened, and do something about it."

It is said that hindsight is twenty-twenty; we always know what should have been done when a catastrophe has already happened. But foresight often stares us straight in the face, warning us of tomorrow's catastrophe, and we choose to close our eyes.

But here was a man who didn't close his eyes. He was standing on the stage beside Esther, and they were meeting for the first time, although they had shared a large home popularly known as Hotel Rwanda back in 1994.

"I am really honoured, I am standing here with General Dallàire," Esther said with a beaming smile. The UNAMIR force commander had refused to abandon the Rwandans after the UN withdrawal. He had done what he could to save as many lives as possible. "Actually, I take the opportunity, General Dallaire, to tell you that during the genocide in Rwanda, I was lucky how I survived in the end. I was able to be brought to this famous Hôtel des Mille Collines, the Hotel Rwanda, where the UN troops were, and they evacuated me with my girls to a safe area, so I am glad I can tell you that. Thank you." Esther stood there because some who cared did what they could to save those abandoned by the world. Her words of wisdom for the illustrious gathering were simple but poignant: "If we want to change, we have to be humble and listen to those who have been through [suffering]...take the body for science, but listen to those that are the relatives of the body."

Éloge was sitting attentively in the audience. I wondered what all of this meant to him, having lost his father and many other loved ones in the genocide. Some years later, he told me the story of his best friend, Samuel. Just as Éloge and his family were turned away from the ETO in Kicukiro, Samuel and his family found shelter in the ETO in Murambi, in the south. They waited in vain for UN soldiers to rescue them, but none ever came. The Interahamwe killed him and his entire family. But now there is a little Samuel, playful and mischievous, sitting on my lap, full of curiosity about the world.

I asked Éloge about his son's namesake. "I think we wanted his memory to live on," he says of his best friend. "We wanted to make his bright and joyful candle to shine again in this world."

I wondered how Samuel would one day recount his father's story to his children. I wondered if he would live in a world free from the scourge of genocide, a world in which people refuse to be bystanders. Cockroaches and butterflies, hatred and love, complacency and compassion; we are born with wings, yet we choose to crawl through this fleeting life.

FOUR

THE ONENESS OF HUMANKIND

OF ONE ESSENCE

"ALL CIRCUITS ARE BUSY. Please try your call again."
On any other day, that would have been an annoying message, made worse by the cordial voice of
that anonymous woman who taunts irritated callers around the world with a mocking tone of polite
ridicule. One of the fundamental rites of passage
in modern society is to suffer the on-hold hell
of automated telephone systems; condescending
recordings telling us that the next available cus-
tomer service agent will be with us "shortly," while
for nearly an hour, we listen to a never-ending
loop of Dolly Parton and Kenny Rogers singing
"Islands in the Stream." But on that day, instead of

exasperation, the impersonal telephone rebuff gave rise to panic and desperation.

"All circuits are busy." I listened to the recording repeatedly, as I obsessively dialled her number again and again. I was in utter disbelief at what had just happened. I was frantic to hear the voice of my wife and two-year-old son so that the nightmare of uncertainty would end. I just wanted to know that they were still alive. I thought of the joyous day he was born. His wondrous eyes were wide open, brimming with curiosity about the new world he had just entered. He had grown so quickly. He was now an adorable toddler, waddling around the house in pursuit of mischief, skillfully deploying his disarming smile with malice aforethought to undermine my fatherly authority. Shortly after I had kissed him goodbye that morning on my way to work, he had taken the train to Manhattan with his mother and grandparents. They were on their way to the World Trade Center, and now their whereabouts were unknown. The date was September 11, 2001, the dawn of a new millennium.

The horror of that day marked a turning point in history. Shocked by the scale of the terrorist attack, America declared a "War on Terror." The narrative that emerged was a clash of civilizations between Islam and the West, of destroying foreign extremists before they destroyed us. But unlike the enemies from wars past, this one was everywhere, from the mountains of Afghanistan to the double-decker buses of London. With drone warfare and suicide bombing, surveillance and xenophobia, apocalyptic survivalism became the new norm. I had witnessed in war zones throughout the world the deceptive power of visceral fear, the immediate need for self-defence blinding us to the search for lasting solutions. Like someone addicted to an unhealthy lifestyle, the world found it easier to fixate on symptoms than to deal with root causes. The single indivisible body that we call humankind was ingesting poison long before the outbreak of 9/11. The toxic combination of divisive ideologies and cynical geopolitical calculations was the perfect breeding ground for the disease of violent extremism. Amidst the hysterical belligerence, the most important narrative — that of inextricable global interdependence — was all but lost. If we appreciate that the oneness of humankind is an inescapable reality rather than a naive ideal, then we will not be surprised that ignoring the suffering of others, let alone causing it, will always come back to haunt us. It's called bad karma.

The absurdity of my predicament on that day was that I had left my job at the UN to end my weary wanderings in war zones. As if the wounds of persecution and exile from Iran weren't bad enough, I had added the extreme anguish of the horrors in Bosnia, Rwanda, and other sites of sorrow I had witnessed around the world as a UN prosecutor. I was fed up with reckless human rights crusading! It had destroyed my life. The birth of my son had come as an epiphany. Holding him in my arms with tears of joy, I had decided to embrace the miracle of life, to put death and despair behind me. It was time, I thought, to rid my tormented soul of those horrible images that haunted me incessantly. So here I was, the human rights saviour, transformed into the well-paid corporate lawyer. I had exchanged bullets and bombs, mass graves and torture victims, for a magnificent office in New York, atop a sleek skyscraper with a panoramic view of Manhattan. Below me, the relentless energy of the city cast a hypnotic spell on the busy people, rushing back and forth on the streets, on the way to this or that meeting, chasing dreams of riches and fame amidst the unforgiving concrete jungle. And now I too was part of the action.

It was a beautiful autumn morning in New York

that day. The sun was shining against a blue sky, and I was full of ambition as I embarked on my daily commute. The anguish of those wounded nations I once frequented seemed a world away. It was now my turn to enjoy the good life, I thought to myself, to give my family the happiness and comfort they deserved. They had suffered enough from the gloom that had consumed me all those years at the UN tribunal in The Hague. But at that moment, when I wondered if my family was dead or alive, it became clear that the dark currents of violence I wanted to escape had followed me to my hedonistic refuge. This time, it wasn't someone else's loved ones suffering in a forgotten war in a forsaken land. Now it was my family caught in the crossfire. I couldn't just take the UN airlift and leave the horrors behind as I had done in the past.

On September 10, the world had looked very different. The terror of extreme violence was someone else's problem. True, those of us with lofty liberal sentiments would occasionally express righteous indignation at some tragedy or other that happened to be headline news. But otherwise, the splendid isolation of Western civilization from the savagery on its fringes allowed for a comfortable and secure existence. My family had left that cauldron of conflict in the Middle East that was once our home and now lived in the "free world." Having escaped persecution, we were seemingly safe from the fanatical monsters lurking in that alien realm beyond. Terror was the fate of others less fortunate than us. That evening, during one of those rare moments when I wasn't measuring my self-worth by billing hours for the law firm, I was reading a moving essay by my friend Mohsen Makhmalbaf, the famous Iranian filmmaker and master of cinéma-vérité. His latest film, *Kandahar*, had just been screened at the Cannes Film Festival. It had received a lukewarm reception. Afghanistan was not yet fashionable.

The film depicted the tragic plight of Afghanistan's forgotten people, with a cast of real refugees as actors. It was a vivid re-enactment of their daily struggle for survival amidst the scourge of war, starvation, and genocide. After the Soviet withdrawal in 1989, ruthless warlords fought for supremacy in the resulting power vacuum. Unleashing the jihadist fury of mujahedin fighters had been useful for winning the Cold War, but once the Soviet Union collapsed, Afghanistan was quickly forgotten. There was no more use for the broken nation; it had already served its geopolitical purpose. Hailing the post–Cold War era as a historic beginning, U.S. president George Bush Sr. had proclaimed a "New World Order." The triumphant gods of liberalism and capitalism were now poised to conquer the planet, and some even celebrated the "end of history."

Angered by the world's callous abandonment of Afghanistan, Makhmalbaf titled his essay "Limbs of No Body: The World's Indifference to the Afghan Tragedy." This ancient nation that nobody cared about was like a limb severed from the body of humankind, because nobody felt its pain. "Those who recognize the name Afghanistan," he wrote, "immediately associate it with smuggling, the Taliban, Islamic fundamentalism, war with the Soviet Union, a long-time civil war, famine, and high mortality." During the previous two decades he noted, "about 2.5 million Afghans have died as a direct or indirect result of war," and yet "I person- ally do not recollect any nation whose population was reduced by 10 percent via mortality, and 30 percent through migration, and yet faced so much indifference from the world." But unknown to Makhmalbaf, the name of Afghanistan would soon be seared into the public consciousness.

"These idols have been gods of the infidels," Mullah Muhammad Omar had declared in March

2001. The notorious one-eyed Taliban leader was determined to destroy all false gods in his quest for Islamic purity. But the history of Afghanistan was one of the fusion of different cultures and civilizations on the mountainous crossroads of caravan routes, a meeting point of diverse peoples and beliefs. One such place was Bamiyan. Situated on the ancient Silk Route that connected China to Europe, it was once a flourishing centre of pilgrimage and learning for Buddhists. In 630 A.D., the Chinese pilgrim Xuanzang recorded that there were no fewer than "ten monasteries and more than a thousand monks" in the ancient caravan city. He was most impressed by the magnificent twin statues of the Buddha chiselled into the side of a sandstone cliff and decorated with gold and fine jewels. Carved in the Greco-Buddhist style that had flourished in the ancient kingdom of Kandahar, the anthropomorphic representation of the Buddha blended Hellenistic art with Indian religious motifs, a unique merging of East and West. At staggering heights of thirty-seven and fifty-five metres respectively, they were the tallest Buddhas in the world, their majesty inspiring awe among those worshipping at their feet. The twin statues survived the turbulence of the centuries, from the Islamic conquests to Genghis Khan's Mongol hordes. But in March 2001, they would finally be demolished with explosives. The fanatical Mullah Omar feared any gods that competed with the angry god he had created in his impoverished imagination.

On August 8, 1998, not far from Bamiyan, the Taliban had captured the city of Mazar-i-Sharif, giving them control of every major city in Afghanistan. They initiated their theocratic utopia by massacring some two thousand men and boys, belonging to the Hazara Shia minority, deemed to be infidels. As these atrocities were committed, there was a deafening silence in the world. The Taliban were useful to certain powers, and most people going about their daily lives elsewhere, far from the horrors unfolding in that desolate place, did not even know that somewhere there was a country called Afghanistan. But while the extreme suffering of people did not elicit a response, the destruction of the twin Buddhas of Bamiyan resulted in a global outcry that momentarily put Afghanistan on the map.

"I reached the conclusion," Makhmalbaf wrote, "that the statue of Buddha was not demolished by anybody; it crumbled out of shame... for the world's ignorance towards Afghanistan. It broke down knowing its greatness did no good."

From the twin Buddhas of Bamiyan, to the twin towers of New York, that fateful day in September was a violent wake-up call, alerting us to the reality that in an interdependent world, we are all connected; that the welfare of one part affects the welfare of the rest. Everyone would now notice this forgotten place called Afghanistan, because our indifference to the extreme suffering of those we had once used as pawns in sinister geopolitical games had come back to haunt us a world away.

Several terrible hours after the collapse of the twin towers, the telephone lines were back in operation. I finally managed to reach my wife to learn that she, my son, and my parents were unharmed. My two-year-old had made a fuss getting dressed in the morning, so they had taken the later train to Manhattan. If they hadn't missed the earlier train, they would have been at the World Trade Center when the aircraft struck. I put the telephone down, relieved, exhausted, horrified, and confused, trying to make sense of it all. The randomness of death was humbling, not least when it affected people in your own neighbourhood. Some who worked at the towers had meetings elsewhere that morning and survived. Others who didn't work at the towers had meetings there that day and died horrible deaths. Children lost their fathers and mothers; husbands and wives, brothers and sisters, best friends and work colleagues lost each other. A lot of people suffered. This city intoxicated with ambition was suddenly wet with tears, a dark cloud of grief cast over its restless denizens. They now retreated from their busy lives to mourn their loss, to ponder the fragility of life. I had seen it before, in Bosnia, in Rwanda, in the many other tragic places I had visited; but I had never expected to see it in New York. There was an outpouring of sympathy across the world, including from nations that had suffered far more than the U.S. I wondered why there had been so little sympathy for these others in their hour of need.

As political leaders unleashed the dogs of war to retaliate against terrorism, the real story of this tragedy was lost. Amidst the frenzied fear and fury that had gripped people traumatized by mass violence, the convenient narrative was that the jihadists were "enemies of freedom." They had suddenly appeared out of nowhere to attack Americans. There was no time for contemplation to understand how the disease of blind rage that had been instrumentalized for strategic gain, the fanaticism that was still exploited for political gain by our allies, had now spread to our shores. Evil had to be destroyed, and the repository of evil was always elsewhere, the responsibility of other, faceless people who had no history, no context, no relation to our choices or destiny; people whose pain was less worthy than ours. Most of all, there was no recognition that this unprecedented act of violence was a unique opportunity to revitalize the United Nations, to make it an effective instrument for addressing global threats and common interests.

I thought back to my first tour of the UN building in New York. It was a more innocent time, when I was on a student internship, dazzled by the glamour of diplomacy and the bureaucracy working towards the betterment of humankind. Being of Iranian origin, I was proud to see the magnificent Persian carpet that decorates the portal of the hall where the General Assembly meets, the one place where all nations gather to solve the pressing problems of the planet. Painstakingly woven from thousands of tiny threads that combine to form enchanting patterns of vivid colours, the carpet itself conveyed the unified beauty of diversity. It was graced by a famous poem that we learned

as children in Iran, the poignant verse of the thir-
teenth-century Sufi mystic Saadi, from the fabled
city of Shiraz. His words spoke to all those that
entered the UN to deliberate in the name of world
peace:

> *Human beings are members of a whole*
> *In creation of one essence and soul*
> *If one member is afflicted with pain*
> *Other members uneasy will remain*
> *If you have no sympathy for human pain*
> *The name of human you cannot retain*

As the towers were reduced to dust that day,
I desperately grappled for an explanation, and I
thought of that poem. I reflected on how prescient
it was about the reality of our oneness, long before
the age of globalization. Afghanistan was not a
detached limb of humankind; it was part of the
single body that inextricably connects us. The fes-
tering wound that had been ignored for so long, the
unspeakable suffering of others a world away, had
now spread like a virulent disease, a pandemic of
hatred afflicting the heedless. Far from a clash of
civilizations, the story of 9/11 was that humankind
is a single, inseparable, indivisible body; ours is a

world in which the welfare of all peoples is inextricably intertwined, a world in desperate need of both attitudes and institutions reflecting the reality of our oneness.

JIHADIST FRIENDS TURNED FOES

Abdullah was a gentleman and a scholar from a distinguished and wealthy family. There were very few Ph.D. candidates at Harvard Law School, and even fewer from the Middle East. We had very different intellectual interests: he was writing on Islamic finance, and I was writing on human rights. But we shared a certain cultural affinity, being confined to a small circle of oriental outcasts in our occidental schoolyard of theoretical speculation. There was no hint in our conversations of the religious prejudice that often informed exchanges between Iranians and Saudi Arabians. Khomeinism and Wahhabism — Islamic sectarianism of the Shia and Sunni varieties, respectively — were divisive creeds; they glorified intolerance by separating the world into believers and non-believers, condemning any deviance from their narrow theological constructs as satanic idolatry. Their hateful ethos was the root of much evil in the region and beyond. In a rapidly changing world grappling with the disruptive transition from tradition to modernity, they offered psychic comfort by casting others as demons. The biggest victims of this delusional dichotomy were other Muslims who did not share such rigid revulsion for diversity.

From the panoramic perspective of the ivory tower, such absolute certainty about the truth seemed the privilege of fools and fanatics. The brilliant intellects in our midst embraced a more enlightened creed; the god we worshiped was the cynical skepticism of postmodern angst. The excited outbursts at academic seminars over the subversive subtext of inscrutable anti-essentialist jargon could best be described as thesaurus therapy, not unlike the Dark Ages scholarship that confused theological hairsplitting with useful knowledge. Some amongst us were intellectual martyrs, choosing a heroic death by deconstruction. Like me, Abdullah was content with a modest slice of specialized knowledge in his chosen field, though that didn't detract from his cosmopolitan erudition. He was well-versed in the sophisticated subtleties of the scholarly mind, the academic meanderings of the curious intellect on the tortuous path to Ph.D.

redemption. But as we exchanged lofty views among colleagues from the armchairs of the student lounge, I wondered what it would be like to have a conversation with Abdullah's half-brother Osama bin Laden.

"Mr. O," as Abdullah called him, was the *enfant terrible* of the bin Laden family. They had last met in 1988 at the funeral of their older brother Salem, the charismatic head of the family fortune. He had died in an airplane crash in Texas, where he counted George W. Bush and family as close friends and business associates. That same year, Osama had created Al-Qaeda to continue the jihadist cause after what seemed like an imminent Soviet withdrawal from Afghanistan. In 1979, the aspiring Islamic warrior had left the lucrative family business in Saudi Arabia to join the training camps of the mujahedin resistance in Pakistan. Like many other young men in the Islamic world, he was enraged at the atrocities against the Afghan people. Upon arrival, volunteers like him were welcomed with open arms. It was recruiting season for jihadists, celebrated as freedom fighters by the Western democracies and their authoritarian allies alike.

It was in 1979, the year Osama left home, that the CIA, in concert with Saudi Arabia and Pakistan, had launched Operation Cyclone, a conspiracy to release the jihadist genie out of the bottle and destroy their common Soviet foe in Afghanistan. The strategy was to exploit an Islamic "arc of crisis" adjacent to the Soviet Union's vulnerable Central Asian underbelly, and thus destabilize Moscow. U.S. officials had talked of "sucking the Soviets into a Vietnamese quagmire." It was yet another sordid episode of the Cold War's ruthless contest for supremacy. On the one hand, this was a relatively peaceful period, because nuclear deterrence had succeeded in keeping the peace among the competing superpowers. The unimpeachable logic of mutual assured destruction had rendered the historic utility of conventional war redundant, arguably avoiding a Third World War. On the other hand, instead of nuclear annihilation, vicious proxy wars were fought on the periphery of these contending empires, at the expense of other peoples, in the global South; people whose lives were somehow expendable, and whose suffering didn't really matter.

The cynical zero-sum politics of the day made for strange bedfellows. The aphorism "the enemy of my enemy is my friend" was nothing new. Even as modern strategists celebrated their own strategic genius, they were simply re-enacting an ancient proverb dating to the dawn of civilization: as early as the fourth century B.C. *Arthashastra*, a Sanskrit treatise on statecraft by the Indian philosopher Kautilya, had offered this utilitarian political wisdom to the rulers of the day. But in the age of revolutionary globalization, such malicious Machiavellian games would have radically different, self-destructive consequences. Justifying all manner of wickedness in the name of this or that ideological deity would lay bare the equally ancient wisdom of another Indian philosopher — the Buddha whose statues adorned the cliffs of Bamiyan: "It is a man's own mind, not his enemy or foe, that lures him to evil ways."

Admittedly, fighting a war against the murderous onslaught of the Soviet army in Afghanistan was not for the faint of heart. It called for fierce warriors with no fear of death. It demanded apocalyptic visions of ultimate victory against overwhelming odds. In this context, religious fanaticism was a prized asset. It was the equalizer between the mujahedin and the vastly superior military power of their Soviet foes. Where one side had modern weapons and a professional army, the other side had the power of absolute faith in a just cause. Radical violence tends to be an ideological game-changer. It transforms idle philosophical musings into a theology of rampant rage. Endurance in extremes does not allow much room for vacillation. Perhaps that is why the furious dichotomy of good and evil, of believers and infidels, was especially appealing in such circumstances. As the academic seminar dragged on at Harvard, the only fury Abdullah and I endured was the conflict between the radical critique of linear conceptions of time and the rapidly approaching lunch hour. As the pangs of hunger made my stomach growl, I thought that existential doubt was the privilege of intellectuals who occupied the stylish cafés of Paris; the outgunned warriors who occupied the stark mountains around Kabul needed absolute certainty in their cause.

The likes of Osama bin Laden were heroic role models in a veritable David and Goliath contest. Many of the poor young men in the Islamic world viewed the Gulf Arab elites with contempt, as corrupt oil-rich tyrants propped up by Western leaders who blindly worshipped their petro-dollars. They were resentful of the extravagant billionaire sheikhs with their private jets and golden Rolls-Royces, frequenting the nightclubs of London and the casinos of Monte Carlo, splurging money to impress glamorous women, while their fellow Muslims lived a wretched life of hunger and misery. These ostentatious displays of wealth aroused anger and bitterness, whether among the devout believers who rejected such corruption or the envious masses who simply wanted a slice of the action. Even the sacred city of Mecca had been transformed from a religious refuge for the pious pilgrim into a fusion of Disneyland and Las Vegas for the mega-rich, its gaudy five-star hotels and shopping malls a godless spectacle of luxury. In the eyes of the Muslim masses, Osama was different. Hailing from one of the richest families, he had given up a life of privilege to wage jihad from the desolate caves of Afghanistan. Instead of paying lip service to Islam like others, he had sacrificed ease and comfort to support his oppressed Muslim brethren. For the alienated young men in search of purpose, he was the superlative Islamic hero, leading by example, inspiring others to follow him on the path of martyrdom. For those on the Arab street in search of purpose and power, he instilled confidence that faith alone could bring an evil superpower to its knees. The motivation of foreign jihadists, however, wasn't necessarily the same as that of the Afghans, who were simply fighting to liberate their own country.

General Ayub Assil was an unlikely warrior when I first met him. He listened attentively
as I lectured in the seminar for the Afghanistan
Human Rights Commission in 2014. As he took
notes on fine points of international law, the mujahedin insurgency in which he was a heroic figure
seemed a distant, surreal world. With the defeat of
the Taliban after 9/11, the world's focus was now on
democratic institution-building and human rights
training, though much of it was undone by rampant corruption among Afghan political elites that
helped keep extremism alive. A lecturer himself,
at Kabul University, and an author of books on
criminal law, the elderly General Ayub was a tall,
distinguished, and affable gentleman who preferred
poetry over politics. Characteristic of the learned
men of his generation, he had committed countless
elegant passages to memory, ready to deploy one
or the other for any imaginable occasion in which
mere mortal words would not suffice to express
his sentiments. While sharing a meal, he would
dwell at length on the delicate nuances of this or
that verse, visibly enchanted by the depth of the
emotion that it conveyed, oblivious that his food
was getting cold. Yet throughout the 1980s, this
same sensitive soul, an affectionate grandfather

to all who crossed his path, was the voice of the mujahedin, bearing witness to the Soviet atrocities before the world community.

"We all had to do what we could," he told me politely. "We had no other choice."

General Ayub's mandate was to expose the atrocities committed by the Soviets and their Afghan allies. Just as the mujahedin leadership held meetings with President Reagan at the White House to seek support for their jihad against the godless communists, Ayub's peripatetic profession brought him to various Western capitals, where he testified about shocking crimes. These included the barbaric torture of suspects in notorious prisons such as Pul-i-Charkhi, a bleak fortress on a dirt road outside Kabul. The thousands who entered its menacing steel doors invariably disappeared, never to be seen again by their families. The more fortunate victims were shot or hanged. Others less fortunate died excruciating deaths, doused with boiling oil, crushed by tanks, or buried alive in mass graves. Women were routinely raped.

The situation was even worse in the countryside. While the Soviets controlled the cities, resistance fighters infiltrated the vast rural areas. There, they could count on ethnic and tribal loyalties for support. In characteristically brutal fashion, the Soviet counter-insurgency tactic was to demoralize the suspect civilian population through indiscriminate bombing, mass displacement, and destruction of food supplies, in what amounted to an extermination campaign. Countless civilians were killed and maimed; numerous towns and villages were reduced to rubble. An estimated five million Afghans — almost a third of the population — became refugees.

One of those refugees whom I had the good fortune to meet was Sima Samar. Her story defied the enduring image of Afghan women as hapless, burqa-clad victims. As a youth, she had seen a time of rapid social change that catapulted the nation from tradition to modernity in a single generation. On the one hand, modern women, many of them educated and accomplished, walked freely in the streets of Kabul in stylish dresses. On the other hand, traditional women were still encumbered by practices, such as arranged marriage, considered indignities in the eyes of the more progressive elements of society. Defiant and ambitious, Sima was determined to study hard and succeed, but she was forbidden by her father to attend university unless she married. At the age of eighteen, she accepted her father's choice of Abdul Chafoor Sultani, a professor of physics who she admired, not least because he was an enlightened man who supported her intellectual ambitions and studies. When her suitor had proposed marriage, she had said that she would be his good friend but not a submissive wife. Things turned out well for her: they had a son together and shared a happy life. He even did the housework while she studied at medical school.

But just as Sima's idyllic life was falling into place, things went from bad to worse in Afghanistan. In December 1979, Soviet troops had invaded the country and installed Babrak Karmal as the president. She remembered being unable to sleep at night, terrified by the sound of screaming jets flying overhead. Then, one fateful night in 1984, her blissful family life would be shattered, and she would be forced to discover her hidden strength. Earlier that day, the authorities had arrested her brother-in-law. Her husband was lying in bed, unable to sleep. He was tormented by the thought of the torture his brother was probably enduring. Suddenly there was a knock on the door. They had now come for him. "I will bring him back in two hours," they said as they took Sima's husband away. She would never see him again.

Professor Sultani probably met his end in that same Pul-i-Charkhi prison where so many others had perished. Just like that, her life was turned upside down, leading her on a long and exhausting journey of redemption.

A twenty-three-year-old widow with a small child, afraid that she too might be arrested, Sima eventually fled to the squalid refugee camps of Quetta, in Pakistan. Her only weapons were righteous rage and a stethoscope. There, she encountered shocking child mortality rates. The majority of children were severely malnourished and many had missing limbs because of land mines, which they often mistook for toys. Even in this misery, the girls were still the worst off. From exile, having lost everything she had, Sima responded to adversity by doing what she could to save the ailing among this suffering sea of humanity. In 1989, towards the end of the Soviet occupation, she established the Shuhada Organization to provide healthcare to Afghan women and girls in the refugee camps. Upon her return to Afghanistan, she would go on to build clinics throughout the country. Now, as chair of the Afghanistan Human Rights Commission, she reflected on all the death threats she had received from the Taliban for promoting women's rights and refusing to cover herself with the burqa.

Just as Sima was building clinics for women and girls and advocating for their education, the Taliban was building Saudi-funded schools — the so-called *madrassas* — where children received ultra-conservative Wahhabist religious instruction and became holy warriors. There they learned that the only righteous path was a particularistic puritanical interpretation of Islam, that anyone with differing beliefs was an infidel, and that pious women had to stay at home and be subservient to men. Sima's project and that of the Taliban were on an obvious collision course. As a woman, a human rights advocate, and a member of the persecuted Hazara Shia minority, she already had three strikes against her.

"Where do you feel the safest?" I asked her.

"Anywhere outside Afghanistan," she responded with a gracious smile.

Abdul Rahman Hotak had a somewhat different view about the schools where the fundamentalist indoctrination took place. For him, the *madrassas* took care of orphans and malnourished children. Empty stomachs ache for food; hungry children are flexible on ideology; and for traumatized young minds, fanaticism provides a comforting clarity. For those scarred children struggling to survive starvation, being brainwashed with Wahhabist ideology was a price well worth paying.

A former official of the Taliban government, rumoured to have been a one-time confidant of Mullah Omar, Hotak was now a member of the Afghanistan Human Rights Commission. A Pashtun with roots in Kandahar, the stronghold of the Taliban, he had witnessed the population of the city drop from 200,000 before the war to just 20,000 in the 1980s from relentless bombardment and mass-exodus. The region was strategically vital because it was adjacent to Pakistan, where for centuries nomadic tribes had made seasonal migrations across the mountains, indifferent to the imaginary border that existed between the two countries. Control of this southern region was crucial to Soviet attempts to cut the mujahedin supply lines for weapons. For several months, Soviet jets engaged in a ruthless carpet-bombing campaign against Kandahar, killing scores of civilians and reducing the city to rubble. The Pashtun tribes became further radicalized just as they received more weapons from their allies. By 1986, supplied with American Stinger anti-aircraft missiles, the mujahedin had dealt a decisive blow to Soviet airpower.

By 1998, having captured 90 percent of the country's territory, the Taliban had established the Islamic Emirate of Afghanistan. In the same year, Osama bin Laden had first emerged on the international stage, having been indicted by the United States for the bombing of U.S. embassies in Nairobi, Kenya, and Dar es Salaam, Tanzania. The Taliban had rebuffed calls to surrender him, just as they would after September 11. After a decade of civil war in the wake of the Soviet withdrawal, the abandonment of Afghanistan to its own fate was becoming increasingly costly. By 1999, the UN Security Council established a committee to impose a ban on Taliban officials and freeze their financial resources. On January 25, 2001, Abdul Rahman Hotak, who at the time was the Taliban's deputy minister of culture, had been put on that list. Following the American invasion after 9/11, he would spend three years as a prisoner at the U.S. air base in Bagram.

Now, over a traditional lunch of rice and kebabs, we were having an intense but respectful conversation about whether and how women's rights could be reconciled with the Sharia.

"Unfortunately," he said, "some people in Afghanistan are hostile to women; some of them are people I used to work with." He added that some of their interpretations of Islam were, in his view, too extreme and inconsistent with the Holy Qur'an.

As others at the table listened in on our conversation, it was clear that there was tension, especially among the more secular Afghans, who associated this religious discourse with a horrid past that still haunted them. For me, however, it was nothing but remarkable to be engaged in a polite dialogue on human rights with the imposing, bearded former Taliban official. At least his theological evolution exposed the fluidity of fanaticism. When the guns fall silent, the same people who were radicalized in the stark struggle to survive can learn to imagine the world differently; or at least they can come to realize that the rules of legitimacy have changed. There is nothing inherent or irreversible about extremism. What was once condemned by the radical religious clerics as a poisonous pluralism could equally become an internalized social value, casually accepted as an obvious moral truth.

The more I understood about what had happened in Afghanistan in those years, the more my admiration for Sima grew. With heroic calm and mild-mannered patience, she noted that transforming the scarred minds of her compatriots was a long and arduous task, not to be achieved overnight. But in a fleeting moment of optimism, she paused and pointed out: "Human rights now have a meaning in Afghanistan." The progress, however painful and slow, was real.

Upon the withdrawal of the Soviets in 1989, it was blindingly obvious to anyone familiar with the grim realities on the ground that without major international assistance for postwar reconstruction and social transformation, the traumatized and radicalized nation, brimming with jihadists and weapons, would soon collapse into a cauldron of terrorism. But having achieved their geopolitical objectives, those in the corridors of power now had little use for Afghanistan. Moving forward, the agony of its people was irrelevant to their ambitions. The once strategic nation was quickly forgotten amidst the post–Cold War euphoria. Instead of a genuine transformation, the misguided triumphalism of a "New World Order" was built on the weak pillar of unipolar supremacy and the still narrow conceptions of self-interest. It failed to grasp the inescapable reality of interdependence and its far-reaching consequences for global security.

When Osama rejected the admonitions of the bin Laden family to renounce his extremism, he was rebuked and disowned by his own flesh and blood, something not to be taken lightly in the tight-knit traditional society of the Arabs. Yet in an interview conducted shortly after 9/11, Abdullah still felt compelled to explain the circumstances that had driven his brother to such madness: "In the West, people don't understand the incensing brutality of the Soviet war in Afghanistan. It had a severe effect on him. It seemed to change him completely...It fomented his radical feelings and it scarred him. At least, this is how I try to understand my brother and come to terms with what he has done." Abdullah's brother was now the most notorious fugitive on earth. It would be a decade before he would be captured and killed.

"Didn't the fox never catch the rabbit, Uncle Remus?" asked the little boy.

The African-American folktale "Tar-Baby" tells the story of the villainous Br'er Fox, who uses a doll made of tar and turpentine to entrap the unsuspecting Br'er Rabbit. When the polite rabbit's roadside greeting to the doll goes unanswered, he becomes incensed and strikes the Tar-Baby; but the more he fights, the more he becomes entangled in this sticky situation. Back in 1979, an American official had explained the strategy in Afghanistan: "If the Soviets decided to strike at this tar-baby, we had every interest in making sure that they got stuck." The tar-baby here was the extinguished life of millions of innocent people, and now those far from the scene of this spectacular superpower entrapment also found themselves in a sticky situation. After the twin towers collapsed, the narrative that emerged was one of crazed terrorists suddenly emerging from nowhere to wage jihad against the West. The sordid sequence of calculations and miscalculations by cynical statesmen was conveniently forgotten. The attack was portrayed as yet another chapter in an epic clash between Western and Islamic civilizations.

The appalling consequences of short-sighted scorn for moral principles, the catastrophic disregard of human rights ideals in the blind pursuit of power, were rationalized with the cold calculus of a chess game in which the pawns were expendable people in foreign lands. Asked if he regretted stirring this hornet's nest of future terrorists, the former national security advisor to U.S. president Jimmy Carter, Zbigniew Brzezinski, famously responded: "What is more important to the history of the world? The Taliban or the collapse of the Soviet Empire? Some stirred-up Muslims or the liberation of Central Europe and the end of the Cold War?" Beyond a conspicuous failure of humanity, Afghanistan's abandonment was criminal negligence. From the moment when the world turned its back on that bleeding nation, 9/11 was only a matter of time.

FALSE GODS

"We have borscht." It was the same routine every day at the Intourist Hotel restaurant, one of the few places in Moscow where foreigners were allowed to eat and stay. A recent university graduate, I had travelled there in September 1990, unaware that I was in fact witnessing the waning days of the Soviet empire. In November 1989, thousands of jubilant youth had used everything from hammers and picks, cranes and bulldozers, to tear down the odious Berlin Wall. Some two million East Berliners had flooded West Berlin in an epic street party, celebrating freedom and the impending reunification of Germany. I'd been thrilled to hear Chancellor Helmut Kohl speak at the Harvard commencement ceremony. He remarked that for Germans, the Second World War had only ended in 1989. The winds of change were now sweeping across the Soviet Union too. The once-forbidden country was gradually opening its doors to foreigners. For those visiting Moscow, the Intourist Hotel was an affordable place to stay, in close proximity to the Red Square, even if it was an architectural eyesore, a concrete-and-glass monstrosity that stuck out amidst the elegant eighteenth- and nineteenth-century buildings on Tverskaya Ulitsa. Muscovites called it *gniloi zub*, or rotten tooth. It would soon be pulled out, demolished to make way for the luxurious buildings adorning post-Soviet Moscow, a disappeared relic of a forgotten era.

There were long queues everywhere in the city. On the street, I met a couple of Afghan students waiting in front of a shop. Like many of their compatriots, they had come to Moscow to attend university.

"Where are you from?" I asked.

"Kabul," they responded.

"What are you waiting to buy?" I asked.

"We don't know what's on sale," they responded, "but if there is such a long line, it must be good."

For the privileged few with foreign currency, the dining establishment at Intourist was a refuge from

these endless queues for food. It boasted a sizeable menu with numerous mouth-watering items.
The problem was that none were actually available. As I studied the various delicious options in
anticipation of a savoury meal, the waiter stood
patiently, pen and paper in hand, ready to take my
order. But with every selection I made, I heard the
repeated refrain: "We don't have today." In fact, the
only thing available was their bland watery version of "borscht," the otherwise tasty Russian beet
soup; but for some reason, instead of informing me
at the outset, the waiter would let me figure that
out through an exhaustive process of elimination.

"Why do you have such a large menu when you
only have borscht?" I asked one day.

"We want you to have choice," he responded with
the glum indifference of a hardened Muscovite.

Ivan Burylov was one among the many who
encountered the Soviet logic of choice. A humble
beekeeper, in 1949 he participated in the farcical
Soviet elections in his district. As everywhere, only
a single Communist Party candidate appeared on
the ballot. In effect, he was exercising his unques-
tionable right to participate in the absurd ritual of
selecting the only available dish; Soviet democracy
was anything but a tasting menu. In a frivolous

protest at this pointless exercise, he had the audacity to write "comedy" on his supposedly secret ballot paper. He would spend the next eight years of his life in a forced labour camp for his heinous "crime" of humour. Blasphemy against the sacred state could not go unpunished; laughter could not be allowed to replace fear.

Even in its last days, as the elaborate illusion of an invincible ideology was about to crumble, there was a surreal feel to the Soviet Union. Instead of revolutionary slogans, the secretary-general of the Communist Party, Mikhail Gorbachev, had popularized the pragmatic discourse of "perestroika" and "glasnost," referring respectively to the restructuring and openness of the increasingly untenable Soviet state. Reeling from military defeat in Afghanistan at the hands of a motley crew of jihadists, the disillusioned Soviets realized it was time to rethink the Marxist orthodoxy of the past and integrate into the liberal global order. It was not easy to accept the failure of the Soviet experiment. For devout communists, the materialist conception of history had been the incontestable truth, and a totalitarian state was the price for realizing the communist utopia.

The enlightened Soviet man was beyond superstitious belief in a sacred universe. His view of reality was scientific. A disciple of Karl Marx, he knew for a fact that the relations of production — technology, labour, capital — defined all human consciousness and social progress. Beliefs were nothing more than the superstructure reflecting these underlying material forces. "Man makes religion, religion does not make man," Marx famously wrote. The mystical longing for other worlds, the search for the sublime, was merely "the sigh of the oppressed creature... the opium of the people." On the path of modern progress, abandonment of this "illusory happiness" was necessary to attain the "real happiness" of materialist ideology. Yet for all its post-Enlightenment rebuke of religious irrationality, there was a distinctly millennial quality to the Marxist vision of the future. All history, Soviet citizens learned, was the history of class struggle, of atonement for the original sin of private ownership, and with the establishment of communism, the redemption of all suffering would come to pass, just as the return of the Messiah would bring salvation to the Christian faithful.

Alexey Stakhanov was the Soviet equivalent of a saint, a hero of socialist labour, worshipping the revolution by toiling in the Donbass coal mines of eastern Ukraine as a jackhammer operator.

His exemplary work ethic embodied the new Soviet man, selfless and disciplined, sacrificing his life for the relentless progress of the communist cause. It was reported that on August 31, 1935, he extracted a record one hundred tons of coal in less than six hours, almost fifteen times his quota. He became an instant celebrity, his name emblazoned in newspapers and posters, the role model all Soviet citizens should follow. His image even graced the cover of *Time* magazine. Henceforth, all workers that exceeded their quotas became known as Stakhanovites.

In the Moscow of 1990, the people I encountered were more interested in buying the Western blue jeans I was wearing than becoming heroes of socialist labour. There was a voracious appetite for consumer goods but nothing decent to buy on the bare shelves of the state-controlled stores. Seventy years of socialist fervour and sacrificial struggle had succeeded in creating proletarian masses yearning for Gucci and Prada. It was the Golden Rolex Revolution, conflating freedom with blind imitation of America's crass consumerism. The prevailing sentiment of shopping envy stood in sharp contrast to the still-ubiquitous Soviet iconography in the streets and buildings, the last vestiges of a quickly disappearing dream of social equality. There were the artistic representations, in the style of socialist realism, of Lenin rallying the oppressed masses in the glorious October 1917 Revolution, the red Soviet flag fluttering in the wind, noble men and women toiling happily in farms and factories, holding up hammers and sickles; heroic soldiers with weapons in hand, defending the dictatorship of the proletariat against its inveterate enemies. These romantic images of a just world filled the unsuspecting idealist with awe and admiration. By comparison, the anti-heroic consumerist ethos of Western liberalism, where all worshipped the god of greed so the obscenely rich could amass even more obscene riches, appeared mediocre and uninspiring. There was something strangely alluring about the displays of communist kitsch, glimpses of a magnificent temple of social solidarity extolling the Marxian mantra "from each according to his ability, to each according to his needs." Like other utopian dreams, however, there was little resemblance between the fantasy and the reality of the Soviet Empire.

Comrade Stalin's murderous purge of millions during the "Red Terror" of the 1930s was conveniently obscured from the idyllic imagery on display. Kulaks and nationalists, saboteurs and spies, traitors and wreckers, foreign agents and imperialists, and especially heretical Marxists — the sacred Soviet state had to be cleansed of this long list of "fifth column" enemies. As the prosecutor put it at the famous Moscow show trials of the old Bolshevik party leaders, "Let the verdict be heard like thunder, like a fresh, purifying thunderstorm of Soviet justice." But it wasn't only the suspect political elites who got a taste of Stalin's paranoid "justice."

Sometime during the Soviet famine of 1932 to 1933, Maria Tchebotareva, the peasant mother of four starving children, returned to her confiscated farm in a desperate search for food. Like many others, she had lost her grain-producing field because of forced collectivization. She allegedly stole a kilogram of rye to feed her starving youngsters. She spent the next twenty years of her life in the gulag, subjected to forced labour followed by exile in the harsh Siberian Arctic. By the time she returned home in 1956, after Stalin's death, there was no trace of her children. She died not knowing what happened to them. The Soviet famine claimed an estimated ten million lives. The Ukrainians called it "Holodomor": death inflicted by hunger. None of these horrors featured in the sanitized narrative in leftist circles that portrayed Stalin as the "Leader of Progressive Mankind." My Russian mentor, Professor Yuri Luryi, had described it best: "In capitalism, man exploits man," he told me with his wry humour, "but in communism, it is the other way around!"

By the twentieth century, romantic ideologies competed with faith as "the opium of the people." Like communism, the various incarnations of modernity's utopian creeds, each vying to be the absolute truth, became substitute religions, filling the vacuum of belief in the wake of Christianity's precipitous decline. While touting the triumph of rationalism over faith, these totalitarian ideologies took a catastrophic toll that made the barbarity of Europe's religious wars seem tame in comparison. The 1648 peace treaties concluded in the Westphalian cities of Osnabrück and Münster had brought to an end the devastating Thirty Years War. The Holy Roman Empire would no longer impose Catholicism on Protestant realms. The new order would achieve peace and progress by enshrining the principle of national sovereignty. Free from external religious hegemony, the state became the vehicle of a particular nation, but since a homogenous people didn't really exist, it had to be created. In pursuit of a territorially bound uniformity, German-speakers in Strasbourg and Italian-speakers in Nice would henceforth become Frenchmen like the Parisians, and Bavarian Catholics and Saxon Protestants would become Germans first and Christians second, just as the squabbling medieval city-states of Florence, Milan, and Venice would have to reconcile and become fellow Italians. New histories would be written of imaginary loyalties existing from time immemorial, myths instilled in the minds of unwitting subjects by absolutist rulers consolidating the power of the modern state.

With the steady progress of modern civilization, instead of killing each other in the name of religion, enlightened European men would now kill each other in the name of nationalism and ideology. And they would do so with increasing efficiency as primeval predatory instincts were exponentially magnified by lethal technologies of mass destruction. The shift from religious to scientific thought, the transition from feudalism to industrialization, the rise of national sovereignty and radical ideologies — these did not alter our dubious distinction as the most murderous mammal on earth. It would take our tremendous talent for self-destruction to learn that we must conceive the world differently. It would be exactly three hundred years of wars and genocide, from the Peace of Westphalia in 1648 to the Universal Declaration of Human Rights in 1948, before we reimagined international law and national sovereignty in light of the core principle of human rights rather than brute force.

Just as European nationalism and communism devised romantic ideologies exalting this or that segment of humankind over others, racialism directed at non-Europeans grappled with reconciling emerging ideals of equality with the colonial domination of half the world. The celebrated Western liberal philosopher John Stuart Mill, an employee of the British East India Company, considered British imperial rule "a blessing of unspeakable magnitude to the population of Hindustan." "Even the utmost abuse of European power," he maintained, "is better...than the most temperate exercise of Oriental despotism...The wider the circumference of British dominion, the more extensive the reign of peace." This self-proclaimed civilizational superiority had far-reaching consequences for the half of humankind that was denied the right to self-determination. In 1943, to mention but one instance, just as Britain fought to liberate Europe from Nazi fascism, up to three million subjects of the British Raj perished in the Bengal famine as food was diverted from India for the war effort, in full knowledge of the catastrophic consequences. "I hate Indians," the celebrated British prime minister Winston Churchill had told the British secretary of state for India. "They are a beastly people with a beastly religion." The famine, he claimed, was the fault of the starving Indians for "breeding like rabbits."

As for those on the other side of the world labelled "Red Indians," the situation was no better. The founding U.S. president, George Washington, had famously said: "Indians and wolves are both beasts of prey, tho' they differ in shape." His contemporary Thomas Jefferson had promoted the "Indian Removal" — the mass deportation of the Cherokee and Shawnee tribes from their ancestral lands — remarking: "If ever we are constrained to lift the hatchet against any tribe, we will never lay it down till that tribe is exterminated, or driven beyond the Mississippi..." In fact, according to a reputable source:

Hitler's concept of concentration camps as well as the practicality of genocide owed much, so he claimed, to his studies of English and United States history. He admired the camps for Boer prisoners in South Africa and for the Indians in the wild West; and often praised to his inner circle the efficiency of America's extermination — by starvation and uneven combat — of the red savages who could not be tamed by captivity.

Against this historical backdrop, the tragic contemporary plight of indigenous peoples becomes less difficult to understand. However much we may wish to distance ourselves from the evil of Nazi ideology through a selectively remembered past, its racist conception of the state was simply an extreme point on a prevalent spectrum of white supremacy, a conception shameful and iniquitous in the past, and even more so today.

European colonialism, however, is not unique. No civilization, nation, or culture has had a monopoly on demeaning, enslaving, and exterminating others. The point is that the substitute religions of modern times have been no less appalling than the savagery of the past. What we imagine as backward barbarity today may in fact be an expression of our contemporary reality. It is fair to say that the Taliban and their ilk were incubated in the modern matrix of ideological violence, not in the *madrassas* of medieval Mecca. Extremism begets extremism. Its stripe and shape is irrelevant, because radical evil is always committed in the name of a greater good, whether clothed as progress or tradition. In an interdependent world, the atrocities beyond our imagined borders do not solely express the cruelty of others; they are also connected with our own beliefs and actions, our glorification of greed, our cynical geopolitical games, which we sanitize and justify with our intellectual sophistication. In ancient times, the Buddhist pilgrims in Bamiyan would have simply called it karma: what we release into the universe now will come back to us in the future.

Instead of embracing the reality of our oneness, the purveyors of political mirages have preyed on base instincts of fear, avarice, and hatred among the masses. The ideologies they have offered as solutions for humankind's divisive afflictions have only exacerbated the illness. They have demonized, dominated, and destroyed others to promote the supremacy of a particular class, nation, race, or creed. The substitution of ideology for empathy; the deification of collective narcissism; the scapegoating of others for self-inflicted woes, severing the limbs of the indivisible body to which we all belong—these are truly the hallmarks of an idolatrous world worshipping at the altar of false gods, their high priests the leaders that sacrifice the lives of the innocent, their incantations odious slogans and demagoguery, their incense the smoke of sorrow from the bleeding hearts of the bereaved. Where is the new world of peace and prosperity that these visionaries promised? How long will we persist in the absurd belief that our welfare is separate from the welfare of others?

BIRTH OF A NEW WORLD

"What hath God wrought?" The date was May 24, 1844. The American inventor Samuel Morse had just dispatched the biblical quote as a telegraphic message from the United States Capitol building in Washington, D.C., to Mount Clare train station in Baltimore, Maryland. The world's first commercial telegraph line was thus inaugurated. Before this revolutionary invention, it would have taken several hours for a horse-drawn carriage to carry mail across that distance, though a homing pigeon, if available, would have been somewhat more efficient. Within a decade, twenty-thousand miles of telegraph cable would criss-cross America, connecting the nation from coast to coast. By August 16, 1858, the first transatlantic submarine cable made it possible for Queen Victoria to send a message to President Buchanan.

"The Queen," she wrote, "is convinced that the President will join with her in fervently hoping that the electric cable, which now connects Great Britain with the United States, will prove an additional link between the two places whose friendship is founded upon their common interests and reciprocal esteem."

The age of the steamship and railroad had also arrived, and the invention of flying machines was not too far off. The world was shrinking as never before, bringing the nations closer together at an alarming speed. In historical terms, it was a hop, skip, and a jump from telegraphs to telephones, televisions, computers, and the Internet. In fact, it was only in 1991, the same year as the Soviet Union's collapse, that the World Wide Web became available to the public, ushering in the Information Age that has changed our world beyond recognition.

"[W]e fully believe that the Lord will come, and that man's probationary state will end at the termination of the prophetic periods ... that ... cannot be far distant — no farther than man's reckoning may vary from the true reckoning." "The Millerite's Confession and Adventist's Apology" was published in the May 1844 issue of the publication *Advent Shield*, the same month that the Morse Code revolutionized communication. It was a time of messianic expectation for the followers of William Miller, a prosperous farmer and Christian preacher from New York, who in 1833 had proclaimed, "Jesus Christ will come again to this earth, cleanse, purify and take possession of the same with all his saints, some time between March 21, 1843, and March 21, 1844." The critical date had come and gone, and now the faithful experienced a great disappointment as they struggled to understand why the second advent of Christ had not passed according to schedule. When, then, would the divine creator return to reveal the heavenly secrets that would make sense of earthly realities?

In anticipating an apocalyptic end to history, the Christian faithful were by no means alone. The devout Muslims too awaited the Mahdi's appearance in advance of the Day of Judgement when, following catastrophic punishments, he would rid the world of all evil. The secular ideologues that ridiculed religious fanatics had prophetic visions too, of imminent occurrences that would abruptly end the existing world order and usher in a new and perfect civilization. Just as the religious zealot and the radical ideologue proselytized their utopias and looked to the heavens for signs of the promised day, they failed to see that all around them the world as they knew it for centuries was, in fact, about to end.

Claudius Ptolemy's *Almagest* was a ground-breaking treatise in ancient Greece. The celebrated astronomer's thesis of geocentric cosmology posited that the Earth is stationary, at the centre of the universe, with the sun and all other planets revolving around it. From around 150 A.D. — when *Almagest* was published in Hellenic Alexandria — until the Renaissance, Ptolemaic astronomy would be the dominant view. In 1543, the mathematician and astronomer Nicolaus Copernicus published his treatise *On the Revolutions of the Celestial Spheres*. Contrary to the accepted wisdom of more than a thousand years, he proposed that, in fact, it was the sun and not the Earth that was at the centre of the universe. Not everybody was enthusiastic about this sudden subversion of the Earth-centric truth as they had known it, but there was no escaping it. The

Copernican Revolution had made a monumental contribution to scientific advancement, fundamentally and irreversibly changing the conception of our place in the wider universe. Of course, the reality of the solar system had never changed; it was simply that our minds had eventually caught up. The consequences of embracing this simple truth would be far-reaching.

"Lift off! We wish you a good flight!" Those were the fateful words of the control room to Soviet cosmonaut Yuri Gagarin.

"Poyekhali!" was Gagarin's famous response: "Let's Go!"

The date was April 12, 1961, just over a century after Morse's telegraph. Four years earlier, in 1957, the Soviet canine space explorer Laika had become the first dog to orbit the Earth. Now it was time for the first human being to achieve the same feat. Within a few hours, the spacecraft Vostok 1 had carried Gagarin around the Earth, launching the space race among the superpowers that would bring American astronaut Neil Armstrong to the moon in 1969. The age of space exploration could have scarcely been possible had we clung to the myth that the Earth was stationery, at the centre of the universe, as Ptolemaic astronomy would have it.

If simple ideas have far-reaching consequences, then that of humankind being a single race occupying a single home is surely the one with the most profound impact on our self-conception. As we stared back from the darkness of space at the blue celestial sphere that we call Earth, we could see for the first time the actual image of one planet with one people; and yet back on Earth we went about our business as usual, holding on to the anachronistic ideas that failed to grasp our fundamental oneness.

We live in an age of extremes. On the one hand, we witness the resurgence of divisive ideologies; the glorification of greed, hatred, and violence; the futile building of boundaries and walls; a delusional descent into the dark abyss of collective narcissism; the stubborn clinging to outworn shibboleths and obsolete doctrines. On the other hand, our destinies have become inextricably intertwined in our hyper-connected global society, our narrow identities surreptitiously converging into a greater, all-embracing sense of belonging. We are being infused with a wider loyalty, witnessing the rise of an unprecedented consciousness that we all belong to a single emerging world civilization, that our survival depends on acceptance of a transcendent ethos of human dignity for all.

One process, of destruction and disintegration, of an old world order manifestly at odds with the reality of our oneness, desperately holds on to the myth that the thin slice of humanity we define as "self" is at the centre of the universe, while those defined as "others" must naturally revolve around its orbit. The other process, of construction and integration, of a new world order consistent with the inescapable fact of our oneness, embraces, whether reluctantly or enthusiastically, the truth that we all revolve around the same sun, that we all depend on its light for our survival, that we all share a common home and common destiny. These twin processes, of destruction and construction, of disintegration and integration, occurring simultaneously, pulling us in opposite directions, stirring confusion and consternation among the masses, are leading inexorably to a world civilization the boundaries of which are the planet itself. For the first time in history, we are forced collectively to reimagine our identities through the inclusion, rather than exclusion, of others, to achieve the consummation of our social evolution as a single species. Those with messianic expectations were right: the world as we knew it for thousands of years has come to an abrupt end.

The question in this new world is whether we can learn the art of dialogue in pursuit of the peace that our ancestors dreamt of for so long. "They yell at each other, one in Spanish and the other in Russian," my friend said of her Dominican mother and Russian father, who retreated to their mother tongue for the occasional spousal squabble. "It's just like the United Nations!"

Listening to the UN debates on Aleppo on December 14, 2016, I recall that conversation from some time ago: "Are you truly incapable of shame? Is there literally nothing that can shame you?" The American ambassador to the UN, Samantha Power, a friend from my law school days, was letting the Russian ambassador, Vitaly Churkin, have it for his country's role in supporting the Assad regime's bombardment of civilians in Aleppo. "Is there no act of barbarism against civilians, no execution of a child that gets under your skin?" she continued.

"The speech by the U.S. representative," her Russian counterpart defiantly responded, "is particularly strange to me; she gave her speech as if she was Mother Teresa herself. Please, remember which country you represent. Please, remember the track record of your country."

A ruthless ally of Moscow, fighting jihadists

backed by Western powers and their Arab allies, with civilians getting massacred in between — it all sounded familiar, except the Cold War was supposedly behind us. As the distinguished delegates exchanged witty barbs before the UN Security Council, playing their geopolitical games in English and Russian, and those in the translation booth diligently conveyed their every word, the reality of the situation was lost.

The UN under-secretary for humanitarian affairs, Stephen O'Brien, desperately tried to inject an element of humanity into the politicized debate: "Let me take you to east Aleppo this afternoon," he began:

> In a deep basement, huddled with your children and elderly parents, the stench of urine and the vomit caused by unrelieved fear never leaving your nostrils, waiting for the bunker-busting bomb you know may kill you in this, the only sanctuary left to you, but like the one that took your neighbour and their house out last night; or scrabbling with your bare hands in the street above to reach under concrete rubble, lethal steel reinforcing bars jutting at you as you hysterically try to reach your young child screaming unseen in

the dust and dirt below your feet, you choking to catch your breath in the toxic dust and the smell of gas ever-ready to ignite and explode over you.

O'Brien called it "our generation's shame": yet another failure by the Security Council to protect innocent civilians against mass atrocities, just as the mass exodus of desperate refugees streaming into Europe gave ammunition to xenophobic hate-mongers on the far right, eager to whip up hysteria about the "Islamic" threat, demonizing those who have once again fallen victim to the ruthless power struggles played out by others at their expense. Yet, within a few weeks after the fall of Aleppo, it was all forgotten, taken over by new events, as the headlines moved on to other matters. Such is the "New World Order" triumphantly proclaimed at the supposed conclusion of the Cold War.

When the UN Charter was first signed, in San Francisco on June 26, 1945, world leaders pledged "to save succeeding generations from the scourge of war" and "to reaffirm faith in fundamental human rights, in the dignity and worth of the human person, in the equal rights of men and women and of nations large and small." Yet there is a certain mocking derision for those words in the corridors of power, where all manner of malice is casually rationalized as an unfortunate expression of political "reality." The most pressing reality, though, is that of interdependence, and not the myopic disregard of moral principles that passes for brilliant statesmanship. When the Berlin Wall fell in 1989 and the Cold War finally came to an end in 1991, world leaders squandered the opportunity to create a genuinely new world order, a global system that was something more than the triumphal domination of the world by a sole superpower in pursuit of its narrow interests. Now we are paying the price for that failure.

A strong and vibrant UN with the capacity to address pressing problems, a unity of purpose among nations to pursue their common interests through multilateralism, the building of a world civilization on the foundation of transcendent human rights ideals — these aspirations that briefly brought a broken world together in 1945 were all swept under the carpet in the name of expedience and arrogant exceptionalism. When walking through the portal of the General Assembly, those emissaries that claim to speak for peace forgot the immortal words of Saadi at the portal: "Human beings are members of a whole / In creation of one essence and soul." The tragic destruction and dis-integration that we confront today are merely a reflection of our failure to understand that far from being a naive ideal, the oneness of humankind is an inescapable reality.

THE UN FUTURE

"We all are a little bit what we were yesterday and a little bit what we are today and also a little bit we're not these things." Published in communist Czechoslovakia in 1963, Václav Havel's play *Garden Party* was written in the style of the theatre of the absurd. It was a biting satire of the content-free speech of obedient communist bureaucrats: "You see, man when he is from time to time a little bit not is not diminished thereby! And if at the moment I am — relatively speaking — rather not, I assure you that soon I might be much more than I've ever been — and then we can discuss this again, but on an entirely different platform!" Following the arrest of the Plastic People of the Universe — a rock band that was also part of Prague's underground cul-ture — Havel helped lead the historic Charter 77 movement, calling for human rights and freedom of expression. Its dissemination was considered a crime by the communist state. The notorious dissident Havel would be persecuted until the 1989 Velvet Revolution, when he became the first democratically elected president of post-communist Czechoslovakia. True to his origins as a champion of human rights, Havel would not allow the temptations of power to eclipse his visionary politics. He well understood that building a better world required something more than the content-free non-speech that he had criticized while a political dissident, not unlike some of the euphemistic empty talk that every so often characterized the annual speeches before the UN General Assembly.

The UN Millennium Summit, held from September 6 to 8, 2000, in New York, was the largest ever gathering of world leaders. It was an occasion to devise a historic agenda for the twenty-first century. No fewer than 149 heads of state and government were in attendance to deliberate on the future of the UN and how it might be reformed to adequately address pressing global challenges. It was not surprising that calls for far-reaching change were dismissed through diplomatic double-talk and halting half-measures. Within a year, the inadequacy of this impoverished political thought would become manifest as 9/11 threw the world into a prolonged period of chaos with a sequential series of disasters. It was still a time of complacency, with no perceived need for radical change, and no conception of a different future. Havel's visionary statesmanship, however, stood out as an extraordinary expression of political courage and candour about the long-term needs of humankind.

"What will this world, and the United Nations, look like a hundred years from now?" he asked the assembled leaders. The possibilities he recognized ranged "from the most horrific to the ideal." For him, the challenge was to change the UN "from a scene of clashes among particular interests of various states into a platform of joint, solidarity-based decision-making by the whole of humankind on how best to organize our stay on this planet." It was a reminder that, after all, the UN Charter begins with "We the Peoples of the United Nations" and not "We the Self-Serving Political Masters of the Universe."

For Havel, a future UN would rest on two pillars: "One constituted by an assembly of equal executive representatives of individual countries … and the other consisting of a group elected directly by the globe's population." These two bodies would become a world legislature, to which the Security Council would be answerable as an executive organ, without a veto power for any single member. The future UN would also have "its own permanent military and police force" and enforce international laws in regard to security, human rights, environment, and a range of other global issues. Havel recognized that such a world commonwealth required, above all, a transcendent global ethos founded on a sense of shared responsibility.

This, he stressed, could be found somewhere "in the primeval foundations of all the world's religions," in which we find "the same set of underlying moral imperatives... for an ethos for global renewal and for the source and energy of a truly responsible attitude towards our Earth and all its inhabitants, as well as towards future generations."

By now, as I celebrated every word of his refreshing speech, I could imagine the cynical cringing among the so-called realists. I could see the annoyed naysayers dismissing such visionary politics as the far-fetched fantasy of foolish idealists. Even on the occasion of a new millennium, in the shadow of the most revolutionary changes throughout all human history, the worldly-wise with pretensions of global leadership held on to the misguided belief that we could just continue, business as usual. I thought to myself that far from naive idealism, Havel's vision of the future UN was the only realistic option. But the courageous moral leadership that it called for was nowhere to be found.

THE LIGHT OF DAWN

For most of history, we have occupied a detached, egocentric political space, as tribes, city-states, and nations, oblivious to what unites us as a single human race. Now, with the revolutionary developments in technology and consciousness, we have awakened to a new world, where we witness the fusion of myriad diverse peoples into a single civilization. The Global Village is not always romantic. It requires tolerance and dialogue, cooperation and sacrifice, the courage to let go of the familiar but divisive ways of the past and to walk into an unknown future of infinite possibilities. Those who turn their back to this irresistible process of integration will surely be relegated to the dustbin of history. The unification of all peoples into a world commonwealth is not only possible; it is inevitable.

It is the next stage in the evolution of humankind. The only question is whether we will achieve it by vision and volition, or after unimaginable calamities leave us with no other choice.

Thus far, our experiments in global governance have been reactions to catastrophes after the fact. The League of Nations emerged from the ashes of the First World War, and the United Nations from the devastation of the Second World War. How will the future world commonwealth that is necessary to secure peace emerge? Will it be because of a Third World War? Or an environmental disaster that will bring the planet to the brink of extinction? Or is it possible that the peoples of the world will arise with foresight and fortitude and bring an end to the self-defeating politics that have left a bleeding humankind stumbling from one nightmare to the next? At this crucial juncture in our collective history, nothing less than a radically new conception of world order will suffice; nothing less will avert the unconscionable catastrophes that our divisive habits will lead to sooner or later.

When I embraced my two-year-old again, I held him tight and kissed his forehead repeatedly. It had been a long and traumatizing day, but finally he had arrived home with his mother and grandparents. They had cheated death because the naughty boy had made a fuss getting dressed, and they had arrived late for the train that would have placed them at the World Trade Centre at the moment of impact. In fact, my son had a seeming habit of arriving late from the very beginning of his life. He was a bit too comfortable in his mother's womb and simply didn't want to come out. But after forty-two weeks of gestation, he was becoming too large to stay any longer, so labour had to be induced.

Even by the already painful standards of childbirth, it was an agonizing delivery for his poor mother as the contractions became sharper and sharper but the stubborn baby refused to leave his happy home. I could only try to imagine how excruciating the pain was as she pushed and pushed over several hours, throughout the night, without success. Sometime around twenty minutes past eleven on the morning of December 29, 1999, at Bronovo Hospital in The Hague, the guest of honour finally arrived. His beautiful eyes were wide open, eagerly absorbing the surprising sights and sounds of this strange new world, just two days before the new millennium. It had been an exhausting ordeal for his mother, but once the nurse placed the baby in her arms, the joyous miracle of life made her forget the suffering she had endured.

Today, we feel the birth pangs of a new world, humankind struggling to emerge from a familiar space of confined consciousness that it has clearly outgrown, still surrounded by darkness, unaware that just beyond, astonishing possibilities await those who open their eyes to the magnificent light of dawn.

FIVE

THE SPIRIT OF HUMAN RIGHTS

THE BONDS THAT MAKE LIFE WORTH LIVING

"I MISS MY MOTHER." It's not what I expected to hear from a suicide bomber. Ahmed Qasim al-Khateb had a boyish face — big brown eyes, long eyelashes, missing front teeth, and a caterpillar moustache — but he spoke with unwavering confidence about his sacred mission. His clumsy arrogance reminded me more of a rebellious teenager than a ruthless terrorist. It took some imagination to realize that he was in fact highly dangerous.

Ahmed had been captured by the Kurdish peshmerga troops, crossing into Iraq at the Syrian border. His suicide vest had failed to explode. Now he was behind bars, deprived of both freedom and the glory of martyrdom. "There is only one Allah," he proclaimed, defiantly holding up his index finger. The salute of ISIS — the so-called Islamic State in Iraq and Syria — symbolized *tawhid*, the oneness of God. From that sublime premise, the narcissistic narrative of the holy warriors leaped to the improbable conclusion that anyone who disagreed with their ultra-conservative Salafist ideology was an infidel who should be killed. Here I was, a law professor from Canada, sitting in Duhok prison with the celebrated journalist Sally Armstrong, getting schooled in Jihad 101 by a youth half my age.

Ahmed's lecture in psychotic theology demonstrated the success of the emirs in brainwashing impressionable youth, exploiting their desperate rage for the diabolical cause of the so-called caliphate. But it didn't take long for him to run out of things to say. As his ideological swagger began to crumble, it exposed a confused and vulnerable adolescent, rethinking his life choices.

"I miss my mother," he muttered as he was being taken back to his prison cell by the guards. "I wish I could turn time back and go to school. I wanted to become a doctor."

How had Ahmed the healer become Ahmed the killer? What would make a young man with

dreams and ambitions choose death over life? The
power of the primal bond with his mother perhaps
offered a clue. Evidently, having lost everything,
it was a lifeline to the most meaningful connection that he knew. Teenage suicide, as I had come
to understand, was about extreme despair, a want
of the bonds that make life worth living. It was a
question of mental health, not religious ideology.
Maybe in another universe, closer to my reality, I
would have encountered Ahmed hanging around
a shopping mall, texting his girlfriend on the latest
iPhone. Instead of fighting a holy war, he would be
fighting boredom with the wide range of electronic
distractions at his fingertips. For him, the scenes of
carnage in Iraq and Syria would be no more than a
Facebook post. But whether afflicted by cataclysmic
terror or consumerist tedium, one way or another
he would have to grapple with what it means to
live and die in a world of extremes. Whether in
the prison or the shopping mall, there would be
no escape from the perennial problem of how the
depth of our connections distinguishes a meaning-
less life from a meaningful death.

Far from the grim reality I encountered in
Iraq's prisons and refugee camps, the blogo-
sphere and television talk shows were buzzing

with commentary. The Internet-savvy ISIS was pushing all the right buttons. Its psychological warfare had successfully invaded Western minds. Politicians and pundits, celebrities and saviours, all chimed in to process the shocking spectacle of beheadings broadcast on social media. The sadistic cruelty on display had created a palpable consternation. Angry condemnations mixed with visceral fear and voyeuristic fascination, and the occasional expression of sorrow for the victims. It resembled group therapy for secondary post-traumatic stress. Reflecting on this righteous storm in cyberspace, it occurred to me that the story wasn't just about what was happening in ISIS territory, but also what was happening at home, among the spectators.

What do our encounters with human rights atrocities say about who we are, as distinct from who we pretend to be? In pursuit of a virtuous self-image, how does the "civilized" world of Western liberalism perceive the suffering of others at its periphery? We no longer define the sublime by turning to the heaven of medieval Christianity, or even to the modern utopias of totalitarian ideologies. Disabused of the catastrophic illusions of the past, in our postmodern search for transcendence we have embraced human rights as the secular sacred. Having shunned absolute truths, we navigate the stormy seas of moral relativism, weary of foundering on the forbidden rocks of individual autonomy and cultural diversity. In this disenchanted universe, belief in the inherent dignity of humankind is the magical island where we can still find refuge amidst moral uncertainty.

Belief in human dignity finds expression in democratic institutions, constitutional rights, principled foreign policy, and so forth, but it is much more than a set of legal concepts and political procedures. By one classical account, liberalism is merely a social contract designed to prevent our descent into anarchic violence. But what we espouse as an unimpeachable truth about human nature, what we enshrine as a fundamental purpose of society, also reflects our most basic self-definition, as individuals, communities, and civilizations. In fact, the conception of human beings as possessing a noble essence is a giant leap of faith. We could equally conclude that our species is incorrigibly selfish and aggressive, doomed to self-destruction. It is this stark contrast that makes it difficult to reconcile worship of the secular sacred with the crass materialism of our consumerist culture. The glorification of greed and the violence that it breeds are fundamentally incompatible with the spiritual reality that the depths of our humanity can only be discovered through altruism. The light of our soul is best mirrored in how we help the suffering, not in how much we consume.

It may seem odd or even an exaggeration to dwell on the mystical roots of human rights. But we live in exceptional times, when the unravelling of our fragile civilization calls for a radical re-conception of reality. The cosmopolitan creed of liberalism has gone from post–Cold War triumphalism to siege warfare, as terrorism and war, indifference and inequality, disillusionment and demagoguery surround our societies and push us to the limits. There is shock and despair in enlightened circles at the unexpected U-turn, or at least the disruptive detour, in what was once a daily commute to historical progress. We bemoan violent extremism and retrograde populism, yet our response is often no more than a recycling of liberal clichés. The incantation of these ideas has conspicuously failed to address the avarice and anger that is devouring our decency. In fact, the fetishistic privileging of liberal ideology over the intimate reality of human suffering is itself part of the problem. At times, it resembles a fundamentalist belief, a poverty of imagination, an inability to ponder a different and deeper truth about our potential.

We live in a postmodern world of unprecedented prosperity and exponential technological advancement. Before us lies a vista of future possibilities scarcely imaginable by our ancestors. Yet, ironically, we are slowly drowning in a rising sea of despair, gripped by an epidemic of stress, anxiety, and depression. We are electronically hyper-connected but experience only the most superficial of human connections, even with our own selves. Conditioned to expect instant gratification, we are told that fulfillment is no more than a chemical cocktail of serotonin and dopamine, oxytocin and endorphin. Happiness is just a pill away. It has nothing to do with our life choices. This mindset reflects the spiritual crisis of our times, with far-reaching implications on how we conceive the struggle for human betterment.

Egotistic emptiness is a terrible affliction. Its bittersweet medicine is selfless sacrifice. The spirit of human rights, embracing the suffering of others, is about the retrieval of our own authenticity. It is about understanding that our healing depends on helping others heal. In responding to injustice with genuine empathy and meaningful engagement, we are nobody's saviour except our own. Liberal lip service and feel-good activism is not a substitute for the hard work necessary for our completion, for the making of a better world. No matter how swiftly we advance in our fast-paced universe of technological wonders, no matter how much our self-indulgence confuses political correctness with real progress, there is no expiry date for the ancient wisdom that if we stand for the truth, there will always be a price to pay.

LOST YOUTH

As Ahmed was escorted to his cell by the prison guards, longing for his mother, I thought about the self-imposed prison of male narcissistic rage, the cause of so much evil in the world. His violent self-expression was a compensation for his emotional vulnerability, yet another instance of how the failure to connect with others is at the root of aggression. It occurred to me that the horrors of war had extinguished the dignity not only of the victims but also that of the perpetrators. Advancing justice, I had learned from other conflicts around the world, was much more than prosecuting a criminal here and there. It was about redeeming a shared humanity.

In 2016, I was on a mission in Iraqi Kurdistan to explore options for holding ISIS accountable for its heinous crimes. Some had proposed trials before the International Criminal Court (ICC) at The Hague, but there was a curious lack of political will at the UN Security Council. I surmised that other Iraqi factions with similarly murderous militias feared that they too could be ensnared by criminal investigations; they preferred to sweep the atrocities under the carpet of power politics. I had also proposed the option of a truth commission that could hear survivor testimony, to promote healing and reconciliation. But for those policymakers who had not listened to the voices of the victims languishing in the refugee camps, the idea of a grassroots catharsis seemed far-fetched and irrelevant.

It was ironic that I would be pursuing justice next door to my native Iran. There, Shia fanatics had killed our loved ones because of their Bahá'í religious faith. The land of my birth, which our family had to abandon years ago, was now a forbidden world. It was tantalizing to be helping the cause of human rights in neighbouring Iraq, unable to do the same next door without facing imprisonment and torture. Having suffered from Shia extremism, I was now confronted by Ahmed, a Sunni extremist who believed that Shia Muslims should be killed. After listening to his odious sermon, it was obvious that the disease of sectarian strife was always the same, whatever the identity of victims and perpetrators may be. Whether it was the Shia or Sunni jihadists, or the resurgent White Crusaders in the West, hatred knew no boundaries, and neither did its self-defeating logic of healing a wounded self by inflicting wounds on others.

Ahmed came from Deir ez-Zour, an ancient city on the shores of the Euphrates River, once part of the Semitic Palmyrene Empire. Its renowned merchants were enriched by both the trade caravans and the diverse faiths that traversed the Silk Route. Rumi had famously said at the time that "in every religion there is love, yet love has no religion." Greco-Roman and Zoroastrian, Mesopotamian and Arabian, Judeo-Christian and Islamic — the gods of all adorned the diverse pantheon of deities that had accumulated over the centuries at this crossroads of civilization. Yet it was that same strategic geopolitical situation that had now ripped the region apart. Those lusting for power exploited toxic, hateful identities, unleashing murderous passions among desperate despondent youth who served as expendable pawns. Leaders playing a ruthless balance-of-power politics vied for violent supremacy at the expense of a whole generation of youth like Ahmed.

"I joined [ISIS] because they were fighting Bashar [al-Assad]," he explained.

With the catastrophic toll of half a million deaths in the Syrian war and another million in Iraq, preceded by decades of tyranny, corruption, and cynical foreign meddling, it came as no surprise that the ISIS death cult was an attractive option for thousands of lost youth. Duhok prison was a world away from my reality, but there was a certain familiarity about the poor choices made by the likes of Ahmed. A train wreck of trauma, rage, and humiliation, these young men had nothing to lose.

"There was a kind of system to get girls," explained Muhammad Fali Mahmood. A decidedly less devout prisoner than Ahmed, he had run away from home as a teenager to join ISIS. "As long as you were a fighter on the front, you could have as many girls as you wanted."

The way he described it, ISIS sounded like a street gang, with male bonding experienced through violent rites of passage. The merger of murderous and misogynous instincts, and their elevation to an expression of righteous belief, created a delusional self-worth for fragile boys in search of manhood, an identity at once sadistic and sanctimonious. ISIS rewarded obedient holy warriors with sex slaves, and Muhammad was entrusted with their distribution. Unlike Ahmed, he was seemingly apologetic and ashamed of his past, or perhaps he was cleverly opportunistic in his expressions of remorse, hoping that we could somehow secure his release.

"I couldn't look at them in the eyes," he said. "All of them in a prison, and you can't free them, you can't do anything for them." He told the story of discovering two Yazidi girls tied up in the home of an emir in Mosul, as if to partially absolve himself. "I untied their hands and told them to run away...Just run and don't tell anybody that I did this...For two days, all of ISIS in Mosul were busy trying to recapture these girls, but as far as I know they never found them." The glimpses of his guilty conscience competed with his yearning for freedom at the prime of his life. "I deserve to be punished," he admitted, "but I don't deserve fifteen years in prison."

How much of his remorse was genuine? Perhaps in the solitude of his prison cell, in the silence of his conscience, he had discovered contrition. Perhaps one day he would apologize before a truth commission to those he had so grievously harmed. He would outgrow his vicious thrill-seeking folly one day, I thought to myself, but the wounds of those girls might never heal.

"We were blindfolded and had our hands chained together." Badia and Bushra were teenage sisters living in the desolate Khanke refugee camp, not far from Duhok, where Ahmed and Muhammad were imprisoned. They were two of the Yazidi girls who were handed out to ISIS fighters after their village was captured on August 3, 2014. At the time, they were aged thirteen and twelve respectively. They lived on Mount Shengal (or Mount Sinjar as the Arabs called it), a sacred place for the Yazidi believers. They claim that after the biblical flood, its highest summit became the resting place of Noah's ark. Long a persecuted minority, they were now drowning in a deluge of anguish; even this historic sanctuary had failed to shelter them from the horrors of blind hatred. Their blended beliefs originated in the ancient religions of Mesopotamia, complemented by elements of Zoroastrianism, Judaism, Christianity, and Islam, an eclectic creed mirroring the bewildering complexity of this cradle of civilization. But in the fanatical eyes of ISIS, the Yazidis were simply devil-worshippers; they were *kuffar*, infidels to be killed and enslaved.

"In the village, they told us, 'Either you convert to Islam or we will kill you,'" Bushra recalled with a gracious tone that was incongruent with her horrid account of suffering. She sat on the floor, wearing a traditional dress and head scarf, playing nervously with her fingers as she spoke. Her older sister observed an intense silence, saying very few words.

After their village was captured, the Yazidi men and boys were killed, many of them beheaded as their family members were forced to watch. The women and girls were taken to another village and distributed among the fighters.

"They sold my sister and cousin to two ISIS fighters... One of the fighters took me for himself," Bushra explained in a gentle voice as her eyes swelled with tears. "In the morning they told all the girls, 'Go and take a shower, wash yourself, be clean,'" she continued. "One of the girls cut her wrists and committed suicide."

I listened to her heartbreaking story surrounded by the stench of the makeshift lavatories in the squalid refugee camp, amidst the unbearable heat and dust of the Iraqi summer. The high temperature was a hellish 50 degrees Celsius in Baghdad, comparatively cooler at 46 degrees Celsius in northern Iraq. Sitting on the floor in the shadow of the tent she and her sister now called home, Bushra recounted her story, as streams of sweat mixed with trails of tears, and Sally carefully took notes. It wasn't the first time we heard about how unwashed, bearded men would pray to a compassionate and merciful God just before raping girls, seeing no contradiction between their hallowed heaven and their disgusting deeds.

Later, the sisters went about their household chores, Badia working in the small kitchen and Bushra rocking a baby to sleep in a crib, glancing over her shoulder our way, visibly distressed. They longed to return to the beautiful orchard they had once called home, in the hope that maybe there they could retrieve their innocence, lost like the other possessions they were forced to leave behind. They longed to know what had become of their loved ones who were still missing, and to know why the world had abandoned them in their hour of need.

Sitting in that refugee camp, surrounded by so much misery, I was humbled by the astonishing resilience of these two sisters. I was overcome by the urge to shower them with affection, to help heal their wounds like a loving brother. But against the enormity of their suffering, I felt powerless. Before leaving, I reluctantly asked them for a photo of the three of us standing together. I wanted them to know in some small measure that they meant something to me, that I was touched by their purity and courage, that I would remember them when I returned to my wayward world of indifference and privilege. It was heartwarming to see the hint of a smile on their beautiful faces as we posed together for the photo, a fleeting moment of friendship amidst the unspeakable pain.

THE POLITICS OF VIRTUE

That same summer, a world away from the Khanke refugee camp, in a parallel dimension called the politics of humanitarian virtue, the speaker of the Canadian House of Commons, Geoff Regan, was admonishing members of Parliament to refrain from shouting and heckling as an Opposition motion to call ISIS atrocities "genocide" was debated. "I just want to remind honourable members that ... screaming across the floor is not [the accepted process]."

The date was June 9, 2016. Rona Ambrose, the leader of the Opposition, took the floor to explain the proposed declaration: "As we speak, the brutal jihadist terrorist regime known as ISIS is systematically exterminating Christians, Assyrians, Yazidis, Shia Muslims, and countless other religious minorities in Syria and Iraq... There is a word for this kind of deliberate slaughter of specific groups of innocent people," she concluded passionately. "It is genocide."

Foreign Minister Stéphane Dion responded: "Today's debate on the Conservative motion is not about the fight [against ISIS], but rather on the determination of whether these atrocities may constitute genocide. Our government strongly condemns the terrorist acts committed by ISIL," he added, "and we are actively supporting the prosecution of perpetrators and the investigations into ISIL crimes to determine if some amount to genocide... While we fully respect the motion tabled by our Conservative colleagues," he concluded, "it gets ahead of these investigations."

With this opening salvo, the stage was set for a spectacle of name-calling as each side attempted to gain the moral high ground by appropriating the voice of the victims while accusing the other side of trivializing atrocities.

Predictably unsatisfied with the foreign minis-ter's response, Ambrose retorted: "It is a dark spot on Canada's record that the prime minister and his government cannot gather the moral courage to name the threat that has driven families from their homes, seen women and girls sold into sexual slav-ery, or murdered outright, and forced thousands of innocent people into refugee camps...Despite all the government's photo ops and press conferences," she continued pointedly, "it forgets to mention that only nine cases of Yazidi families have been pro-cessed since Canada's refugee plan was put in place."

"When it comes to the process of getting Syrians into this country," a Liberal member of Parliament angrily countered, "there is one party that opened the doors and there is another party that tried to keep those doors as closed as it possibly could." It was a rebuke of the former Conservative prime minister Stephen Harper's reluctance to accept Syrian asylum seekers. "Now to lecture us on humanitarian values is, my God, unbelievable to listen to."

In the familiar pattern of political theatre, as the debate became increasingly heated, the finger-pointing exercise escalated with flourishes to the oratorical arsenal.

"I find the prevarication of this government on this point not just regrettable but shameful, and it is for a reason," a Conservative member of Parliament said with contempt. "The Liberal Party, which took great pride in advancing the notion of the responsibility to protect at the UN, is opposing the recognition of ISIL's genocide for one reason: its recognition would lead to the inevitable conclusion that we must combat it." The verbal assault was aimed at the Liberal government's decision to stop aerial bombardment of ISIS, a policy that the previous Conservative government had supported; but the parliamentarian also seized the opportunity to reopen old wounds from other fights: "I accuse the government of denying the basic facts for one clear reason: it does not want to fight a genocidal regime. That is why it is denying history. Quite frankly, the reason the Liberal government denied the Armenian genocide in 2004 was that it did not want to upset Turkish diplomats."

In this rhetorical rivalry, the G-word was the weapon of choice for champions of righteousness: "This place recognized the genocidal nature of the Holocaust," the Conservative Party member continued. "It recognized the Rwandan genocide... and it recognized the [Ukrainian] Holodomor as genocide... This place has consistently read history for what it is and has not waited for putative groups of lawyers to tell us what history means, what genocide is."

The competition to win the trophy of ultimate torment, privileged the sorrow of some as genocide, while that of others fell into a black hole of second-best. Reducing the enormity of what had transpired on Mount Shengal to a debate on an abstract taxonomy of evil seemed hopelessly out of touch with the reality of the survivors in the refugee camps. The controversy over legal labelling, the dramatic wielding of distinctions as displays of virtue, appeared to be a settling of political scores by exploiting the suffering of others.

As the Oppression Olympics got underway, the exchanges became even more absurd: "Mr. Speaker, the members opposite seem to think that if they say the word 'genocide' three times, spin around in a circle, and click their heels, suddenly something stops," scoffed a Liberal Party member. "It is as empty a set of rhetorical arguments as the notion that saying 'Get out of Ukraine' suddenly solved the crisis in that part of the world," he continued, in a jab at Stephen Harper's tough talk with Vladimir Putin on the annexation of Crimea.

"Mr. Speaker," yet another Conservative Party member protested indignantly, "in fifty years, when some future government stands here and apologizes to the world for inaction on this, I hope the... comment, that if one calls it genocide and clicks their heels, that level of glibness, is remembered. I hope the disgusting trivializing of hundreds of thousands of people dying and being raped and how he treats it are remembered by his constituents."

As if things weren't bad enough in this mud-throwing contest between the Liberals and Conservatives, a parliamentarian from the New Democratic Party joined the fray. "Saudi Arabia beheads people," she pointed out didactically. "If we look at the list of crimes under ISIS and its punishment and look at what is happening in Saudi Arabia, we see it is the same. Yet we are selling arms to Saudi Arabia. I am sorry, but I fail to understand."

Despite the bad blood, this was at least one issue on which the Liberals and Conservatives found common cause. What followed was a loud silence on weapons sales to the Saudi kingdom in which people are beheaded for crimes such as witchcraft and sorcery. Wahhabism, its official religion, is a puritanical version of Sharia, rather similar to the

ISIS ideology. There is a long-standing policy of exporting it through a network of radical preachers at myriad mosques throughout the world. It seemed that for the parliamentarians, chopping off the heads of infidels was a barbaric cultural practice only if big money wasn't at stake. There were limits, even to shedding crocodile tears for the victims of fanatical violence. In politics, principles are sold to the highest bidder.

LOFTY SUMMITS

Davos is a charming village in the Swiss Alps, a fabled ski resort with spectacular scenery and fabulous fondue. As the gondola rises to the summit of Jakobshorn at 2,590 metres, the village becomes smaller and smaller until it disappears from sight. Here, at the highest point, there are snow-covered mountains as far as the eye can see, their majestic peaks gleaming under the sun against a clear blue sky. Here, there is a euphoric feeling of invincibility, as if you are on top of the world without being a part of it. At least that is what I tell myself as the young snowboarders barrel down the slopes at reckless speeds, making a mockery of the more prudent middle-aged skiers in their midst. But on this occasion, the action was back in the village, at the annual meeting of the World Economic Forum.

"Look, it's Angelina!" Hollywood actress Angelina Jolie was being followed by a frantic pack of cameramen and adulating admirers in a feeding frenzy on her glamorous image. But she was by no means the only high-power celebrity at this most exclusive of gatherings. Walking about the conference centre, I saw a dizzying array of Hollywood superstars, billionaire bosses, and prominent politicians, with a small sprinkling of academics and activists like me who somehow made it onto the invitation list. We knew we weren't rich and famous, because we arrived by shuttle bus rather than private helicopter. This was truly a who's who of the global elite, a schmooze-fest like no other. Oh look, there is the founder of Google talking to the inventor of Skype, next to the CEO of Coca-Cola shaking hands with the CEO of Cisco; and there is the Israeli prime minister, Shimon Peres, rubbing shoulders with the Arab League secretary-general, Amr Moussa, trailed by a crown prince or two. There goes Bill Clinton chatting with Bill Gates, and Richard Branson having a drink with Bono, who's sporting shiny leather pants.

I found myself on the foremost site of the adrenaline sport known as extreme networking, a kind of speed-dating on steroids for corporate lobbyists and social climbers. Everybody looked carefully at the name badges to gauge whether the person in their proximity was at least worthy of a business card exchange, if not a more lengthy conversation. What mattered most at this Rolodex-enriching endurance contest was the efficient use of scarce time to optimize on myriad seminars and receptions and huddles and breakaway meetings. At the Davos Club, everyone is presumed to be interesting, but some more than others. Not to be outdone by the VIPs, I took off my badge to create an air of mystery. Eventually, I accepted the painful reality that for most people, a widely cited academic publication was less impressive than winning an Oscar. Later that evening though, at the Bollywood-themed gala night hosted by the Indian delegation, I delivered an Oscar-worthy performance, lip-syncing an addictive song on unrequited love before a captive audience of notable public figures.

The date was January 2006, a decade before my encounters with the devastated youth in northern Iraq. The 2008 market crash, the scandalous impunity of Wall Street, the impoverishment of the masses, disillusionment with smooth-talking, self-serving liberal politicians, the alarming spread of corrosive corruption, the cynical petroleum politics of a militarized Middle East, the Arab Spring, the mass exodus of Syrian refugees, the horrors of ISIS, the rise of the hate-mongering far-right, Brexit, Trumpocalypse, and all manner of other angry revolts against the heedless establishment would unfold under the watch of those same elites.

The Davos buzz was relentless, and scheduling overload a recurring problem. It was difficult to choose between parallel panels featuring leading figures — one on the emergence of China and India, another on world trade, another on the impact of globalization. With all the masters of the universe scurrying about from this to that seminar, it was telling that one of the most popular sessions was entitled "All You Ever Wanted to Know about Relationships but Were Afraid to Ask." Intimacy and happiness, it seemed, were also issues for the global elite — perhaps especially so. But despite the prominent leaders and eminent thinkers, the most oversubscribed session seemed to be "Celebrity-Inspired Action," with Michael Douglas and Peter Gabriel. The year before, megastar Sharon Stone had chosen malaria over diarrhea as her favourite cause, and now the question was which charitable theme would emerge from this year's superstar panel.

"Improving the State of the World," the banner for the World Economic Forum ambitiously proclaimed; at least it was clear that I was improving the state of my vocabulary as I absorbed a bewildering array of cutting-edge jargon from the connoisseurs of Davos Talk. I learned about "horizontal synergies," "resilient dynamism," "tech-enabled peer norming," and "catalyzing multi-stakeholder platforms." As I struggled to figure out the rhyme and reason of this opaque language, I felt like a newly arrived immigrant in an intensive language-immersion course. *Either I am really stupid,* I thought, *or I am being bamboozled by gobbledygook.* There were a lot of impressive and accomplished people, but there was also a decided lack of humility. As I listened to the grand ideas of the global jet set on the mountaintop, it seemed as if they had it all figured out: there was a brilliant technocratic solution for all the ills afflicting humankind. We could all relax, the status quo was fine. It just needed a few adjustments here and there to make the machine run even more smoothly.

It was easy to get swept up by the Davos buzz. But the idea that was conspicuously absent was how the rich and famous could help change the same neo-liberal order that had allowed them to amass obscene fortunes to the exclusion of the 99 percent; how globalization could be reframed in terms of empathy and empowerment rather than the "profit before people" principle. When all was said and done, the unspoken truth seemed to be that what mattered most were big money and political power, legitimized by the discourse of human betterment. Groundbreaking paradigm shifts and sexy slogans were welcome so long as they didn't threaten the racket that privileged the chosen few. Looking down from the sublime summits of Davos at the world below enabled narcissistic self-deception — in the billionaire class, carrying on business as usual; in their political servants, glorifying greed with this or that liberal euphemism; and in the fashionable Hollywood glitterati, glamourizing it all for public consumption.

Eight years later, on June 10, 2014, the *Daily Mail* wrote: "David Cameron and William Hague looked more like a pair of awestruck schoolboys than senior politicians as they met Angelina Jolie yesterday." The British prime minister and foreign secretary were apparently fighting to fawn over the superstar during her visit to London. Angelina was wearing a white blazer and flared skirt designer outfit, another publication wrote, while another celebrity accessorized with a $20,000 Hermès Birkin bag. The high-profile event, the subject of extensive media coverage and celebrity gossip, was the Global Summit to End Sexual Violence in Conflict. The use of rape as a systematic weapon of war throughout history was nothing new, but the attention to the issue was unprecedented; and seemingly it took attention-grabbing Hollywood stars for people to momentarily look up from their iPhones and notice the grim reality of brutalized girls in distant lands. It was, of course, a welcome initiative to break the deplorable silence of the past, but there was more to the Summit than met the eye.

A particular area of concern that year was the shocking scale of sexual violence in the Democratic Republic of Congo. In the decade between 1998 and 2008, following the spillover of the 1994 Rwandan genocide, up to six million people had died in the Second Congo War. In 2010, following years of violence and lawlessness, the UN special representative on sexual violence in conflict, Margot Wallström of Sweden, had dubbed Congo "the rape capital of the world." The year before, more than

eight thousand women and girls had been raped,
primarily in South Kivu, where 60 percent of the
victims had been gang-raped by armed militiamen,
mostly in their own homes. "If women continue to
suffer sexual violence," Wallström had remarked,
"it is not because the law is inadequate to protect
them, but because it is inadequately enforced."

The Global Summit was doubtless about a worthy cause, but beyond the celebrity spectacle, the
bigger picture of the root causes of these atrocities and the dubious politics of humanitarian virtue
were lost.

The travail of the hapless women in Kivu had
a historical context that was probably best forgotten by those wanting to demonstrate sympathy
without rocking the boat. Belgian Congo, as it was
known during the colonial period, had been ruth-
lessly exploited. A latecomer to the colonial race,
King Leopold II of Belgium was in a particular rush
to catch up with the campaign of unjust enrich-
ment by the European powers. At the 1884–85
Berlin Conference that formalized the "Scramble
for Africa," the Belgian monarch persuaded the
European powers to grant him sovereign rights
over the Congo Free State under the pretext of
philanthropic efforts to "civilize" the "natives."

The United States had been the first to recognize Leopold's claim, expressing "sympathy with and approval of [his] humane and benevolent purposes." Such was Belgium's altruistic activism that it also hosted the 1889–90 Anti-Slavery Conference. In a familiar pattern that would extend into the development aid era, what little good was done in Africa was grossly outweighed by outflows of wealth to Europe. In this instance, a shocking policy of exploitation inflicted catastrophic damage on the Congolese for generations to come.

Having secured his personal fiefdom with humanitarian pretenses, King Leopold II moved quickly to terrorize the Congolese population into forced labour for the extraction and export of rubber, a commodity in high demand in the late nineteenth century. The lucrative trade enriched him but decimated the indigenous population: countless Congolese were either murdered or worked to death; the amputation of hands was a widespread practice used to impose obedience among reluctant workers. Other elements of this purportedly altruistic "civilizing mission" included the looting and burning of villages and the kidnapping and rape of women by sadistic colonial administrators. Between 1885 and 1908, in what became known as the "Congo Horrors," up to ten million people perished from atrocities and disease, an African Holocaust conveniently blotted out of historical memory, like so many other colonial misadventures.

After the Congo achieved independence in June 1960, Belgium and America helped overthrow Prime Minister Lumumba, installing in his place the notoriously corrupt President Mobutu. For decades, Mobutu facilitated the pillage of the Congo's natural resources by multinational corporations, leaving few benefits, if any, for the local population. Amid the familiar cycle of domination and violence, exploitation and impoverishment, fragile institutions and failed states, and armed conflict in which women and girls were invariably the biggest victims, marauding militias of violent youth raped with impunity in the lawless desolation of Kivu. But this bigger picture of ongoing exploitation and indifference did not figure in the search for meaningful solutions. Instead, the generosity of the global elite was confined to the language of charitable concern, an expression of noblesse oblige for those suffering unspeakable horrors at the margins of the unjust world created by the rich and powerful.

One of the central issues at the Global Summit was the prosecution of rape in the Congo. Eager to appease public opinion, the Congolese president, Joseph Kabila, promised justice for the victims. But once the attention dissipated, nothing much happened in the form of criminal trials, except that the few women who had the courage to testify in court faced threats and reprisals by their tormentors.

"Funding is very low for tackling sexual violence," one human rights NGO complained. "Major donors have dropped out of this area and it's become very difficult to even get minimal coverage."

The 2014 Global Summit had cost the British government £5 million, but only a negligible fraction of that amount was on offer to help those fighting for justice on the front lines, far away from the limelight.

Later in 2014, at a ceremony in London, the Canadian foreign minister, John Baird, awarded the British foreign secretary, William Hague, a prestigious human rights prize for his work on the Global Summit. Earlier, in the name of "efficiencies and savings," the government had shut down the reputable Canadian agency Rights and Democracy, whose activities included assistance to victims of sexual violence in the Congo. At the reception, as I

feasted on the tasty canapes and heard the congratulatory speeches, I thought about the recent capture
of Mount Shengal by ISIS. Little did I know then
that I would soon meet two teenage sisters named
Bushra and Badia, the suffering of whose people
would become the new *cause célèbre* as the plight of
the Congolese girls became yesterday's news.

GLAMOROUS SUFFERING

> You may bethink you of the spell
> Of that sly urchin page;
> This to his lord did impart,
> And made him seem, by glamour art,
> A knight from Hermitage.

Upon Sir Walter Scott's death in 1832, his poem on
the sly urchin had introduced the Scottish word
"gramarye" into the English language. Derived from
the occult learning of medieval grammarians, it
signified a magic spell that made things appear
better than they really were. In modern usage, it
emerged metaphorically to describe a trance cast
by that which is enchanting and exciting, attractive and alluring. The "glamour of Hollywood" has

become synonymous with a magical world of beautiful people, with an irresistible if cosmetic appeal.

The glamourization of suffering is especially attractive because it creates the illusion of involvement, a pretense of concern without the need to feel the pain of others, let alone to sacrifice anything for their well-being. In the attention-seeking universe of the glitterati and their hypnotized fans, philanthropy is also a branding exercise, an image-enhancing marketing tool, a spell of virtue that with the wave of a magic wand transforms spectacle into sympathy and entertainment into empathy. Like the cinema, it allows us to indulge in effortless fantasies of fighting for justice as romanticized saviours of nameless victims in exotic lands.

Jamie was the face of the less mysterious everyday inequity in our own backyard. Instead of Sir Walter's "sly urchin," he could have been best described in his childhood as a "shy urchin." A vulnerable bedwetter, poor, afflicted with learning disabilities, he didn't lead a life that could be considered glamorous. With an absent father and an alcoholic mother, he was a virtual orphan on the streets, and it was only a matter of time before he ran into trouble with the police. By age seven, he was sent to a home for delinquent children, where he became a tragic character in a brutal contemporary version of *Oliver Twist*. At first, Jamie's cockney slang made me think of an affable bloke in a pub, entertaining his mates with anecdotes over a pint of beer. (A sixty-year-old white military man, he didn't immediately fit into the conventional conception of victimhood.) But his story was a powerful reminder that all human beings suffer alike. Like many whom we come across in our daily lives without knowing about their painful pasts, just beneath the surface of normalcy he concealed a shattered soul.

"Uncle Ted" was the headmaster's brother, Jamie began to recount. His wife sat by his side, gently holding his hand as he told his heartbreaking story.

"He abused me and then pimped me out." Jamie tapped his foot nervously as he spoke, at times grimacing as if his anger was about to explode, but his wife's soothing touch calmed him down. "I worked at railway stations by age eleven. I was taken to the gent's toilets; he dropped me off there and picked me up at the end of the day with the money. I was terrified and conditioned to do whatever he wanted."

Predictably, during his adolescence, Jamie suffered chronic illness and missed a lot of school. By age sixteen he had dropped out, psychologically destroyed. "I became a thing" is how he described it.

Tragically, he was but one among an alarming number of children in Britain who were victims of sexual abuse, betrayed by a culture of privilege that allowed the elite to prey on the vulnerable with impunity. In 2015, following shocking revelations about well-known public figures and extensive pedophile rings, the government established the Independent Inquiry into Child Sexual Abuse. It was a long overdue step towards breaking the silence that had allowed sexual predators to terrorize so many children for so long. But Jamie and many others were profoundly mistrustful of an inquiry run by the same establishment that had repeatedly covered up these crimes; an establishment that preferred to protect reputations rather than vulnerable children.

A group of survivors had asked the few of us, volunteer lawyers and therapists and social workers, to set up a grassroots "people's tribunal" to listen to their stories and speak as advocates on their behalf. Their plight was a familiar abuse of authority to prey on the weak, but the extent of this abuse was truly wicked.

"They were members of Parliament and diplomats," Jamie said about some of Uncle Ted's clients. "I was warned to keep quiet."

As I listened to his story, my grief and anger mixed with admiration, if not astonishment, at how he had survived all these years, carrying such deep wounds.

"I had mental health problems and made suicide attempts," he explained. A young man in desperate search of a new beginning, he joined the British army in Northern Ireland during the Troubles in the 1970s. "I would take on the most risky jobs," he said, explaining how he had eagerly volunteered for bomb disposal. "I had no worries about being blown up. Part of me wanted to die."

When he finished his story, we all sat in silence. He lowered his gaze, staring at the floor, his adoring wife gently stroking his back. There was nothing we could say in response.

It was exhausting to listen to the testimony of these broken souls, enraging to think how the poor at the margins had been betrayed by a prosperous society flaunting its virtue. As I walked through the bustling streets of London on my way home, I was overwhelmed by what Jamie had said, by the incongruity between the courageous soldier and the wounded child. I had fancied myself as an international human rights lawyer. I was on a quixotic quest for global justice in war zones halfway around the world. Now I was humbled to learn about the gross injustice in our own midst, just around the corner.

I thought again about the Global Summit to End Sexual Violence a few months earlier. It was perplexing that while high-profile conferences were being held on rape in the Congo, the staggering scale of sexual violence against children at home had been covered up for so long. There was also a dark side to public displays of virtue, I thought, an exploitation of the woes of victims as a platform for self-promotion and political subterfuge, a pretending and performing on stage rather than truly seeking justice. There were, of course, good and bad people everywhere — or, better yet, good and bad attitudes, including among the global elites. But to me it seemed utterly foolish for people to think that somehow the unholy trinity of the mega-rich, political opportunists, and fashionable entertainers would do the right thing; that they would act with selflessness to achieve meaningful change.

Amidst a rising tide of despair, the only thing those desperate for hope could reliably count on were the recycled broken promises of leaders in the trash can of politics as corporate capitalism

devoured both people and the planet to sustain
its voracious appetite. *When will we learn our lesson?* I asked myself. If the masses were asleep at
the switch, ignorant and indifferent to injustice,
blindly consuming goods in the elusive search for
happiness, if they didn't arise and speak truth to
power and transform their own communities from
the ground up, then the future would fall into the
wrong hands. Compassion kitsch by the 1 percent
was surely not the way to build a better world.

My encounter with Jamie made me reflect on my
experience among the Davos crowd. As a former
UN prosecutor, I had been an interesting anomaly,
with a certain prestige. Putting war criminals on
trial was intriguing and exciting; it validated me
among the global elite. But it occurred to me then
that healing the wounds of the bereaved, bringing
human dignity to the surface, wasn't some Indiana
Jones adventure. Embellishing my CV wasn't the
same thing as helping others. I thought of what
it had meant to Jamie, abused and forgotten for
so long, to have simply had a listening ear in an
uncaring world. I thought of the amazing pro bono
lawyers, volunteer therapists, and die-hard social
workers, and the friends, neighbours, and random
strangers who had showed compassion to him over

the years and convinced him not to take his own life. I thought of those on the ground in Kivu, helping the devastated Congolese girls day in and day out with meagre resources, giving survivors hope and healing amidst the extreme misery as best as they could. Whether at home or halfway across the world, the mega-stars and superheroes were those giving of themselves freely, sincerely, daily, in ways large and small, not for reward or recognition, but with humility and gratitude, because the depth of their conscience left them with no choice but to help those in need, as sure as we breathe the air to survive.

I tried to fight cynicism as I thought of "limousine liberals" and "champagne socialists" hijacking human rights for their own purposes. But I also thought of the foolishness of those at the top playing their game of smoke and mirrors so they could increase their fame or hoard more and more money in their already overflowing pockets. Avoiding authenticity, being possessed by your possessions, I realized, was a profound form of spiritual self-harm. Those indulging in hypocrisy and tokenism were merely denying their own potential to experience meaningful transformative connections. For all their cunning and intelligence, they failed to see the obvious truth that lusting for power was the greatest sign of weakness. Serving humanity with joy and sincerity was, I thought, the most genuine conception of power, the deepest understanding of happiness, of freedom from the prison of egotism. There was something paradoxically liberating, profoundly touching, about soothing the pain of those who suffer rather than indulging in self-centred feel-good activism. Breaking the glamorous spell with gracious sacrifice was an act of embracing our true self, of discovering in our inner universe the magical power to infuse transient words with transcendent worth.

ADVOCATES OF AWESOME

"Peekaboo!" My three-year-old loved to play hide-and-seek. "I will hide behind the sofa so you can find me," he would say with his beaming smile and cartoonish voice. "Look at me, look at me, I'm hiding!" He was in plain sight, but because he had his eyes tightly covered with his little hands, he imagined that I could not see him. His arrival had been a challenge for his older brother, who at four years of age had to deal with the grim reality of sharing both attention and toys with someone else. A few days after the baby came home from the hospital, my elder son decided that the new addition to the family wasn't such a threat after all: "He's cute," he reluctantly admitted. "Can we keep him?"

The famous Swiss child psychologist Jean Piaget observed that preschool children are fundamentally self-centred, unable to perceive a situation from another person's point of view. In their egocentric minds, they assume that everybody else sees the world exactly as they do. It is an adorable trait in children, but one we expect them to outgrow once they become adults. By this measure, it would seem that our culture of self-absorption is not conducive to maturity. It is true that public awareness and grassroots activism are crucial for social progress. But our expressions of concern for human rights often appear focused more on our own need for validation than on the needs of victims.

"You are an advocate of awesome," declared the website, but only if you bought the "action kit." The wristband was the "ultimate accessory," and the T-shirt was really cool. The brisk trade in "awareness products" revolved around a viral video trending on Twitter, a marketing miracle with more than a hundred million views on YouTube.

"We have maxed out our limits . . . we don't have enough merchandise," the executive explained with excitement.

Indeed, the products had quickly sold out, and some observers complained that principles had also been sold out, quite literally. The catchy video had convinced young people surfing cyberspace that with a single credit-card transaction, they could purchase both goods and goodness.

"It's not about the money," the awareness campaign insisted. But the NGO had raked in more than $30 million. Promoting the plight of child soldiers in Uganda was obviously a good cause. Never mind that more than 80 percent of those funds went to cover costs for media, mobilization, and marketing; and never mind that the Ugandan charities were not asked about their real needs.

The American NGO Invisible Children had launched Kony 2012 as a grassroots campaign to hunt down Joseph Kony, the ruthless commander of the Lord's Resistance Army (LRA), a messianic cult revolving around his self-proclaimed prophetic powers. Since the 1980s, the notorious militia had terrorized the population of Acholiland, in northern Uganda, forcibly recruiting thousands of children as soldiers. Those abducted were often forced to kill their own families so they would have nothing and nobody to return to. They were routinely subjected to rape, torture, and mutilation so that the boys would become obedient killers and the girls obedient "wives," serving as sex slaves and domestic servants. Norman was twelve years old when he was captured in his village.

"The first time you kill, it's difficult," he explained. "But then you change."

The Kony 2012 video showed images of the so-called "night commuters," children who flowed into towns to sleep in shelters, fearful of LRA's nocturnal raids on their villages. It showed images of suffering children talking to the film director and co-founder of Invisible Children, Jason Russell.

"We are going to stop them," he tells a distraught Ugandan boy, followed by the narration: "I made that promise to Jacob." From there, things became even more interesting: "2012 is the year that we can finally fulfill [the promise]," he says, adding that "time is running out" because "this movie expires on December 31, 2012." It was an incredibly clever gimmick, telling young people in search of meaning that the time to make a contribution was now, before the expiry date for capturing Kony.

The problem with the video was that the war in

northern Uganda had ended six years earlier. The images of the night commuters were all from the past. Joseph Kony was now a shadow of his former self, hiding in the bush in the Democratic Republic of Congo as a multinational force hunted him down. U.S. photojournalist Glenna Gordon, who had covered the story for several years before it went viral, disparaged the video as an "emotionally manipulative... irresponsible act of image-making." Ugandan peace activist Victor Ochen noted that while "Invisible Children is invisible on the ground," they are visible elsewhere because of "good access to international media [though] they have no connection with the community they claim to represent." Two thousand twelve came and went and nothing happened. They didn't get Kony, but they did get lots of money, and for a little while, a lot of young people could tell their Facebook friends that they were "advocates of awesome."

Back in 2003, abductions in Acholiland had reached a peak. Thousands of children had been stolen from their villages, swelling the ranks of the LRA, strengthening its murderous campaign in the north. In search of a solution, I had proposed to the government of Uganda that the newly established International Criminal Court could serve to isolate the LRA leadership. It was a match made in heaven: the court needed a compelling first case, and Uganda needed to eliminate Kony. The strategy was to issue arrest warrants against the top LRA leadership while offering an amnesty to the thousands of child soldiers to encourage defections. Forcibly recruited and brutalized, most were eager to escape if they could, especially if they had assurances that upon surrendering they would be rehabilitated rather than imprisoned. The timing was auspicious because the government of Sudan and the southern Sudan People's Liberation Movement (SPLM) were at an advanced stage of a prolonged peace process. During the North-South Sudanese war, the government in Khartoum had supported the LRA to destabilize Uganda, while Uganda had supported the SPLM. But now the incentives for this wicked political game were gone.

The dual strategy of isolation and defection was so successful that even LRA negotiators defected. The Ugandan mediator, Betty Bigombe, was left with the predicament of not having anyone to negotiate with. Vincent Otti, Kony's number two, had explained that they could not attend the talks because "we are afraid of the ICC indictment on us... The ICC is just like a landmine... which I will not accept to step on." Similarly, the paranoid Kony had said, "I will not go to The Hague because [Ugandan president] Museveni has a lot of connections with the British and the Americans...They will hijack me on the way to The Hague and kill me."

By 2007, the distrustful Kony had killed Otti, fearing that his support for a peace agreement carried the risk of defection and collaboration with the enemy. By then, the LRA insurgency in northern Uganda had come to an end. Kony's dwindling band of followers was forced to flee to Garamba National Park in the Congo, with Ugandan and other military forces in hot pursuit. They continued to commit atrocities, but on a vastly smaller scale. In July 2015, Dominic Ongwen, the last survivor other than Kony among the five leaders indicted by the ICC, defected from the LRA and surrendered to local forces. He was flown to The Hague to stand trial. By then, Acholiland was at peace. In fact, it was going through an economic boom. The once-terrified children were back at school. The nighttime was now an occasion for people to gather in bars and restaurants rather than cowering in fear. The former child soldiers, now older youths, had returned to their homes and entered rehabilitation programs, hoping for a new start in life. They were gradually integrating into their local communities in a painful process of healing and reconciliation.

Against this backdrop, the misleading portrayal of reality in the Kony 2012 campaign provoked anger among many in Uganda. This was yet another "outsider trying to be a hero, saving Africa," my journalist friend Rosebell Kagumire complained. "We have seen these stories a lot." Brilliant and outspoken, she was incensed by the patronizing narrative that subordinated local initiatives and needs to the triumphant agenda of foreign saviours. For her, the portrayal of Africans as victims waiting to be saved was more about the needs of the human rights industry than about the empowerment of those whose plight was being invoked for legitimacy.

"If you are showing me as hopeless, as voiceless, you shouldn't be telling my story," she said. Another of the Ugandans complained, "It is a slap in the face to so many of us who want to rise from the ashes of our tumultuous past and the noose of benevolent, paternalistic, aid-driven development memes...To be properly heard we have to ride the coattails of the self-righteous idiocy train." Yet another who had survived the LRA's horrors wrote: "I am a visible child from northern Uganda. Who are the 'invisible children'?"

For the do-gooders on the outside, it was difficult to understand why Ugandans would react with such contempt to what were ostensibly well-intentioned efforts. One Hollywood director, Jon Turteltaub, rebuffed the criticism, saying that there was nothing wrong with "three middle-class white guys risking their lives to stop a genocidal madman instead of hanging out at home and playing Angry Birds...The story," he maintained, was that "even some goofballs from San Diego can change the world using media, the internet, and their hearts." This assumed that viral videos translated into meaningful change for child soldiers. It also assumed that what mattered most was not the needs of battle-scarred African youth but the needs of bored American youth to do "something" rather than nothing at all.

Youthful idealism is at the core of the search for a better world. But our materialistic culture of instant gratification is not conducive to either genuine empathy or meaningful engagement. Why make a serious effort when validation is a click of a button away? Real virtue in the world of virtual reality is expressed through "slacktivism." The postmodern tech-savvy wisdom is that with a good headset on your shoulders and some pixel persistence, anything is possible. After all, what is the difference between inner meaning and an immersive interactive experience? Helping others is a great idea, so long as it fits into a bespoke make-believe universe of adventure games, tailored to meet our whims and desires.

The "selfie syndrome" perhaps says it best: Look at me, I am special, I crave affirmation, the universe revolves around my needs. YOLO: you only live once, so you may as well kill the boredom with some really sick fun. This noxious combination of nihilism and narcissism has introduced to our lexicon the once-unthinkable term "Yolocaust," inspired by the Internet image of girls snapping selfies at Auschwitz while pouting for their online audience. When you can't feel anything anymore, when nothing is sacred, dark tourism, like drugs and other distractions, is an easy way to escape the numbness, at least for a while. "Milking the macabre," trivializing torture, reflects the fear of a slow and agonizing death by mediocrity.

In the 1980s, world leaders like U.S. president Ronald Reagan transformed greed from a moral transgression to a policy goal. My generation of youth were told that self-absorbed consumerism was one and the same as the pursuit of happiness.

We were made to believe that revolutionary shopping would create a better world. That is the
cancerous creed of materialism, eating away at
our soul, that we have bequeathed to the millennial generation. Should we be surprised that they
suffer from an entitlement epidemic, that they live
in an emotional wasteland, robbed of the joys of
selflessness and sacrifice? The yearning for transcendence is definitely there but difficult to find in
a culture that equates ecstasy with a pill. As parents and teachers, leaders and thinkers, have we set
a befitting example for those who must build the
better world of tomorrow? How can we tell them to
bring about change if their role models are behaving like arrogant adolescents?

When we speak of compassion fatigue, when we
claim that we have already done enough, it is often
because we are motivated by guilt rather than love.
We write cheques to charities so we can sleep better
at night. We want the terrible images on our television screens to go away. Instead of getting off the
couch and becoming intimately involved, we prefer
to outsource the pleasure and privilege of helping
others. It is one thing to open the wallet, and yet
another to open the heart. Beyond obscene inequality and the poisoning of the earth, the gospel of

greed has also brought a tsunami of despair, as the psychic pestilence of stress, anxiety, and depression spreads like a pandemic. As in the Black Plague of medieval times, there is widespread illness but ignorance about the cause. We consume more and more, but we are less and less happy. We reach for spiritual lifeboats amidst the flood of emptiness: yoga, self-help books, and Headspace apps. But somehow we miss the obvious truth that our salvation comes from giving to others, not because we are doing them a favour but because we are fulfilling our inherent purpose. The formula is rather simple: self-worth comes from doing something worthy with our self.

The idea of building a spiritualized culture in which human dignity can be realized isn't a surfeit of psychobabble; it is a matter of survival. Ours is a highly complex, interdependent, and vulnerable civilization prone to collapse without deep-seated moral values and social solidarity. In an age when robotization and artificial intelligence are combined with increasing inequality and climate change, the choices are stark. A deep-seated ethos of the oneness of humankind is the only thing that stands between a flourishing, just civilization of unimaginable possibilities and a dystopian future with shrinking islands of privilege amidst a rising sea of rage and violence. Quite simply, we need to grow up and stop behaving like self-centred fools before it is too late.

The stubborn clinging to obsolete beliefs and odious behaviours that we witness today is the last gasp of an arrogant adolescence. A toxic egotism is lashing out at an ever-expanding consciousness, terrified of deeper, more mature bonds. Faced with the daunting responsibilities of adulthood, infantile regression is appealing, until we realize that it is impossible to return to the comfort of our mother's womb. At this historical juncture, the wise will walk willingly into the future, in pursuit of the profound pleasures of purpose and inner peace, while the foolish will stumble upon maturity kicking and screaming. Better then to let go of the colossal stupidity of the past and embrace the next stage of humankind's evolution to a higher spiritual consciousness, our collective coming of age.

THE SOUNDS OF SILENCE

Songs are thoughts, sung out with the breath when people are moved by great forces and

ordinary speech no longer suffices. Man is moved
just like the ice floe sailing here and there out in
the current. His thoughts are driven by a flowing
force when he feels joy, when he feels fear, when
he feels sorrow. Thoughts can wash over him like
a flood, making his breath come in gasps and his
heart throb...And then it will happen that we,
who always think we are small, will feel still
smaller. And we will fear to use words.

Orpingalik was a Netsilik Inuit spiritual healer
from Kitikmeot. His oral meditation was recorded
in 1927 by the Danish-Inuit Arctic explorer and
anthropologist Knud Rasmussen. The *angakkuit*
shaman priests were said to possess special powers:
they cured the sick; they interpreted dreams; they
could run as fast as caribou and fly like the birds;
they were impervious to wounds. Some among
them were orphans who had survived hardships,
helped by the spirit of those among the dead who
loved them. They had acquired their healing powers through intimate knowledge of suffering.

The Canadian Arctic is an extraordinary place,
not least during the winter months of constant
darkness and bewildering temperatures. My first
trip to Baker Lake (Qamani'tuaq in Inuktitut) in

what is now Nunavut was in December 1984. When the small airplane landed after a long journey, I naively asked about the weather, only to be told, "It doesn't matter." With the wind chill at a shocking minus 54 degrees Celsius, it was incomprehensible how anyone could have survived here for so long. But the unforgiving cold was tempered by the magical green glow of the northern lights, a stunning cosmic curtain fluttering in the heavens, reminding us that we are but an insignificant speck in an infinite universe. It wasn't difficult in that vast space to understand the purposeful silence that I witnessed among the Inuit elders. It was a silence that spoke, a wisdom that could not be put into words, like the wind that carried mysterious messages from other worlds. They used very few words, but what words they used carried great meaning.

As an immigrant teenager from Toronto trying to gain acceptance in "white culture," I had learned much about cultural adaptation, but learning Inuit social etiquette was unlike anything I had encountered before. It took some time to understand how people communicated. Here, instead of being the misunderstood minority in the schoolyard, I too felt like a *kabloona*, a white person from the south, a stranger to the Inuit experience. But in one important respect, I did feel at home: the tragic displacement, the loss of a way of life, the deep wounds yearning for spiritual healing—these were somehow familiar, even if their cultural expression was different.

"My sister went to the south. She never came back." Those words came out of nowhere. I didn't know how to respond. There had been no introduction, no pleasantries, no conversation; just a prolonged silence. Then suddenly, someone who was a stranger had revealed something very personal, very tragic, just like that.

Shelley was a teenage mother, around my age. At first, I didn't notice the pouch in the back of her parka, where her little girl was ensconced. She would occasionally emerge from her secret hideout to take a peek at the grown-ups with her big, beautiful brown eyes before disappearing again. Very few words were exchanged as Shelley and I sat there, staring into empty space, avoiding eye contact. Given my cultural penchant for small talk with strangers, I found the silence rather awkward. But then, for some inexplicable reason, she suddenly decided to open up and tell me about her missing sister, and to show me the burn marks on her forearm made with cigarette butts by some despicable men. Little did I know then that she had offered me but a small glimpse of the plight of thousands of indigenous women and girls, many of whom were murdered or missing, forgotten in an uncaring world.

For an outsider, the stark contrast between the spiritual ways of the elders and the despair among the youth was difficult to grasp. It was easy to make friends with the other teenagers, to hear them talk about sniffing glue or attempting suicide. For someone whose family had sought refuge in Canada from religious persecution, it was difficult to reconcile this grim reality with the image of a human rights paradise.

Almost thirty years later, on June 21, 2012, in Saskatoon, Leona Bird appeared before the Canadian Truth and Reconciliation Commission to offer her witness testimony.

And then we seen this... army truck outside the place. And as we were walking towards it, kids were herded into there like cattle... Then in the far distance I seen my mother with my little sister. I went running to her, and she says, "Leona," she was crying, and I was so scared. I didn't know what was going on, I didn't know what was happening. My sister didn't cry because she didn't understand... what's gonna happen to us.

Like thousands of others, she told the painful story of forcible separation from her home. She was six years of age, taken together with her younger sister to the Indian Residential Schools as her mother watched helplessly.

It was time for me and her to go, and … when we got in that truck, she just held me, pinched me, and held me on my skirt. "Momma, Momma, Momma." And then my mother couldn't do nothing, she just stood there, weeping. And then I took my little sister, and tried to make her calm down, I just told, "We're going bye-bye, we're going somewhere for a little while." Well, nobody told us how long we were gonna be gone. It's just, like, we were gonna go into this big truck, and that's how … it started.

That's how it started, not just for Leona, but for generations of indigenous children who endured humiliation in the boarding schools whose supposedly "civilizing mission" was to "kill the Indian in the child." I thought about how much she must have missed her mother, of what it meant to be suddenly ripped away from her loved ones; I thought of the catastrophic toll of such wounds across the generations.

Now, at long last, there was a commission to help Canadians reckon with this traumatic past, what it called cultural genocide, by uncovering the historical truth as a first step towards healing and reconciliation. The heartbreaking testimony of the survivors brought me back to that formative experience among the Inuit in my youth; the despair I had witnessed then began to make more sense.

When we lecture less and listen more, we learn that there is always a story behind people's wounds. Reconciliation, the righting of past wrongs, I thought, wasn't about feeling sorry for the victims; it was about listening and learning from their struggle to reclaim a lost humanity, because in their cry for healing we also hear the echo of a greater universe that teaches us who we really are. Unlike the noisy modern culture that had tried to erase their ancient wisdom, the traditional healers that I had encountered still understood the eternal language of silence — the magical art of listening with humility, and feeling the unspoken presence of others. They remained in my mind inspiring masters of intuitive knowledge, heroic defenders of the deeper dignity that our frantic civilization left behind in its mad rush towards progress. It was time, I thought, for the so-called civilized to become spiritualized, to listen and learn from those they once dismissed as ignorant and inferior, to rediscover the ancient soul that binds us together, so we can all find our way home.

WONDROUS JOURNEY

On June 11, 2008, in Winnipeg, Manitoba, four years before Leona's testimony, there was a knock at Donovan Fontaine's front door. That is what many indigenous families heard just before their children were taken away; but on that occasion, the knocking held a different meaning. It had been a historic day for the chief of the Sagkeeng Nation and other indigenous Canadians. Prime Minister Harper had issued an official apology for the Indian Residential Schools and agreed to set up a Truth and Reconciliation Commission as part of a legal settlement with the survivors. It was all over the news. As Chief Fontaine opened his front door, he found his next-door neighbours, an elderly immigrant couple, standing with a plate of muffins. They had seen the news; they wanted to reach out and do something.

"They were offering it in recognition of what happened," Chief Fontaine told me. "A gesture of peace."

It was also a gesture of peace that had inspired me as a teenager to make that unlikely voyage to the Arctic at a dark time for my family, in search of understanding the transcendent bonds that bring together people from different worlds.

"My quiet little sorrow": that is how she described enduring childhood abuse at her home in Qu'Appelle Valley, Saskatchewan, in an interview years after I'd met her. I didn't know at the time that Buffy Sainte-Marie was a famous singer-songwriter, or that she had such a painful past. But her striking presence, her willingness to share in my grief, left a deep and lasting impression on me. As a youth growing up in Toronto, I couldn't quite grasp why an indigenous woman from a different planet than mine would reach out to comfort Iranian Bahá'í refugees mourning the loss of their loved ones. Years later, I would begin to understand how the wounded who wander on the path of redemption have an unusual talent for finding one another.

Nineteen eighty-three had been a turning point in my life. Like most teenagers, I was enthralled with the newly released music video of Michael Jackson's "Thriller." My moonwalking skills were rather appalling, but that didn't dilute my enthusiasm to be trendy and cool. But then my life was turned upside down as we were forced to watch helplessly while our loved ones in Iran were executed for their religious beliefs. Now I found myself on the set of another music video, "Mona with the Children," sharing anguish on a stage with Buffy Sainte Marie, other performance artists, and a bunch of refugees. We had all volunteered to tell the world the story of Mona Mahmudnizhad, my sixteen-year-old contemporary from the persecuted Bahá'í minority, a high school student hanged by Iran's fanatical rulers for daring to speak out in defence of human rights.

Despite months of brutal torture, Mona's spirit did not break. No matter how hard her tormentors tried, they couldn't extract a forced confession, because their cowardly violence was no match for the resilience of her spirit. She knew what awaited her, and she was determined to meet her end with dignity. When the moment came, with the hangman's noose around her neck, her last wish was that the youth of the world would arise and build a better world. Her heroic example had shattered my complacent world of trivial illusions, forcing me to rethink the purpose of my life. As we recreated that scene of her final moments in a film studio north of Toronto, there was a stunned silence. No words could suffice. Tears streamed from Buffy's eyes, for a foreign girl she never knew. Touched by the depth of her sincerity, I felt that I too should reciprocate, to make an effort and understand the grief of her people, for it was her own grief that had opened her to sharing ours.

In a world of dizzying distractions and endless entertainment, where even suffering has been reduced to a spectacle, we must rediscover the profound power of the everyday, of heartfelt compassion, of the transcendent healing connections that transform our impoverished culture of indifference from the bottom up. The political pendulum swings intermittently from the superficial sentimentality of liberals to the populist rage of demagogues, and we imagine foolishly that we can trust those in power to bring about meaningful change. Such apathy is the best accomplice of evil in the world. We need to take seriously the immense impact of our own empathy, of our own engagement — of our responsibility both to comfort those who suffer and to awaken those who suffer from too much comfort. Just as the oppressed must be made whole, so too must the complacent. As we overdose on crass materialism and corrosive narcissism, somewhere within our alienated being we long for the deep connections that make life worth living, to cut through the layers of numbness so we can feel the joy of genuine feelings. The cure that a world groaning from emptiness needs most is a grass-roots conspiracy of authenticity, implemented by transactions of selfless beauty.

Having survived a winter trip to the Arctic, I returned to Baker Lake the following summer to revisit my friends. Going from constant darkness to constant light, the contrast was bewildering. I could barely recognize the place I had seen before. A per-plexing, luminous day had arrived. The universe was dancing in ecstasy; longing and belong-ing had merged into one. It made the wisdom of patience and purposeful silence as resplendent as the twenty-four-hour sun. I would come to learn that in times of gloom, when we have done what we can, our only choice is submission to the rhythm of the seasons. Those were heartbreaking years, when the innocent world of my childhood was forever shattered. We had entered what seemed like an all-consuming darkness, a long, never-ending night. Yet now I understand that if in times of grief we persevere with indomitable hope, if we embrace our wounds and walk the path of love with unflinching determination, we will one day look back and laugh at how the seasons of the soul come and go, at how sorrow prepares us for joy.

Over a quarter century of struggling for justice, my human rights odyssey has brought me to once-unimaginable places and spaces, far from the familiar home I once knew. I have witnessed unspeakable suffering, but I have also witnessed the astonishing, inextinguishable light of the human spirit. I have learned much from the fellow travellers I have seen along the way, but most of all I have learned that just as Mona fundamentally changed the course of my life, the journey always begins with feeling the searing pain of injustice. To become worthy of serving humanity, we must first be broken open, so the invincible light can enter the depths of our being. Without knowledge of suffering, without kindling a raging fire in our hearts, we will never set out on that wondrous journey, in search of a better world.

Oh sweet bitterness
I will soothe you and heal you
I will bring you roses
I, too, have been covered with thorns.

NOTES

The Hafez epigraph is from "My Brilliant Image," *I Heard God Laughing: Poems of Hope and Joy*, trans. Daniel Ladinsky (New York: Penguin, 2006), 7.

CHAPTER 1: THE KNOWLEDGE OF SUFFERING

The Rumi parable on journeys appears in "The Three Fish," *The Essential Rumi*, ed. and trans. Coleman Barks (San Francisco: HarperCollins, 1995), 194. The author uses a somewhat different translation from the Persian original.

Max Weber's quote on the "fate of our times" is from "Science as a Vocation," a 1918 speech at Munich University, published in 1919 by Duncker & Humblot, Munich.

The Universal Declaration of Human Rights was adopted by the United Nations General Assembly on December 10, 1948. For the full declaration, see UN General Assembly, "Universal Declaration of Human Rights," General Assembly Resolution 217 (III), part A, 1948.

Edward Gibbon's quote on history being "little more than the register of the crimes, follies, and misfortunes of mankind" is from *The History of the Decline and Fall of the Roman Empire,* vol. 1 (London: Strahan & Cadell, 1776).

The term "Westoxication," an English translation of the Persian *gharbzadegi,* was popularized by Iranian secular intellectual Jalal al-e Ahmad in his 1962 clandestine publication, *Gharbzadegi.*

Cyropaedia, written by Xenophon of Athens around 370 B.C., is a partly fictional biography of Cyrus the Great, king of Persia and founder of the Achaemenid Empire (550–330 B.C.).

The Hebrew Bible verses praising Cyrus are Ezra 1:1 and 1:2.

Known as the 50/50 Agreement, the deal concluded on December 30, 1950, between Aramco and the government of the Kingdom of Saudi Arabia set the precedent of equal sharing of income from oil in the Middle East.

On Mohammad Mossadegh as the "Iranian George Washington," see Sam Sasan Shoamanesh, "Iran's George Washington: Remembering and Preserving the Legacy of 1953," MIT *International Review,* 2009 online exclusive, http://web.mit.edu/mitir/2009/online/mossadegh. htm.

On Mossadegh as *Time* magazine's 1951 "Man of the Year," see *Time,* January 7, 1952, http://content.time.com/time/covers/ 0,16641,19520107,00.html.

Post-revolutionary Iran's position on the 1948 Universal Declaration of Human Rights was articulated in 1981 by the Iranian ambassador to the United Nations, Said Rajaie-Khorassani, following the United Nations Human Rights Commission's condemnation of mass executions in Iran under Khomeini's totalitarian theocracy.

For more on the teachings of Bahá'u'lláh, see *The Summon of the Lord of Hosts,* a compilation of Bahá'u'lláh's work, available online at the Bahá'í Reference Library, http://www.bahai.org/library/authoritative-texts/ bahaullah/summons-lord-hosts/.

Bahá'u'lláh's quote "Whither can a lover go but to the land of his beloved?" is from *The Hidden Words*, a work consisting of short passages revealed by Bahá'u'lláh in Persian and Arabic in 1857 and 1858 during His exile in Baghdad. Translated by Shoghi Effendi and available through the Bahá'í Reference Library, http://www.bahai. org/library/authoritative-texts/bahaullah/hidden-words/.

The quote "Knowledge is a single point but the ignorant have multiplied it" is from the Hadíth (a record of acts and utterances attributed to the Prophet Muhammad), reproduced in Bahá'u'lláh's *The Seven Valleys*, a work describing the stages of the soul's journey to union with its Creator. Translated by Marzieh Gail for the Bahá'í Reference Library, http://www.bahai.org/library/authoritative-texts/bahaullah/ seven-valleys-four-valleys/#r=svfv_en-1.

Abd'ul-Bahá's quote on "two wings equivalent in strength" is from *The Promulgation of Universal Peace: Talks Delivered by Abdu'l-Bahá during His Visit to the United States and Canada in 1912*, comp. Howard MacNutt, 2nd ed. (Wilmette, IL: Bahá'í Publishing Trust, 1982), 375.

Khomeini's rejection of equality of women and men was pronounced in an address before the people of Qom on June 3, 1963, entitled "In the Name of God, the Compassionate, the Merciful." See Maryam Dadgar, "Shi'ite Clerics and the 'Problem' of Baha'ism," Iran Press Watch, August 26, 2015, http://iranpresswatch.org/post/12856/ shiite-clerics-and-the-problem-of-bahaism/.

George Curzon's quotes are from his *Persia and the Persian Question* (London: Longmans, Green, & Co., 1892), 499–502.

The accounts of the pogrom against Bahá'ís in Yazd in 1903 are from Haji Mirza Haydar-Ali Isfahani, *Bahá'í Martyrdoms in Persia in the Year 1903 AD*, trans. Youness Afroukhteh (Chicago: Baha'i Publishing Trust, 1917; originally published in Persian in 1904).

Michel Foucault's quote on Khomeini's utopian ideology as a "political spirituality" was first published in "What are the Iranians Dreaming About?" *Le Nouvel Observateur*, October 16–22, 1978, and later as an excerpt in Janet Afary and Kevin B. Anderson, *Foucault and the Iranian Revolution: Gender and the Seduction of Islamism* (Chicago: University of Chicago Press, 2005), 203–9.

On Khomeini's secret message to Washington, see Kambiz Fattahi, "Two Weeks in January: America's Secret Engagement with Khomeini," BBC News, June 3, 2016, http://www.bbc.com/news/world-us-canada-36431160.

Ayatollah Khalkhali's quote about the "many more" victims who "deserved to be killed" is from his autobiography, *Ayatollah Khalkhali Remembers* (Tehran: Nashr-e Sayeh, 2000), quoted in Nazila Fathi, "Sadegh Khalkhali, 77, a Judge in Iran Who Executed Hundreds," *New York Times*, November 29, 2003.

For more on the context of Khomeini's dismissal of fair trials as a "Western absurdity," see Shaul Bakhash, *The Reign of the Ayatollahs: Iran and the Islamic Revolution* (New York: Basic Books, 1984), 62.

Khomeini's quote "Criminals should not be tried; they should be killed" is mentioned in Steven O'Hern, *Iran's Revolutionary Guard: The Threat That Grows While America Sleeps* (Washington: Potomac Books, 2012), 19.

During the Cold War, the "arc of crisis" was considered to be the last major region of the "free world" directly adjacent to the Soviet Union. It consisted of the Indian subcontinent to the east, extending west up to the Horn of Africa. See George Lenczowski, "The Arc of Crisis: Its Central Sector," *Foreign Affairs*, Spring 1979, http://www.foreignaffairs.com/articles/russian-federation/1979-03-01/arc-crisis-its-central-sector.

William Shakespeare's quote on "bloody instructions" is from *Macbeth*, act 1, scene 7, lines 5–10.

On Khomeini equating Zionism with a "cancerous tumour" and invoking Shia fury against the "godless" Baathists, see David Hirst,

Beware of Small States: Lebanon, Battleground of the Middle East (London: Faber & Faber, 2010), 178–79.

The "thirteen-year-old child who threw himself against the enemy," as memorialized by Khomeini, was Mohammad Hossein Fahmideh; the quote is from Joyce Davis, *Martyrs: Innocence, Vengeance, and Despair in the Middle East* (New York: Palgrave Macmillan, 2003), 49.

On Khomeini's forced acceptance of UN Security Council Resolution 598, see Ervand Abrahamian, *A History of Modern Iran* (New York: Cambridge University Press, 2008), 181.

On Khomeini's fatwa, see *Deadly Fatwa: Iran's 1988 Prison Massacre* (New Haven, CT: Iran Human Rights Documentation Center, 2009), http://www.iranhrdc.org/english/publications/reports/3158-deadly-fatwa-iran-s-1988-prison-massacre.html.

On Khomeini's declaration that the Bahá'í religious minority was a treasonous "political party" see Eliz Sanasarian, *Religious Minorities in Iran* (Cambridge: Cambridge University Press, 2000), 30; on his condemnation of all Bahá'ís as "spies," see 119.

The Iranian officials' justification for the killings of prominent Bahá'ís — that it was "binding upon religious judges to punish them accordingly" — is quoted from the judgement against Jinus Ni'mat Mahmudi, convicted of espionage on December 27, 1981. See the president's statement confirming the execution, available through Human Rights & Democracy for Iran, a project of the Abdorrahman Boroumand Foundation, http://www.iranrights.org/memorial/story/-4018/jinus-nimat-mahmudi.

For the 1985 report referring to the killing of Iranian Bahá'ís as "genocide," see Benjamin Whitaker, "Revised and Updated Report on the Prevention and Punishment of the Crime of Genocide," UN Economic and Social Council Commission on Human Rights, Sub-Commission on Prevention of Discrimination and Protection of Minorities, E/CN.4/Sub.2/1985/6, July 2, 1985, http://www.preventgenocide.org/prevent/UNdocs/whitaker/.

Firuz Naïmi's story is from the recollection of the author's family. For Naïmi's last will and testament, see "Text of the Will of the Bahá'ís Killed in Hamadan" (in Persian), *Iran Wire*, December 5, 2014, http://iranwire.com/fa/features/1275. For an account of the execution of the Bahá'í leaders in Hamadan, see Ayda Ghajar, "Execution of the Bahais of Hamadan: Zhinous's Memories of the Seven Martyrs," *Iran Press Watch*, September 8, 2014, http://iranpresswatch.org/post/10792/execution-of-the-bahais-of-hamadan-zhinouss-memories-of-the-seven-martyrs/.

Much of Mona's story has been taken from the recollections of Olya Roohizadegan, a survivor among the Bahá'ís executed in Shiraz, in her book, *Olya's Story – A Survivor's Dramatic Account of the Persecution of Bahá'ís in Revolutionary Iran* (Oxford: Oneworld, 1994). See also *Community Under Siege: The Ordeal of the Bahá'ís of Shiraz*, (New Haven, CT: Iran Human Rights Documentation Center, 2007), http://www.iranhrdc.org/english/publications/reports/3151-community-under-siege%3A-the-ordeal-of-the-baha%E2%80%99is-of-shiraz.html.

Ruhi Jahanpour's recollections of the persecution she and other Bahá'í women of Shiraz suffered are also detailed in Roohizadegan, *Community Under Siege*.

The Hafez quote is from "Love is the Funeral Pyre," *The Gift: Poems by Hafiz, the Great Sufi Master*, trans. Daniel Ladinsky (New York: Penguin, 1999), 69.

Rumi's quote "I know you are tired, but come" is from "Drumsound rises in the air . . ." *Rumi: The Book of Love*, ed. and trans. Coleman Barks, (New York: HarperCollins, 2000), 8.

CHAPTER 2: THE PURSUIT OF GLOBAL JUSTICE

Dražen Erdemović's testimony is quoted from the Sentencing Judgement of the ICTY, *Erdemović* (IT-96-22), November 29, 1996, paragraph 10, http://www.icty.org/x/cases/erdemovic/tjug/en/erd-tsj961129e.pdf.

For more on the Nuremberg judgement, see International Military Tribunal Nuremberg, *The Trial of Major War Criminals before the International Military Tribunal*, vol. 22, *Nuremberg: 14 November 14 1945 – 1 October 1946*. Each volume can be accessed through the Library of Congress online database: http://www.loc.gov/rr/frd/Military_Law/NT_major-war-criminals.html.

Radovan Karadžić's order to "create an unbearable situation of total insecurity ... for the inhabitants of Srebrenica" was given on March 8, 1995, in a directive for the upcoming operations of the Krajina Corps of the Bosnian Serb Army at Srebrenica: *Supreme Command of the Armed Forces of Republika Srpska*, Ref. No.: 2/2-11 (March 8, 1995), 10, http://www.documentcloud.org/documents/251259-950308-directive-7.html.

Erdemović's account of the blunt choice his military commander gave him at Srebrenica is also taken from the November 29, 1996, ICTY Sentencing Judgment, para. 10.

Judge Fouad Abdel-Moneim Riad's description of the first genocide on European soil since World War II as the "darkest pages of human history" is from his confirmation of the International Criminal Tribunal for the former Yugoslavia's indictment of Radovan Karadžić and Ratko Maldić on November 14, 1995, http://www.icty.org/en/press/radovan-karadzic-and-ratko-mladic-accused-genocide-following-take-over-srebrenica.

Kaiser Wilhelm II's skepticism in reaction to the Russian tsar's invitation to the Hague Conference in 1899, prompting him to keep his "dagger at [his] side during the waltz," is summarized in Robert K. Massie, *The Dreadnought: Britain, Germany, and the Coming of the Great War* (London: Pimlico, 2004), 429–30.

The quote from the Treaty of Versailles (June 28, 1919), is from part VII, article 227. For the full treaty, see the Avalon Project, Lillian Goldman

Law Library, Yale Law School, http://avalon.law.yale.edu/imt/parti. asp.

Albert Speer's quote on the "time of tremendous suffering" for the German people is from the International Military Tribunal Nuremberg, *The Trial of Major War Criminals before the International Military Tribunal*, vol. 22, *Nuremberg: 14 November 1945 – 1 October 1946*, 405.

Speer's quote "It would be ridiculous if I complained about the punishment" is from G. M. Gilbert, *Nuremberg Diary* (Boston: Da Capo Press, 1995, originally published in 1947), 433.

Joseph Keenan's quote on war criminals is from a press statement he issued during the Tokyo trials, which took place between May 3, 1946, and November 12, 1948. For more on the International Military Tribunal for the Far East and the Tokyo war crimes trials and its chief prosecutor, see Joseph Berry Keenan Digital Collection, Harvard Law School Library, http://hls.harvard.edu/library/digital-collections-and-exhibitions/ joseph-berry-keenan-digital-collection/.

Robert Jackson's quote on "the most significant tributes that Power has ever paid to Reason" was part of his opening statement at Nuremberg before the International Military Tribunal, delivered on November 21, 1945. For the full statement, see the Robert H. Jackson Center, http://www.roberthjackson.org/speech-and-writing/ opening-statement-before-the-international-military-tribunal/.

Jackson's description of the Nuremberg Tribunal as establishing "incredible events by credible evidence" is from his June 6, 1945, report to the U.S. President upon his return from the International Conference on Military Trials in London. For the full report, see the Avalon Project, Lillian Goodman Law Library, Yale Law School, http:// avalon.law.yale.edu/imt/jack08.asp.

For Hannah Arendt's writing on the Nazi crimes that "explode the limits of law," see Hannah Arendt and Karl Jaspers, *Correspondence 1926–1969* (New York : Mariner Books, 1993), 54.

Auguste Champetier de Ribes's remark on the Holocaust as "monstrous" was recorded on July 29, 1946, during the Nuremberg trials. For his full address, see the International Military Tribunal Nuremberg, *The Trial of Major War Criminals before the International Military*, vol. 19, *14 November 1945 – 1 October 1946*, 531.

Polish jurist Raphael Lemkin first coined the term "genocide" in chapter 9 of his 1944 publication *Axis in Occupied Europe – Laws of Occupation, Analysis of Government, Proposal for Redress* (Washington: Carnegie Endowment for International Peace, Division of International Law, 1944), 79–95.

Lemkin's description of the Genocide Convention as "an epitaph on my mother's grave" is quoted in John Cooper, *Raphael Lemkin and the Struggle for the Genocide Convention* (New York: Palgrave Macmillan, 2008), 72.

The request for an International Law Commission study on "the desirability and possibility of establishing an international judicial organ for the trial of persons charged with genocide" was formally announced in the United Nations General Assembly Resolution 260, A/Res/3/260, December 9, 1948.

Meša Selimović's quote "I call to witness time" is from the opening passage (loosely based on verses from the Qur'an) of his novel *Death and the Dervish*, trans. Bogdan Rakić and Stephen M. Dickey (Evanston, IL: Northwestern University Press, 1966).

British statesman David Owen's comment "Don't live under the dream that the West is going to come and sort this problem out" was made in December 1992 at the Sarajevo airport. It is cited in Timothy Waters, *The Milošević Trial: An Autopsy* (New York: Oxford University Press, 2014), 95.

For more on Dame Anne Warburton's report on the estimated number of rape victims during the war, see *Report on Rape in Bosnia-Herzegovina — EC Investigative Mission into the Treatment of Muslim Women in the Former Yugoslavia: Report to EC Foreign Ministers*

(Copenhagen: Ministry of Foreign Affairs, 1993), para. 17. On the UN investigation, see Tadeusz Mazowiecki, "The Situation of Human Rights in the Territory of the Former Yugoslavia," UN Doc A/48/92-S/25341, February 26, 1993, 69, http://repository.un.org/handle/11176/51391.

The UN Human Rights Commission quote describing the Markale open-air market bombing as a "horrible massacre" and condemning the "policy of genocide" is from "Situation of Human rights in Bosnia and Herzegovina," E/CN.4/RES/1994/75, March 9, 1994, para. 1, http://www.refworld.org/docid/3b00fod82o.html.

For Slobodan Milošević's June 28, 1989, Gazimestan monument speech on "resolve, bravery, and sacrifice," see "History of Kosovo: Primary Documents," EuroDocs: Online Sources for European History, Harold B. Lee Library, Brigham Young University, http://eudocs.lib.byu.edu/index.php/History_of_Kosovo:_Primary_Documents.

The anti-war leader who called the Yugoslav army's brutal siege of Vukovar the "Hiroshima" of national madness was Vuk Drašković, quoted in Dubravka Stojanović, "The Traumatic Circle of the Serbian Opposition," in *The Road to War in Serbia: Trauma and Catharsis*, ed. Nebojša Popov, English version ed. Drinka Gojković (Budapest: Central European University Press, 2000), 474.

Radovan Karadžić's poem "Sarajevo" is published in his collection *Pamtivek* (Sarajevo: Svjetlos, 1971).

Karadžić spoke publicly about the "annihilation" of the "Muslim people" when he addressed the parliament of the Republic of Bosnia and Herzegovina on the night of October 14–15, 1991. See Institute for War and Peace Reporting, *Karadzic Witness Says Serbs "Provoked" into War*, November 15, 2013, http://www.refworld.org/docid/528b4obe4.html.

The description of Ratko Mladić as a "charismatic murderer" is by Richard Holbrooke, chief negotiator of the Bosnia Peace Accord, from his book *To End A War* (New York: Random House, 1998), 149.

Mladić's quote "Borders have always been drawn with blood" is from a 1994 interview with *Der Spiegel*, a German weekly news magazine, cited in Michael Mann, *The Dark Side of Democracy: Explaining Ethnic Cleansing* (Cambridge: Cambridge University Press, 2005), 405.

Mladić's description of defending his nation as "a holy duty" is from an interview with Robert Block, cited in "The Madness of General Mladic," *New York Review of Books*, October 9, 1995, http://www.nybooks.com/articles/1995/10/05/the-madness-of-general-mladic/.

Mladić's vow to take "vengeance against the Turks" was made on the occasion of the Serb takeover of Srebrenica on July 11, 1995. For more, see Sonja Biserko, "We'll Take Vengeance on the Turks," *Bosnia Report*, May 11, 2006, http://www.bosnia.org.uk/news/news_body.cfm?newsid=2200.

Samuel Huntington's quote on the "fault lines between civilizations" is from a lecture he delivered at the American Enterprise Institute on October 19, 1992, later published as "The Clash of Civilizations?" *Foreign Affairs*, Summer 1993, http://www.foreignaffairs.com/articles/united-states/1993-06-01/clash-civilizations.

Warren Zimmermann's observations on "racial and historical tinder" are from his book *Origins of a Catastrophe: Yugoslavia and Its Destroyers* (New York: Three Rivers, 1999), 210.

Erdemović's description of the reluctance of his friends to participate in warfare is from *Erdemović* (IT-96-22), November 20, 1996, 340, http://www.icty.org/x/cases/erdemovic/trans/en/961120ED.htm.

For the *Time* magazine cover of Fikret Alić, see *Time*, August 17, 1992, http://content.time.com/time/covers/0,16641,19920817,00.html. The story of the Bosnian concentration camps was initially revealed to the press by British reporter Ed Vulliamy.

Edin Ramulić's reaction to the news of Karadžić's arrest was quoted in "Karadzic Arrest: Celebrations in Sarajevo," *Balkan*

Insight, July 21, 2008, http://www.balkaninsight.com/en/article/karadzic-arrest-celebrations-in-sarajevo.

Erdemović's statement on "the peace of my mind" is from *Erdemović* (IT-96-22), November 20, 1996, 341, http://www.icty.org/x/cases/erdemovic/trans/en/961120ED.htm.

For the exchange between Erdemović and Karadžić during Erdemović's cross-examination at Karadžić's trial, see ICTY, *Karadžić,* IT-95-5/18, February 28, 2012, 25410, http://www.icty.org/x/cases/karadzic/trans/en/120228ED.htm.

For the sentence pronounced on Karadžić by Judge Kwon, see *Karadžić,* IT-95-5/1, March 24, 2016, 48160–61, http://www.icty.org/x/cases/karadzic/trans/en/160324IT.htm.

Ratko Mladić's words to his daughter — "Come on, my angel" — are quoted in Erich Follath, "Portrait of a Man Possessed: The Search for the Real Ratko Mladic — Part 3: A Family Tragedy," *Der Spiegel,* September 30, 2011, http://www.spiegel.de/international/europe/portrait-of-a-man-possessed-a-search-for-the-real-ratko-mladic-a-784851-3.html.

The description of Mladić as a "broken man" is from Zoran Stanković, chief military pathologist, former Serbian defence minister, and one of Mladić's closest confidants, quoted in Dan Bilefsky, "Karadzic's general, Ratko Mladic, may be tougher to apprehend," *New York Times,* August 3, 2008, http://www.nytimes.com/2008/08/03/world/europe/03iht-serb.4.14971730.html.

.

CHAPTER 3: THE WILL TO INTERVENE

"A cockroach cannot give birth to a butterfly" was a phrase first employed by the Hutus in 1993 to dehumanize the Tutsi people. See Manus I. Midlarsky, *The Killing Trap: Genocide in the Twentieth Century* (New York: Cambridge University Press, 2005), 177. See also *Prosecutor v Ferdinand Nahimana, Jean-Bosco Barayagwiza, and Hassan Ngeze,* ICTR-99-52-T, December 3, 2003, 122, para. 179, http://unictr.

unmict.org/sites/unictr.org/files/case-documents/ictr-99-52/trial-judgements/en/031203.pdf.

Éloge's story is taken from an interview conducted by the author in 2016.

RTLM was the first to report the news of the death of Rwandan president Juvénal Habyarimana on April 6, 1994. For a more detailed account, see Dina Temple-Raston, *Justice on the Grass: Three Rwandan Journalists, Their Trial for War Crimes, and a Nation's Redemption* (New York: Free Press, 2005), 4.

Esther Mujawayo's story is taken from an interview conducted by the author in 2017.

For President Clinton's full speech at the opening of the United States Holocaust Memorial Museum in 1993, see William J. Clinton, "Remarks at a Reception for the Opening of the United States Holocaust Memorial Museum," April 21, 1993, American Presidency Project, ed. Gerhard Peters and John T. Woolley, http://www.presidency.ucsb.edu/ws/?pid=46461.

On the dismissal of Trygve Lie's proposed "UN Guard" as a "terrible idea," see Brian Urquhart, preface to *A United Nations Emergency Peace Service to Prevent Genocide and Crimes against Humanity*, ed. Robert C. Johansen (New York: World Federalist Movement, 2006), 7.

For Boutros Boutros-Ghali's proposal for a UN "rapid reaction force," see his "Supplement to an Agenda for Peace: Position Paper of the Secretary-General on the Occasion of the Fiftieth Anniversary of the United Nations," A/50/60-S/1995/1, January 3, 1995, http://www.un.org/documents/ga/docs/50/plenary/a50-60.htm.

Heinrich Himmler's use of the "lice" metaphor in occupied Soviet Ukraine in 1943 was published in a collection of documentary evidence prepared for presentation before the International Military Tribunal at Nuremberg. See Office of United States Chief Counsel for Prosecution of Axis Criminality, *Nazi Conspiracy and Aggression*, vol. 4, (Washington: United States Government Printing Office, 1946), 574, http://www.loc.gov/rr/frd/Military_Law/pdf/NT_Nazi_Vol-IV.pdf.

For Jean-Paul Sartre's famous quote on anti-Semitism, see Jean-Paul Sartre, *Anti-Semite and Jew*, trans. George J. Becker (New York: Schocken, 1948), 8.

For more on the Einsatzgruppen, see Richard Rhodes, *Masters of Death: The SS-Einsatzgruppen and the Invention of the Holocaust* (New York: Vintage, 2002). Otto Olhendorf's trial is available at http://avalon.law.yale.edu/imt/01-03-46.asp.

Charles Darwin's most famous work, *On the Origin of Species*, originally published in 1859, establishes his theory on natural selection. See Charles Darwin, *On the Origin of Species*, ed. Jim Endersby (Cambridge: Cambridge University Press, 2009), chapter 4.

For the origins of the concept of "survival of the fittest", see Herbert Spencer, *The Principles of Biology*, vol. 1 (London: Williams & Norgate, 1864), 444–45.

For David Hume's quote on "all other species of men . . . [as] naturally inferior to the whites," see "Of National Characters" in his *Essays, Moral, Political and Literary*, rev. ed. (Indianapolis: Liberty Fund, 1987; originally published 1758), 198–99.

For more on the Hamitic hypothesis, see Edith R. Sanders, "The Hamitic Hypothesis: Its Origins and Functions in Time Perspective," *Journal of African History*, vol. 10, no. 4 (1969), 521–32.

The Bible quote is from Exodus 24:12 (King James Version).

For the "Hutu Ten Commandments," see "Appeal to the Bahutu Conscience (with the Hutu Ten Commandments)," *Kangura*, no. 6 (December 1990), Rwanda File — Primary Sources for the Rwanda Genocide, ed. Jake Freyer, http://www.rwandafile.com/Kangura/k06a.html.

For the full February 1993 *Kangura* article, see "Editorial: A Cockroach (Inyenzi) Cannot Bring Forth a Butterfly," *Kangura*, no. 40 (February 1993), Rwanda File — Primary Sources for the Rwanda Genocide, ed. Jake Freyer, http://www.rwandafile.com/Kangura/k40r.html.

The song with the lyrics "cockroaches are no more" was originally broadcast on RTLM on July 2, 1994, and was later produced as evidence in *Nahimana*, ICTR-99-52-T, December 3, 2003, 122, para. 357, http://unictr.unmict.org/sites/unictr.org/files/case-documents/ictr-99-52/trial-judgements/en/031203.pdf.

The quote on there being "no difference between the RPF and the *inyenzi*" is taken from an RTLM interview with Ferdinand Nahimana, conducted by Gaspard Gahigi on November 20, 1993, and quoted in the judgement and sentence of *Nahimana*, ICTR-99-52-T, 122, para. 357.

The quote on forbidding Hutus to share meals with Tutsis is from a second RTLM interview by Gaspard Gahigi, this time with Jean-Bosco Barayagwiza on December 12, 1993, and also used as evidence in *Nahimana*, ICTR-99-52-T, 118, para. 345, http://unictr.unmict.org/sites/unictr.org/files/case-documents/ictr-99-52/trial-judgements/en/031203.pdf.

The passage beginning "Dawn is when the day breaks" quotes Ananie Nkurunziza, as broadcast on RTLM on June 5, 1994, and cited in *Nahimana*, ICTR-99-52-T, 137–38, para. 405, http://unictr.unmict.org/sites/unictr.org/files/case-documents/ictr-99-52/trial-judgements/en/031203.pdf.

The passage on the Tutsis' "arrogance and contempt" quotes Kantano Habima, as broadcast on RTLM on May 31, 1994, and cited in *Nahimana*, ICTR-99-52-T, 138, para. 408, http://unictr.unmict.org/sites/unictr.org/files/case-documents/ictr-99-52/trial-judgements/en/031203.pdf.

For Kantano Habimana's exhortations to kill all *inyenzi*, broadcast on RTLM on May 18, 1994, see *Nahimana*, ICTR-99-52-T, 144–45, para. 427, http://unictr.unmict.org/sites/unictr.org/files/case-documents/ictr-99-52/trial-judgements/en/031203.pdf.

For Kantano Habimana's instructions to take drugs to "prevent any cockroach passing", broadcast on RTLM between May 26 and 28 1994, see *Nahimana*, ICTR-99-52-T, 146, para. 433, http://unictr.unmict.org/sites/unictr.org/files/case-documents/ictr-99-52/trial-judgements/en/031203.pdf.

For the full lyrics of the quoted Simon Bikindi song, see "Nanga Abahutu" ("I Hate These Hutus"), version D, 1993, Rwanda File — Primary Sources from the Rwandan Genocide, ed. Jake Freyer, http://www.rwandafile.com/other/bikindisongs.html.

For the full interview with Jean-Paul Samputu and Payam Akhavan, see "Rwanda Reconciliation," *Ideas*, CBC Radio, April 9, 2014, http://www.cbc.ca/radio/ideas/rwanda-reconciliation-1.2604244. Samputu's quote on drinking to forget is at 9 minutes, 0 seconds; his quote on forgiveness is at 13:20; his advice on education and love is at 18:00.

The term "butterfly effect" was coined by American mathematician Edward Lorenz, a pioneer of chaos theory; he introduced the concept during a December 29, 1972, speech at the American Association for the Advancement of Science entitled "Predictability: Does the Flap of a Butterfly's Wings in Brazil Set a Tornado in Texas?"

For more on the effects of the coffee economy on the Rwandan genocide, see Meera Warrier, ed., *The Politics of Fair Trade: A Survey* (London: Routledge, 2011), 199. See also Isaac A. Kamola, "The Global Coffee Economy and the Production of Genocide in Rwanda," *Third World Quarterly*, vol. 28, no. 3 (2007), 571–92.

On the World Bank and the International Monetary Fund's pressure for "structural adjustment" in Rwanda, see Michel Chossudovsky, *The Globalization of Poverty and the New World Order* (Pincourt, QC: Global Research, 2003).

CHAPTER 4: THE ONENESS OF HUMANKIND

For George Bush Sr.'s proclamation of a "New World Order," see George Bush, "Address Before a Joint Session of the Congress on the State of the Union," January 29, 1991, American Presidency Project, ed. Gerhard Peters and John T. Woolley, http://www.presidency.ucsb.edu/ws/?pid=19253.

On the "end of history," see Francis Fukayama, *The End of History and the Last Man* (New York: Maxwell Macmillan International, 1992).

Mohsen Makhmalbaf's article on Afghanistan is entitled "Limbs of Nobody: The World's Indifference to the Afghan Tragedy," *Monthly Review*, vol. 53, no. 6 (November 2001), 28.

Mullah Muhammad Omar's condemnation of the Buddhas of Bamiyan is quoted in Francesco Francioni and Federico Lenzerini, "The Obligation to Prevent and Avoid Destruction of Cultural Heritage: From Bamiyan to Iraq," in *Art and Cultural Heritage: Law, Policy and Practice*, ed. Barbara T. Hoffman (New York: Cambridge University Press, 2006), 32.

For Chinese pilgrim Xuanzang's records of the ancient caravan city of Bamiyan, see Sally Hovey Wriggins, *The Silk Road Journey with Xuanzang* (Boulder, CO: Westview, 2004), 144.

Makhmalbaf's quote on the statue of Buddha crumbling "out of shame" is from his "Limbs of Nobody: The World's Indifference to the Afghan Tragedy," *Monthly Review*, vol. 53, no. 6 (November 2001), 33.

For the narrative of jihadists as "enemies of freedom," see George W. Bush, "Address Before a Joint Session of the Congress on the United States Response to the Terrorist Attacks of September 11," September 20, 2001, American Presidency Project, ed. Gerhard Peters and John T. Woolley, http://www.presidency.ucsb.edu/ws/?pid=64731.

The Saadi quote is translated by M. Aryanpour from *The Gulistan or Rose Garden* (1258 A.D.), ch. 1, story 10.

The quote on the "Vietnamese quagmire" is from Robert Gates, *From the Shadows: The Ultimate Insider's Story of Five Presidents and How They Won the Cold War* (New York: Simon & Schuster, 1996), 145.

For the full Sanskrit treatises by Indian philosopher Kautilya, see *Kautilya's Arthashastra,* trans. Rudrapatna Shamasastry (Bangalore: Government Press, 1915), http://dharmarajya.swarnayug.org/uploads/1/2/1/8/12185983/arthashastra_of_chanakya.pdf.

For the Buddha's teachings on "a man's own mind," see Bukkyō Dendō Kyōkai, *The Teachings of Buddha* (New Delhi: Sterling, 2004), 119.

Sima Samar's story is taken from an interview conducted by the author in 2016.

The exchange with Abdul Rahman Hotak is from the author's recollections of a conversation in 2014.

For Abdullah bin Laden's explanation of his half-brother Osama bin Laden's "radical feelings," see "My Brother Osama," *Telegraph* (London), December 16, 2001, http://www.telegraph.co.uk/news/worldnews/asia/afghanistan/1365453/My-brother-Osama.html.

The quote on the Soviets getting "stuck" on "this tar-baby" (Afghanistan) is from Walt Slocombe, in a September 8, 2011, interview with John Bernell White. See White's "The Strategic Mind of Zbigniew Brzezinski: How a Native Pole Used Afghanistan to Protect His Homeland," (master's thesis, Louisiana State University, May 2012), http://etd.lsu.edu/docs/available/etd-04252012-175722/unrestricted/WHITE_THESIS.pdf.

Zbigniew Brzezinski's quote "What is most important to the history of the world?" is from an interview published as "The CIA's intervention in Afghanistan," *Le Nouvel Observateur*, January 15–21, 1998, http://www.globalresearch.ca/articles/BRZ110A.html.

Karl Marx's quote on "the opium of the people" is from his *Critique of Hegel's 'Philosophy of Right,'* trans. by Annette Jolin and Joseph O'Malley (Cambridge University Press, 1970; reprinted 1982), 131.

For more on Alexey Stakhanov, the Soviet labour hero, see Richard Overy, *The Dictators: Hitler's Germany and Stalin's Russia* (New York: W. W. Norton, 2004).

The Marxian mantra "from each according to his ability, to each according to his needs" is from Karl Marx, *Critique of the Gotha Programme* (London: Electric Book Company, 2001; originally published in 1875), 20.

The exhortation "Let the verdict be heard like thunder" is from prosecutor Andrey Vyshinsky, as quoted in Laura Hill, "The Great Purge of Stalinist Russia," Boston University "Guided History" blog, Spring 2013, http://blogs.bu.edu/guidedhistory/moderneurope/laura-hill/.

John Stuart Mill's description of British imperial rule as "a blessing of unspeakable magnitude" is quoted in Jennifer Pitts, *A Turn to Empire: The Rise of Imperial Liberalism in Britain and France* (Princeton: Princeton University Press, 2009), 125–26.

Winston Churchill's description of Indians as "beastly people with a beastly religion" is quoted in Madhusree Mukerjee, *Churchill's Secret War: The British Empire and the Ravaging of India During World War II* (New York: Basic Books, 2010), 78.

George Washington's quote on "Indians and wolves" is from a September 7, 1783, letter to James Duane, available online at Founders Online (National Archives), http://founders.archives.gov/documents/Washington/99-01-02-11798.

Thomas Jefferson's quote "If we are ever constrained to lift the hatchet against any tribe" is from an August 28, 1807, letter to statesman Henry Dearborn, available online at Founders Online (National Archives), http://founders.archives.gov/documents/Jefferson/99-01-02-6267.

For the idea that Adolf Hitler's conception of concentration camps owed much to his studies of English and United States history, see John Toland, *Adolf Hitler* (New York: Anchor, 1992), 702.

For more on the first-ever telegraphic message, sent by Samuel Morse on May 24, 1844, see "First Telegraphic Message — 24 May 1844," Library of Congress, http://www.loc.gov/item/mmorse000107/.

On Queen Victoria's telegraphic message to the president of the United States, see Robert Monro Black, *The History of Electric Wires and Cables* (London: Peter Peregrinus, 1983), 26.

"The Millerite's Confession" was published in the *Advent Shield and Review*, vol. 1, no. 1 (May 1844), 6, http://adventistdigitallibrary.org/adl-367101/advent-shield-and-review-may-1-1844.

William Miller's proclamation that "Jesus will come again to this earth" is from a February 9, 1844, letter to Joshua Himes, printed in Sylvester Bliss and Joshua Himes, *The Memoirs of William Miller* (Boston: Joshua V. Himes, 1858), 180, http://archive.org/details/memoirswilliammooblisgoog.

Yuri Gagarin's famous exclamation *"Poyekhali!"* ("Let's Go!") is quoted in Graham Smith, "The Main Thing Is That There Is Sausage: Gagarin's Extraordinary Last Words before Making History with First Manned Space Flight 50 Years Ago Today", *Daily Mail* (London), April 13, 2011, http://www.dailymail.co.uk/sciencetech/article-1376008/Yuri-Gagarins-sausage-remark-Last-words-1st-manned-space-flight.html.

Samantha Power's rhetorical question "Are you truly incapable of shame?" and Vitaly Churkin's response are documented in the UN Security Council's 7834th meeting, UN Doc. S/PV/7834, December 13, 2016, 7, http://www.securitycouncilreport.org/atf/cf/%7B65BFCF9B-6D27-4E9C-8CD3-CF6E4FF96FF9%7D/s_pv_7834.pdf.

Stephen O'Brien's full statement to the Security Council on the situation in Aleppo is available online at http://www.unocha.org/sites/unocha/files/dms/Documents/ERC_USG%20Stephen%20OBrien%20

Statement%20on%20Syria%20to%20SecCo%2026OCT2016%20
CAD.pdf. See also Julian Borger, "UN Chief Calls Security Council's
Failure on Aleppo 'Our Generation's Shame,'" *Guardian* (Manchester),
October 27, 2016, http://www.theguardian.com/world/2016/oct/26/
aleppo-bombings-syria-un-stephen-obrien-vitaly-churkin.

The pledges to "save succeeding generations from the scourge of war"
and "to reaffirm faith in fundamental human rights" are taken from the
preamble of the Charter of the United Nations, 1 UNTS XVI, October
24, 1945, http://www.un.org/en/sections/un-charter/preamble/
index.html.

The quotes from Václav Havel's play *Garden Party* (originally published
in 1963) are from *Garden Party and Other Plays*, trans. Vera Blackwell
(New York: Grove, 1993), 50–51.

For Havel's address at the Millennium Summit, see "Address of the
President of the Czech Republic at the Millennium Summit of the
United Nations, New York, September 8, 2000," UN Doc A/55/PV.8,
http://www.un.org/en/ga/search/view_doc.asp?symbol=A/55/PV.8.

CHAPTER 5: THE SPIRIT OF HUMAN RIGHTS

For more on the conversations with Ahmed Qasim al-Khateb
and Muhammad Mahmood, during which the author was
present, see Sally Armstrong, "The real faces of ISIS," *Maclean's*,
August 11, 2016, http://www.macleans.ca/news/world/
the-real-faces-of-isis-sally-armstrong-reports-from-iraq/.

For more on the conversation with Badia and Bushra, during which
the author was present, see Sally Armstrong, "Yazidi women tell their
horrific stories," *Maclean's*, August 30, 2016, http://www.macleans.ca/
news/yazidi-women-tell-their-horrific-stories/.

For the Canadian parliamentary debate on ISIS and genocide, see
House of Commons Debates, vol. 148, no. 69, June 9, 2016, http://

www.ourcommons.ca/DocumentViewer/en/42-1/house/sitting-69/
hansard.

On David Cameron and William Hague meeting Angelina Jolie, see
Tom McTague, "Starstruck Schoolboys: How the Prime Minister
and Foreign Secretary Fought to Fawn Over Angelina Jolie," *Daily
Mail* (London), June 10, 2014, http://www.dailymail.co.uk/news/
article-2653807/Angelina-Jolie-dedicates-crisis-summit-end-rape-
war-victim-met-felt-abandoned-world.html.

For Margot Wallström's account of sexual violence in Congo, see
"Women, Peace and Security: Sexual Violence in Situations of Armed
Conflict," Security Council Open Meeting, New York, April 27, 2010,
3–4, http://www.un.org/sexualviolenceinconflict/wp-content/
uploads/2012/07/Statement_SVC_Open_SC_Meeting_27_
April_20102.pdf; see also "UN Official Calls DR Congo 'Rape Capital
of the World,'" BBC News, April 28, 2010, http://news.bbc.co.uk/2/
hi/8650112.stm.

The United States' recognition and approval of King Leopold's claim of
sovereignty over Congo is cited in Michael Patrick Cullinane, *Liberty
and American Anti-Imperialism: 1898–1909* (New York: Palgrave
Macmillan, 2012), 165.

The statement that funding is low for tackling sexual violence
is from Tamah Murfet of the International Rescue Committee's
women's protection unit in the Congo, quoted in Mark Townsend,
"Revealed: How the World Turned Its Back on Rape Victims of Congo,"
Guardian (Manchester), June 13, 2015, http://www.theguardian.com/
world/2015/jun/13/rape-victims-congo-world-turned-away.

On the cost of the 2014 Global Summit and the reported minimal
distribution of funds to those "fighting for justice on the frontlines,"
see Mark Townsend, "William Hague's Summit against Warzone
Rape Seen as 'Costly Failure,'" *Guardian* (Manchester), June 13, 2015,
http://www.theguardian.com/global-development/2015/jun/13/
warzone-rape-congo-questions-uk-campaign.

For John Baird's speech awarding the Diefenbaker Award to William Hague, see "Address by Minister Baird Presenting the John Diefenbaker Defender of Human Rights and Freedom Award to William Hague, London," December 1, 2014, http://www.canada.ca/en/news/archive/2014/12/address-minister-baird-presenting-john-diefenbaker-defender-human-rights-freedom-award-william-hague.html.

On the Harper government's shutdown of the Canadian agency Rights and Democracy for "efficiencies and savings," see "Troubled Rights and Democracy Agency to Be Closed," CBC News, April 3, 2012, http://www.cbc.ca/news/politics/troubled-rights-and-democracy-agency-to-be-closed-1.1185276.

The Sir Walter Scott verse excerpt is from "The Lay of the Last Minstrel," *Poetical Works of Sir Walter Scott, Bart.*, vol. 1, ed. William Minto (Edinburgh: Adam & Charles Black, 1887), 138.

Jamie's story is taken from the author's recollection of and notes from an interview in 2015.

On the "advocates of awesome," see *Rhetorics of Whiteness: Postracial Hauntings in Popular Culture, Social Media, and Education*, ed. Tammie M. Kennedy, Joyce Irene Middleton, and Krista Ratcliffe (Carbondale, IL: Southern Illinois University Press, 2017), 96–97.

Jason Russel's insistence that the Kony 2012 campaign was "not about the money" is from a March 8, 2012, interview with MSNBC's Lawrence O'Donnell on *The Last Word*. See http://www.msnbc.com/the-last-word/watch/kony-2012-creator-its-not-about-the-money-44148803938. The Kony 2012 video can be viewed online at http://invisiblechildren.com/kony-2012/.

For the interview with Glenna Gordon, who described the Kony 2012 video as an "irresponsible act of image-making," see Elizabeth Flock, "Invisible Children Founders Posing with Guns: An Interview with the Photographer," *Washington Post* "blogPost" blog, March 8, 2012, http://www.washingtonpost.com/blogs/

blogpost/post/invisible-children-founders-posing-with-guns-an-interview-with-the-photographer/2012/03/08/gIQASX68yR_blog.html?utm_term=.4b3c114e2e86.

The quote on Invisible Children being "invisible on the ground and in communities" is from Rosebell Kagumire's March 9, 2012, blog post entitled "More perspective on Kony2012," http://rosebellkagumire.com/2012/03/09/more-perspective-on-kony2012/.

Vincent Otti's description of the ICC as a "landmine," and Kony's explanation of why he would not go to The Hague, are quoted in Mark Kerstern, *Justice in Conflict: The Effects of the International Criminal Court Interventions on Ending Wars and Building Peace* (Oxford: Oxford University Press, 2016), 94.

Rosebell Kagumire's quotes are from her YouTube video "My Response to Kony2012," embedded at http://rosebellkagumire.com/2012/03/08/kony2012-my-response-to-invisible-childrens-campaign/.

The quote on "rising from the ashes of our tumultuous past" is from TMS Ruge, "A Peace of My Mind: Respect My Agency 2012!" Project Diaspora, March 8, 2012, http://projectdiaspora.org/wp-content/2012/03/08/respect-my-agency-2012/.

The quote "I am a visible child from northern Uganda. Who are the 'invisible children'?" is the title of a March 8, 2012, post on the personal blog of Maureen Agena, http://maureenagena.com/society/i-am-visible-child-from-northern-uganda/.

On Hollywood director Jon Turteltaub's rebuff of the Kony 2012 criticism, see Erika Morphy, "Why the Kony Video Could be a Hoax (But It's Not)," *Forbes*, March 11, 2012, http://www.forbes.com/sites/erikamorphy/2012/03/11/why-the-kony-video-could-be-a-hoax-but-its-not/#773644d3622c.

For more on the term "Yolocaust," see the recent BBC article by Joel Gunter, "'Yolocaust': How should you behave at a Holocaust memorial?" BBC News, January 20, 2017, http://www.bbc.com/news/world-europe-38675835.

For the Danish anthropologist Knud Rasmussen's recordings of Orpingalik's oral meditation, see Penny Petrone, ed., *Northern Voices: Inuit Writing in English* (Toronto: University of Toronto Press, 1992), 23.

Shelley's story is taken from the author's recollection of a conversation from 1984.

For Leona Bird's testimony before the Canadian Truth and Reconciliation Commission, see *The Survivors Speak*, vol. 3 (Winnipeg: Truth and Reconciliation Commission of Canada, 2015), 24–25, http://www.trc.ca/websites/trcinstitution/File/2015/Findings/Survivors_Speak_2015_05_30_web_o.pdf.

The official "Statement of Apology – to former students of Indian Residential Schools on behalf of the Government of Canada by The Right Honourable Stephen Harper, Prime Minister of Canada," given on June 11, 2008, is published in *Honouring the Truth, Reconciling for the Future: Summary of the Final Report of the Truth and Reconciliation Commission Canada* (Winnipeg: Truth and Reconciliation Commission of Canada, 2015), 369, http://www.trc.ca/websites/trcinstitution/File/2015/Honouring_the_Truth_Reconciling_for_the_Future_July_23_2015.pdf. The term "civilizing mission" is found at p. 46.

For Rumi's poem "Oh sweet bitterness," see *The Love Poems of Rumi*, trans and ed. Deepak Chopra and Fereydoun Kia (New York: Harmony Books, 1998), 27.

BIBLIOGRAPHY

CHAPTER 1: THE KNOWLEDGE OF SUFFERING

Abrahamian, Ervand. *A History of Modern Iran*. New York: Cambridge University Press, 2008.

_____. *Iran Between Two Revolutions*. Princeton: Princeton University Press, 1982.

_____. *Tortured Confessions: Prisons and Public Recantations in Modern Iran*. Berkeley: University of California Press, 1999.

Alston, Philip, and Ryan Goodman. *International Human Rights*. Oxford: Oxford University Press, 2012.

The Bahá'í International Community. *The Bahá'í Question Revisited: Persecution and Resilience in Iran; A Report of the Bahá'í International Community*. New York: The Bahá'í International Community, 2016. https://www.bic.org/sites/default/files/pdf/thebahaiquestionrevisited_final_160930e.pdf.

Ebadi, Shirin, with Azadeh Moaveni. *Iran Awakening: A Memoir of Revolution and Hope*. London: Rider, 2007.

Hatcher, William S., and J. Douglas Martin. *The Bahá'í Faith: The Emerging Global Religion*. San Francisco: Harper & Row, 1985.

Iran Human Rights Documentation Center. *A Faith Denied: The Persecution of the Baha'is of Iran*. New Haven, CT: Iran Human Rights Documentation Center, 2006. http://www.iranhrdc.org/english/publications/reports/3149-a-faith-denied-the-persecution-of-the-baha-is-of-iran.html.

Iran Human Rights Documentation Center. *Community Under Siege: The Ordeal of the Bahá'ís of Shiraz*. New Haven, CT: Iran Human Rights Documentation Center, 2007. http://www.iranhrdc.org/english/publications/reports/3151-community-under-siege%3A-the-ordeal-of-the-baha%E2%80%99is-of-shiraz.html.

Iran Human Rights Documentation Center. *Crimes Against Humanity: The Islamic Republic's Attacks on the Bahá'ís*. New Haven, CT: Iran Human Rights Documentation Center, 2008. http://www.iranhrdc.org/english/publications/reports/3155-crimes-against-humanity%3A-the-islamic-republic%E2%80%99s-attacks-on-the-bah%C3%A1%E2%80%99%C3%ADs.html.

Kazemzadeh, Firuz. *Russia and Britain in Persia: Imperial Ambitions in Qajar Iran*. New York: I.B. Tauris, 2013.

Kinzer, Stephen. *All the Shah's Men: An American Coup and the Roots of Middle Eastern Terror*. Hoboken: J. Wiley & Sons, 2003.

Molavi, Afshin. *The Soul of Iran: A Nation's Journey for Freedom*. New York: W.W. Norton, 2002.

Momen, Moojan. *The Babi and Bahá'í Religions, 1844–1944: Some Contemporary Western Accounts*. Welwyn, U.K.: George Ronald Publisher, 1981.

_____. *An Introduction to Shi'i Islam*. Oxford: George Ronald Publisher, 1985.

Mottahedeh, Roy. *The Mantle of the Prophet: Religion and Politics in Iran*. Oxford: Oneworld Publications, 2009.

Roohizadegan, Olya. *Olya's Story: A Survivor's Dramatic Account of the Persecution of Bahá'ís in Revolutionary Iran*. London: Oneworld Publications, 1993.

Smith, Peter. *An Introduction to the Bahá'í Faith*. New York: Cambridge University Press, 2008.

CHAPTER 2: THE PURSUIT OF GLOBAL JUSTICE

Akhavan, Payam, and Robert Howse. *Yugoslavia, the Former and Future: Reflections by Scholars from the Region*. Washington, DC: Brookings Institution Press; Geneva: United Nations Research Institute for Social Development, 1995.

Arbour, Louise. *War Crimes and the Culture of Peace*. Toronto: Toronto University Press, 2002.

Armatta, Judith. *Twilight of Impunity: The War Crimes Trial of Slobodan Milosevic*. Durham, NC: Duke University Press, 2010.

Bass, Gary Jonathan. *Stay the Hand of Vengeance: The Politics of War Crime Tribunals*. Princeton: Princeton University Press, 2000.

Borger, Julian. *The Butcher's Trail: How the Search for Balkan War Criminals Became the World's Most Successful Manhunt*. New York: Other Press, 2016.

Fleck, Dieter, ed. *The Handbook of International Humanitarian Law*. 3rd ed. Oxford: Oxford University Press, 2013.

Glenny, Misha. *The Fall of Yugoslavia: The Third Balkan War*. New York: Penguin Books, 1996.

Goldstone, Richard J. *For Humanity: Reflections of a War Crime Prosecutor*. New Haven, CT: Yale University Press, 2000.

Kemal Kurspahic. *Prime Time Crime: Balkan Media in War and Peace*. Washington, DC: United States Institute of Peace Press, 2003.

Maček, Ivana. *Sarajevo Under Siege: Anthropology in Wartime*. Philadelphia: University of Pennsylvania Press, 2009.

Malcolm, Noel. *Bosnia: A Short History*. New York: New York University Press, 1994.

Rohde, David. *Endgame: The Betrayal and Fall of Srebrenica, Europe's Worst Massacre Since World War II*. New York: Farrar, Straus and Giroux, 1997.

Roland, Paul. *The Nuremberg Trials: The Nazis and Their Crimes Against Humanity*. London: Arcturus Publishing, 2010.

Scharf, Michael P. *Balkan Justice: The Story Behind the First International War Crimes Trial Since Nuremberg*. Durham: Carolina Academic Press, 1997.

Waters, Timothy William. *The Milošević Trial: An Autopsy*. New York: Oxford University Press, 2014.

Williams, Paul R., and Michael P. Scharf. *Peace with Justice? War Crimes and Accountability in the Former Yugoslavia*. Lanham, MD: Rowman & Littlefield, 2002.

Zimmerman, Warren. *Origins of a Catastrophe: Yugoslavia and Its Destroyers — America's Last Ambassador Tells What Happened and Why*. New York: Times Books, 1996.

CHAPTER 3: THE WILL TO INTERVENE

Barnett, Michael N. *Eyewitness to a Genocide: The United Nations and Rwanda*. Ithaca, NY: Cornell University Press, 2002.

Browning, Christopher. *The Origins of the Final Solution*. New York: Random House, 2014.

Cruvellier, Thierry. *Court of Remorse: Inside the International Criminal Tribunal for Rwanda*. Translated by Chari Voss. Madison: University of Wisconsin Press, 2010.

Dallaire, Roméo, with Brent Beardsley. *Shake Hands with the Devil: The Failure of Humanity in Rwanda*. New York: Carroll & Graf, 2005.

Des Forges, Alison. *Leave None to Tell the Story: Genocide in Rwanda*. New York: Human Rights Watch, 1999.

Gahima, Gerald. *Transitional Justice in Rwanda: Accountability for Atrocity*. New York: Routledge, 2013.

Gourevitch, Philip. *We Wish to Inform You That Tomorrow We Will Be Killed with Our Families: Stories from Rwanda*. New York: Farrar, Straus and Giroux, 1998.

Hatzfeld, Jean. *Machete Season: The Killers in Rwanda Speak*. New York: Farrar, Straus and Giroux, 2006.

_____. *Life Laid Bare: The Survivors in Rwanda Speak*. New York: Other Press, 2007.

Joris, Lieve. *The Rebels' Hour*. New York: Grove Press, 2010.

Melvern, Linda. *A People Betrayed: The Role of the West in Rwanda's Genocide*. Cape Town: NAEP / New York : Zed Books, 2000.

_____. *Conspiracy to Murder: The Rwandan Genocide*. London: Verso, 2006.

Mujawayo, Esther, and Souad Belhaddad. *La fleur de Stéphanie: Rwanda entre réconciliation et déni*. Paris: Flammarion, 2006.

Mujawayo, Esther, and Souad Belhaddad. *SurVivantes*. La Tour-d'Aigues, Fr.: Éditions de l'Aube, 2004.

Power, Samantha. *"A Problem from Hell": America and the Age of Genocide*. New York: Basic Books, 2002.

Prunier, Gérard. *The Rwanda Crisis: History of a Genocide*. New York: Columbia University Press, 1995.

Rhodes, Richard. *Masters of Death: The SS-Einsatzgruppen and the Invention of the Holocaust*. New York: Vintage Books, 2003.

Rusesabagina, Paul. *An Ordinary Man: The True Story Behind Hotel Rwanda*. London: Bloomsbury, 2007.

CHAPTER 4: THE ONENESS OF HUMANKIND

Armstrong, Sally. *Bitter Roots, Tender Shoots: The Uncertain Fate of Afghanistan's Women*. Toronto: Viking, 2008.

_____. *Veiled Threat: The Hidden Power of the Women of Afghanistan*. Toronto: Viking, 2002.

Coll, Steve. *Ghost Wars: The Secret History of the CIA, Afghanistan, and bin Laden, from the Soviet Invasion to September 10, 2001*. New York: Penguin Press, 2004.

Crews, Robert D., and Amin Tarzi, eds. *The Taliban and the Crisis of Afghanistan*. Cambridge: Harvard University Press, 2008.

Gall, Sandy. *War Against the Taliban: Why It All Went Wrong in Afghanistan*. London: Bloomsbury, 2012.

Goodson, Larry P. *Afghanistan's Endless War: State Failure, Regional Politics, and the Rise of the Taliban.* Seattle: University of Washington Press, 2001.

Marsden, Peter. *The Taliban: War, Religion and the New Order in Afghanistan.* New York: Zed Books, 1998.

Nojumi, Neamatollah. *The Rise of the Taliban in Afghanistan: Mass Mobilization, Civil War, and the Future of the Region.* New York: Palgrave, 2002.

Riedel, Bruce. *What We Won: America's Secret War in Afghanistan, 1979–89.* Washington, DC: Brookings Institution Press, 2014.

Service, Robert. *A History of Twentieth-Century Russia.* Cambridge: Harvard University Press, 1998.

Siegelbaum, Lewis H., and Andrei K. Sokolov, eds. *Stalinism as a Way of Life: A Narrative in Documents.* New Haven, CT: Yale University Press, 2000.

CHAPTER 5: THE SPIRIT OF HUMAN RIGHTS

Allen, Tim, and Vlassenroot, Koen. *The Lord's Resistance Army: Myth and Reality.* New York: Zed Books, 2010.

Axe, David, and Tim Hamilton. *Army of God: Joseph Kony's War in Central Africa.* New York: Public Affairs, 2013

Brooks, Rose. *The Scars of Death: Children Abducted by the Lord's Resistance Army in Uganda.* New York: Human Rights Watch, 1997. https://www.hrw.org/legacy/reports97/uganda/.

Cockburn, Patrick. *The Rise of Islamic State: isis and the New Sunni Revolution.* New York: Verso, 2015.

Fisher, Cate, and Claire Soares. *The Impacts of Child Sexual Abuse: A Rapid Evidence Assessment.* Independent Inquiry into Child Sexual Abuse, 2017. https://www.iicsa.org.uk/key-documents/1534/view/IICSA%20Impacts%20of%20Child%20Sexual%20Abuse%20Rapid%20Evidence%20Assessment%20Full%20Report%20%28English%29.pdf.

Fontaine, Phil, Aimée Craft, and Truth and Reconciliation Commission of Canada. *A Knock on the Door: The Essential History of Residential Schools.* Winnipeg: University of Manitoba Press / National Centre for Truth and Reconciliation, 2016.

Gerges, Fawaz A. *ISIS: A History.* Princeton: Princeton University Press, 2016.

Hochschild, Adam. *King Leopold's Ghost: A Story of Greed, Terror, and Heroism in Colonial Africa.* Boston: Houghton Mifflin, 1999.

Kisangani, Emizet F. *Civil Wars in the Democratic Republic of Congo, 1960–2010.* Boulder, CO: Lynne Rienner Publishers, 2012.

Lavell-Harvard, D. Memee, and Jennifer Brant, eds. *Forever Loved: Exposing the Hidden Crisis of Missing and Murdered Indigenous Women and Girls in Canada.* Bradford, ON: Demeter Press, 2016.

Macklem, Patrick, and Douglas Sanderson, eds. *From Recognition to Reconciliation: Essays on the Constitutional Entrenchment of Aboriginal and Treaty Rights.* Toronto: University of Toronto Press, 2016.

The Macur Review. *The Report of the Macur Review: An independent review of the Tribunal of Inquiry into the abuse of children in care in the former county council areas of Gwynedd and Clwyd in North Wales since 1974.* House of Commons, 2016. https://www.gov.uk/government/uploads/system/uploads/attachment_data/file/517098/The_Report_of_the_Macur_Review__Redacted_version__PRINT.pdf.

McKegney, Sam. *Magic Weapons: Aboriginal Writers Remaking Community after Residential School*. Winnipeg: University of Manitoba Press, 2007.

Niezen, Ronald. *Truth and Indignation: Canada's Truth and Reconciliation Commission on Indian Residential Schools*. Toronto: University of Toronto Press, 2013.

Oloya, Opiyo. *Child to soldier: Stories from Joseph Kony's Lord's Resistance Army*. Toronto: University of Toronto Press, 2013.

Saul, John Ralson. *A Fair Country: Telling Truths about Canada*. Toronto: Viking Canada, 2008.

Stern, Jessica, and J. M. Berger. *ISIS: The State of Terror*. New York: Ecco, 2015.

Truth and Reconciliation Commission of Canada. *Final Report of the Truth and Reconciliation Commission of Canada*. Winnipeg: Truth and Reconciliation Commission of Canada, 2015.

_____. *What We Have Learned: Principles of Truth and Reconciliation*. Winnipeg: Truth and Reconciliation Commission of Canada, 2015.

Turner, Thomas. *The Congo Wars: Conflict, Myth, and Reality*. New York: Zed Books, 2007.

UN Independent International Commission of Inquiry on the Syrian Arab Republic. *"They came to destroy": ISIS Crimes Against the Yazidis*. UN Doc. A/HRC/32/CRP.2.

United Kingdom Child Sexual Abuse People's Tribunal. *Healing and Justice: In Defense of the Survivors of Child Sexual Abuse*. London: Hugh James, 2016. https://www.hughjames.com/wp-content/uploads/2016/03/Healing-and-Justice-in-defence-of-the-survivors-of-child-sexual-abuse-preliminary-report-of-the-United-Kingdom-Child-Sexual-Abuse-Peoples-Tribunal.pdf.

ACKNOWLEDGEMENTS

This book is based on the 2014 Vancouver Human Rights Lecture "Beyond Human Rights: Building a World on Empathy," which I delivered at the kind invitation of Farid Rohani, Chair of the Laurier Institution. It was broadcast on CBC Radio's *Ideas* as part of a memorable interview with Paul Kennedy that helped me realize the importance of sharing my experiences with the wider public.

I am grateful to Esther Mujawayo, Éloge Butera, Sima Samar, Chief Donovan Fontaine, and others who shared their moving stories with me. In writing this book, I have benefited greatly from the encouragement and advice of Greg Kelly, Executive Producer of *Ideas*; the superb editorial guidance of Producer Philip Coulter of the CBC and Editorial Director Janie Yoon and Managing

Editor Maria Golikova of House of Anansi Press; the diligent design work of Alysia Shewchuk; the thoughtful comments of Sally Armstrong, Gerald Filson, and Kathleen McFarland on early versions of the manuscript; and the capable assistance of Emilie de Haas in preparing the endnotes and bibliography.

Since this book is about a human rights odyssey of many years, I also wish to recognize Sarira Vahman, who so selflessly raised my beautiful children while I was either away from home in distant lands, or at home but away in distant thoughts; my older brother Dariush for teaching me the importance of serving humanity by his example; and my parents, Sa'id and Behrokh Akhavan and Fereydun and Shomais Vahman, for showing me what it means to carry on with dignity in times of loss and despair.

INDEX

(THE CBC MASSEY LECTURES SERIES)

The Triumph of Narrative
Robert Fulford
978-0-88784-645-8 (p)

Becoming Human
Jean Vanier
978-0-88784-809-4 (p)

The Elsewhere Community
Hugh Kenner
978-0-88784-607-6 (p)

The Unconscious Civilization
John Ralston Saul
978-0-88784-731-8 (p)

On the Eve of the Millennium
Conor Cruise O'Brien
978-0-88784-559-8 (p)

Democracy on Trial
Jean Bethke Elshtain
978-0-88784-545-1 (p)

Twenty-First Century Capitalism
Robert Heilbroner
978-0-88784-534-5 (p)

The Malaise of Modernity
Charles Taylor
978-0-88784-520-8 (p)

Biology as Ideology
R. C. Lewontin
978-0-88784-518-5 (p)

The Real World of Technology
Ursula Franklin
978-0-88784-636-6 (p)

Necessary Illusions
Noam Chomsky
978-0-88784-574-1 (p)

Compassion and Solidarity
Gregory Baum
978-0-88784-532-1 (p)

Prisons We Choose to Live Inside
Doris Lessing
978-0-88784-521-5 (p)

Latin America
Carlos Fuentes
978-0-88784-665-6 (p)

Nostalgia for the Absolute
George Steiner
978-0-88784-594-9 (p)

Designing Freedom
Stafford Beer
978-0-88784-547-5 (p)

The Politics of the Family
R. D. Laing
978-0-88784-546-8 (p)

The Real World of Democracy
C. B. Macpherson
978-0-88784-530-7 (p)

The Educated Imagination
Northrop Frye
978-0-88784-598-7 (p)

Available in fine bookstores and at www.houseofanansi.com